Landscape and Culture

Landscape and Culture
Geographical and Archaeological Perspectives

Edited by J. M. Wagstaff

Basil Blackwell

Copyright © Basil Blackwell 1987

First published 1987

Basil Blackwell Ltd
108 Cowley Road, Oxford, OX4 1JF, UK

Basil Blackwell Inc,
432 Park Avenue South, Suite 1503
New York, NY 10016, USA

British Library Cataloguing in Publication Data
Landscape and culture: geographical and
archaeological perspectives
1. Geography   2. Archaeology
I. Wagstaff, T. Malcolm
910   GB21
ISBN 0–631–13729–7
ISBN 0–631–15288–1 Pbk

Library of Congress Cataloging in Publication Data
Landscape and culture.
Bibliography: p.
Includes index.
1. Anthropo-geography.   2. Archaeology.
3. Environmental archaeology.   4. Land settlement
patterns.   5. Landscape assessment.   I. Wagstaff,
J. Malcolm (John Malcolm), 1940–   .
GF21.5.L36   1987   304.2   86–26851
ISBN 0–631–13729–7
ISBN 0–631–15288–1 (pbk.)

Typeset in 10 on 12 pt Sabon
by Columns, Reading, Berks
Printed in Great Britain by T. J. Press Ltd, Padstow, Cornwall

Contents

1 Introduction

J. M. Wagstaff

Geography and archaeology are concerned with two dimensions of a single field. The primary objective of both is to study the effects of human behaviour. Geography concentrates upon the spatial dimension. It takes as its starting point the notion that all human activity has location, takes place within a framework of spatial relations and generates spatial forms, whether ephemeral and episodic (like journeys to work) or semi-permanent (like the built environment of cities). From this base, as Goudie indicates in chapter 2, geographers have tended to return time and again to a set of fundamental themes. These are: the analysis of distributions and locations; environmental influences on human activity; the nature of ecosystems; the role of man as an agent of ecological change; the reconstruction of past landscapes and landscape development; and the characterization of regions.

Human activity takes place in time, as well as space. It has antecedents, duration and consequences. The time dimension is the joint concern of archaeology and history. The basic difference between the two is that historians rely largely upon written sources, while archaeologists depend mainly on other types of artefact. The two subjects evidently overlap, but have evolved different methodologies and tend not to share a common philosophy. 'Archaeology is, among other things, the time dimension of anthropology and ethnology' (Clarke, 1968: 13). As Hodges points out in chapter 8, it is concerned with settlement systems, production and distribution, social organization, and problems of cognition. Like geography, archaeology investigates phenomena at the micro-, as well as the meso-scale. Both are concerned with individual places – the single site or a particular city, for example. They are also interested in wider patterns, often defined on the basis of operational or functional criteria.

A shared background in nineteenth-century positivism, accounts, perhaps, for both geography and archaeology relying on physical evidence. For the archaeologist there is no alternative; the data are embedded in the site, created and moulded by the interplay of human actions and physical processes. They are artefacts – created and used by people – then preserved. The voices from the past are heard only through an incomplete and fragmentary physical record. The physical geographer is obviously in a similar position. The landscape itself contains the evidence needed. It is found, for example, in the configuration of hill slopes and the detail of river channels, masked (in part at least) by various deposits and types of vegetation (chapter 4). It is less obvious that the human geographer often starts from purely physical evidence. Nonetheless, the case for this can be made (chapter 3). One example may be quoted: different sectors or zones in cities are recognized on the basis of physical evidence concerning the quality and character of the built environment before those impressions are confirmed by socio-economic indices constructed from census or survey material.

A reliance upon physical evidence and the grounding in natural sciences of many early geographers and archaeologists, encouraged in both subjects what Vidal de la Blache (1902) called a natural-science approach to their material. This was manifested in the early efforts put into systems for classification and categorization – of pottery and settlements, for example. It was perpetuated through the traditions of the two disciplines as they were established in universities and institutes. The elaborate statistical descriptions produced over the last two or three decades are manifestations of the same approach. While classification has often seemed an end in itself, the hope was always that the detection of pattern, of structure or regularity, would produce explanations (chapter 6).

Although geography and archaeology dealt with the results of human activity, social theory was poorly developed and both subjects remained detached from the developing social sciences. As Cherry points out in chapter 10, for example, geography still has no theory of the state, despite the state's acknowledged role in many of the questions dealt with by human geographers.

As a result of the importance attached to classification, both subjects have relied heavily upon typology, though geographers may be surprised to learn that this is what they have been doing when recognizing such things as glacial features, urban settlements or underdeveloped regions. Both disciplines now recognize that much of the patterning found in any set of phenomena arises from two characteristics of the research process. One is the way in which typologies are constructed and, ultimately, in the diagnostic criteria adopted – it is a matter of judgement whether these are significant or not. The second characteristic is the adequacy of the data themselves. Several of the contributions to this book (especially chapters 4, 5 and 6) stress the importance of establishing the limits of the data in terms of precision and comparability before any analysis is attempted. In this respect, there is no more salutary exercise than the construction of a regional distribution map. The pattern which emerges is soon seen to reflect the extent of research coverage, as well as other 'controls', whether physical or social. The problem is acute in landscape archaeology (chapter 6). As Roberts observes, the survival of relict features is due to the underlying geology, the different systems of land use practised over many generations and the degree to which society has consciously or unconsciously allowed the preservation or destruction of landscape elements. Even within individual sites, intensity of research and the differential survival of material, in both the vertical and the horizontal plane, combine to produce daunting problems of interpretation. Geographers and archaeologists gradually came to realize over the last decade or so, that 'facts' do not speak for themselves. The very acts of designation, selection and observation, let alone the conscious search for order and pattern, arise from assumptions about meaning and significance, whether those assumptions are clearly articulated or not. Realization of the problem, as well as the apparent failure of the natural-science approach to produce satisfactory explanations, has encouraged an interest in what might be explained as 'the intention behind the act' which eventually produced the physical object for the geographers and archaeologists to study (chapter 5). As Hodder argues (chapter 9), this development is not so much the result of direct contacts between the two disciplines, but the consequence of reading the same authors from other fields. That in turn was the result of running into similar types of problem, itself at least partly the outcome of having to deal with similar sorts of data.

Geographers now appreciate that 'in the reproduction of social *life* (through systems of interaction) actors routinely draw upon interpretive schemes, resources and norms which are made available by existing structures of signification, domination and legitimation and that in so doing they thus immediately and necessarily reconstitute these structures' (Gregory 1981a: 8–10). There is a growing interest in the world of experience and the meanings attached to it. These are part of the context, just as much as functional relationships (chapter 9).

The geographer often has an advantage here, having recourse to written sources, including diaries and letters, which reveal the attitudes, value systems and perceptions of the writers. In studying present-day situations, he can conduct questionnaire surveys and even play the role of participant observer. The prehistoric archaeologist has no direct evidence about experience and meaning; he is dependent upon inference. Signs, symbols and iconography become important, though interpretation depends upon recurring associations in repeated contexts (Renfrew, 1985: 11–26; Cherry, below, pp. 168–72; Hodder, below, pp. 136–39).

Despite the similarities between geography and archaeology at the intellectual level, each has frequently cast the other discipline in the role of handmaid (chapter 5). In its early days particularly, geographers expected archaeologists to provide at least part of the data for an evolutionary explanation of the patterns of human phenomena in which geographers were primarily interested. This attitude lapsed as processual geography flowered in the 1960s with its ahistorical emphasis on the structure of present-day spatial systems and the processes which sustained them, rather than upon their antecedents. These expectations of archaeologists have recently begun to revive, however, among both physical and human geographers. Evolution and development are now once again seen as important in explanation. Archaeology, for its part, has long used that essentially geographical tool, the distribution map, as a means of integrating its own data. As Clarke put it (1977: 1–32), the map is an aid to the study of the relationships between things (covariability, covariation, correlation, association, change and process). That is why spatial models deriving from the work of von Thünen, Weber and Christaller were taken into the subject, usually through geography. Serious criticism of the applicability of these models to societies before the advent of capitalism was slow to develop, though the models were very much products of their era. One of the most widely used spatial models was a combined effort between an archaeologist, E. S. Higgs, and a physical geographer, Claudio Vita-Finzi, in which they formulated site catchment (or site territory) analysis. This offers a means of defining the area that might have been exploited, largely for subsistence purposes, by a community occupying a particular point site. It is also a method for assessing the potential use of the land within the defined perimeter (Higgs and Vita-Finzi, 1970: 1972). Distance was represented as a major constraint on exploitation. Site catchment analysis has attracted much discussion (e.g. Bailey and Davidson, 1983; Roper, 1979) and two contributions to this book (chapters 5 and 6) continue the debate with important criticisms of some of its underlying assumptions.

Around the time that site catchment analysis was being applied, directors of archaeological projects began to bring geographers into their work. Their role as 'experts' was not only to attempt some kind of territorial analysis (e.g. Lukerman, 1972) but to assist in the reconstruction of the physical environment of – usually – particular sites (e.g. Wagstaff, 1972; 1973). The involvement of geographers, and especially of geomorphologists was the culmination, in Britain anyway, of two long-developing trends. The first, which started in the 1920s, was the study of plant and animal remains from sites and (in the case of pollens) their surroundings, with a view to reconstructing subsistence patterns. The reconstruction of vegetation was an obvious extension. The other trend was a growing interest in the economies of prehistoric settlements and societies (Trigger 1978: 135–6). A boost to geographical involvement was the result of the publication by the physical geographer Karl Butzer, of *Environment and* Archaeology (first British edition, 1965). A type of contextual archaeology is the most recent development (chapters 2 and 3) embracing both human and physical systems, and making great use of ecological ideas as the basis for synthesis (Butzer, 1982).

The geographical input to archaeology has been greater, in recent times, than any counterflow of ideas, techniques and data. Chapter 3 offers some reasons for this. One of the effects has been the ignorance of the average human geographer about the modifications to central-place theory proposed by the anthropologist, Carol Smith (1976a, b) and outlined in chapter 8. Another has been the lack of involvement by geographers in the debate within archaeology over the recognition of regions – a fundamentally geographical concept – using material evidence (Green and Haselgrove, 1978). A third has been that most geographers have left untouched the exceptionally rich data that archaeologists have assembled from an immense span of time and against which many geographical models could and should be tested – especially if these are claimed to have any kind of universal application. As Cherry points out forcibly (chapter 10), geographers have frequently made the extraordinary assumption that the socio-political systems of capitalist nation states embedded in the world economy over, at most, the last two hundred years produce norms of behaviour which are replicated in space and time, irrespective of context. They overlook the diversity of present-day systems on a world scale, and then wonder why their models do not work in, say, the Third World. The rediscovery of the time dimension and the importance of context should help cure such myopia.

The past has left a legacy of forms. These act as constraints upon present-day processes, both physical and social, and it is important to understand their role. Inherited forms, though, have sometimes been produced in contexts different from those in which modern processes operate. For example, the increasing impact of man since the last Ice Age in exploiting and managing his environment has had considerable effects upon the operation of geomorphological systems (chapter 4), while the disappearance of continental ice sheets from the northern hemisphere has transformed the entire context within which processes operate in middle latitudes. On the human side, it is generally acknowledged that the emergence of capitalism, first in western Europe, transformed both social and value systems. A full understanding of present-day spatial forms thus requires some knowledge not only of how the relicts of past activity were created but also how they were preserved. Some processes at work in human, as well as physical, systems operate more quickly than others. In both relatively long periods of virtual stability may be succeeded by short phases of rapid change. The preservation of datable artefacts within time-related levels in an archaeological site thus becomes important in calibrating the development of physical forms and the processes creating them (chapter 4). The same materials from the same context may also allow inferences to be made about the transformation of society over time, as well as its organization at one moment. The archaeologists' long perspective offers an opportunity to geographers to make assessments on a firm basis of the real significance of the processes at work in the physical and human environment. This book is an attempt to take a step in that direction. That aim explains the order of words in its title.

Assembled here is a collection of commissioned essays, each of which seeks to explore the relationships between geography and archaeology. The topics were chosen by the editor in order to cover the wide field in which the two disciplines are currently working and to focus on the many opportunities for mutual enrichment.

At one end of the field is interest in the reconstruction of physical environments, and specifically a concern about the palaeo-ecology of erosion. In chapter 4 J. B. Thornes presents a new approach to the problems of erosion and alluviation in relation to vegetation cover and its modifications by man. The relationships between geography and archaeology are implicit throughout the discussion. This is a major contribution to the long-running debate over how much significance to attach to the anthropogenetic factor, as opposed to climatic change, in varying rates of erosion and sedimentation, which thus modify the shape of the land (chapter 2).

At the opposite end of the field is Ian Hodder's essay on meaning, subjectivity and experience (chapter 9). Hodder points out the different sources of insight into these questions drawn upon by the two disciplines. Archaeology has drawn more upon structuralist ideas, whereas the major inspiration in geography has come from phenom-enology and hermeneutics. In each discipline, however, the concern with experience and meaning developed as a reaction to the positivism which seem to dominate both. Similarly, each subject has sought to focus on *context*. Meanings are time-specific; they develop within historical frameworks. In recognizing this, geography and archaeology are beginning to converge.

The history of the relationship between geography and archaeology down to the present is outlined in chapter 2. Andrew Goudie sees the early associations of the two subjects in Great Britain as lying in the activities of 'local antiquaries' and 'travelled dilettanti'. They grew together during the nineteenth century as the result of shared interests in the evolution of cultures. Environmental reconstruction provided a further close bond between them. While archaeological investigation assisted geomorphological and Quaternary studies, work in physical geography allowed the prediction of site location and the retrodiction of types of land use. Another central link between geography and archaeology is the map, and this helped to foster common methodologies of spatial analysis, at first simple visual correlation between human phenomena and elements in the physical environment and later the use of more rigorous statistically based techniques (Hodder and Orton, 1976).

The use of spatial models is examined specifically in chapter 8. Here Richard Hodges outlines the challenges that faced the early use of models which had been developed by the classical economists of the nineteenth century. But he also draws attention to the important work of Carol Smith and her associates in meeting some of the criticism. A critique of Smith's own assumptions (that the pre-capitalist world was like present-day Mesoamerica and that exchange was always imbalanced or exploitative) is followed in Hodges's essay by some suggestions for further modification. He then explores the idea that archaeology is fundamentally the past tense of anthropology, a notion that owes much to American traditions in the subject (Trigger, 1978, 1984b), and suggests that it also involves the distinctly geographical concept of man–land relationships and the study of the use of place through time ('sequent occupance', in Whittlesey's (1929) term).

Divergence, followed by growing convergence and mutual discovery are the themes of chapter 3 which examines the development of geography and archaeology from the 1960s to the mid-1980s. 'New' approaches and methods emerged but led to the temporary neglect of some central questions. In geography these included regional differentiation and the interplay between physical conditions and human activity. In archaeology, socio-economic change tended to be neglected at first, along with the larger question of what – in the long term – it means to be human. A reaction eventually developed in the two disciplines. It had similar origins: the growing recognition that statistical analysis and probability theory had limitations. Questions were raised about the diachronic validity of some of the new models. Positivism in general came under attack as inappropriate for human sciences. While techniques continue to be improved and refined, a second generaton of new approaches aimed to be less mechanistic and to give social context and meaning to data. Discussion of these will be found throughout the book.

Points of convergence between geography and archaeology are exemplified in chapters 5, 6 and 7. In chapter 5, R. W. Dennell takes up the case argued by Goudie in chapter 2 that geographers can make their greatest contribution to the resolution of archaeological problems through the analysis of off-site data, and in so doing help to elucidate context. While Dennell is concerned mainly with context in terms of the social environment, this cannot be wholly divorced from physical conditions. Dennell mentions some specific topics where mutual assistance would be beneficial, the study of colonization, for example, and the effects of seasonality on human and physical data surviving on particular sites and how these should be interpreted.

In chapter 6, B. K. Roberts is concerned with landscape archaeology, where the collaboration of geography and archaeology is particularly close. Landscapes, he says pragmatically, 'may be defined as assemblages of real world features . . . (which) give character and diversity to the earth's surface, and form the physical framework within which human societies exist'. Roberts brings out the palimpsest nature of landscape. He outlines the potential utility of the different components of landscape (hedgerows and settlement plans, for example) in reconstructing previous forms and for tracing change. The ability to recognize forms typologically is obviously basic to the enterprise. However, the techniques of morpholological analysis which have been developed to deal with landscape relics have recently been criticized: Roberts considers these problems and he produces a valuable reassessment of the techniques, arguing for sensitivity and skill in their application.

Chapter 7 is devoted to industrial archaeology, a field somewhat neglected by both academic archaeologists and geographers. Historical geographers have shied away from the study of industrial activity over recent decades, while archaeologists have left the subject to specialists – often dedicated amateurs – more concerned with the reconstruction of individual structures and site plans than in understanding the cultural basis of the activities within them. E. G. Grant reviews the different approaches that might be adopted to the study of the location of past industrial activity. He considers the relative utility of structural and Marxist approaches to the study of the past (other contributors also touch on these). Industrial activity cannot properly be isolated from the society within which it takes place, for the configuration of that society calls industrial production into being, constrains the particular forms it takes, and is itself affected by the organizational arrangements produced. Grant points out, too, that while the Industrial Revolution is one of the great divides in cultural history, earlier industrialization was an important element in the emergence of complex societies. In view of the crucial role of industry in transforming society, Grant calls for closer collaboration between geographers and archaeologists in studying its past. Understanding industrialization may help us grapple with the problems of the emerging post-industrial societies of the world.

The relative neglect by geographers of major transitions in the history of human society (e.g. in food production and urbanization) is taken up by Cherry in his review essay on power in space. This deals with five aspects of power. The first is the state and the efforts made by archaeologists to discover its origins. In these studies, states have often been conceptualized as power structures which require certain patterns of circulation for matter, energy and information. The recognition of states as territorial units is Cherry's second theme. Geographers usually have no difficulty in this task, but the archaeologists encounter considerable problems owing to the nature of their evidence. Nonetheless, there has been a shared interest in the complex processes which develop at frontiers and boundaries. Cherry's third subject, the growth of states and empires, is a field where the new models being developed by archaeologists should be of considerable interest to geographers. Core–periphery relations, his fourth subject, are at the heart of much applied geography and it is not surprising to find themes common to both the archaeological and the geographical literature. Cherry is concerned finally with legitimation, and deals with the structure of symbols and iconography used to display political relationships and how the material evidence left behind can be used as the basis for discovering how states worked. These perspectives surely could be applied to the contemporary world.

The practical problems of conservation and preservation provides a theme for the concluding chapter. Here P. J. Fowler argues that the cultural heritage of sites and monuments is analagous to the natural heritage. The importance of what survives – and of what is rapidly disappearing – has been realized only comparatively recently. Principles of conservation and preservation are being worked out and complex structures of management have emerged. It is not simply a matter of saving what we have inherited, or even of recording it before its destruction by modern developments. The relics of the past are a resource. As such they can be exploited not only to produce scientific information for scholars but also to deepen general awareness of past cultures and societies and of the tension between change and continuity. Remains are, in addition, a source of mystery, delight and entertainment. Orchestrated to some extent by interest groups, there is now considerable public pressure to retain individual sites or structures, assemblages of buildings and streets, as well as whole cultural and natural landscapes. There is also a growing demand for these sites, buildings and preserved landscapes (or townscapes) to be interpreted and explained – to become more accessible to the understanding as well as to the senses. The resulting problems of planning and education are formidable. As Fowler points out, archaeologists have played a central role in trying to resolve the problems. The role played by geographers should not be overlooked, even if it is the often anonymous one of the planner in a local authority.

Management involves choice. That, in turn, raises questions about the perceptions, the ideologies and the power of the decision makers. Politics is inseparable from any debate over the conservation and preservation of relicts and over acceptable forms of access and explanation. Choices concerning what to keep and how to present it result in concrete expressions of the ideological and cognitive aspects of power. Considerations of past and present thus become reflexive. No matter what the immediate concerns of their practitioners, geography and archaeology are to this extent interdependent. Recognition of that should lead to greater mutual knowledge and greater achievement.

2 Geography and Archaeology: The Growth of a Relationship

A. S. Goudie

Introduction

Geographers have sometimes likened themselves to slash-and-burn agriculturalists, staying but briefly in any one area as they maximize short-term returns only to exploit the same quickly-exhausted field some decades later. However, there have in reality been certain, major themes or traditions that have persisted. Though 'new' geographies come and go, and, like threatened buffalo, their practitioners rush first in this direction and then another, there has been a durability when it comes to the study of certain fundamentals: the analysis of distributions and of locations; the exploration of environmental influences; the investigation of ecosystems; the establishment of the role of man as an agent of ecological change; the reconstruction of past environments; and landscape development and the characterization of regions. The relative importance of these fundamentals within geography has varied through time, and this variation has influenced the nature of the long-standing links between geography and archaeology. Both in terms of problems and personalities these links have been close and largely harmonious. For example, Lord Curzon, a geographer whose interests ranged from singing sands to the political geography of the world's frontiers (Ronaldshay, 1928), resuscitated the Archaeological Survey of India and helped to conserve some of the sub-continent's most remarkable archaeological treasures. Huntington, the greatest of the American environmental determinists, roamed the margins of Curzon's empire and helped to revolutionize the history and prehistory of Central Asia (Chappell, 1970a). Three British professors of geography, Fleure, Forde and Estyn Evans, have made significant contributions to the development of archaeology and anthropology, *sensu lato*, while some individuals, including Crawford, an erstwhile Demonstrator in geography at Oxford, and Harris, another Oxford-trained geographer, have made an almost complete transition from one discipline to the other. Still other geographers have contributed their expertise to archaeological expeditions and projects, a contribution that is revealed as both substantial and long-standing.

Explorers and Antiquaries

Some of the first links between geography and archaeology involved what Daniel (1967: 35) has described as 'local antiquaries' and 'travelled dilettanti'. Among the British exponents of this type he instances Camden (1551–1623), Rowlands (1655–1723) and Stukeley (1687–1765). They stimulated an interest in the remote past of man, but until geologists in the early nineteenth century demonstrated that the world was not created in 4004 BC and hinted at the depth of the human past, relatively little progress was made. The development of scientific geology based less on Mosaic creation, the Noachian deluge and sundry catastrophes, was a major development. The understanding of stratigraphic principles and of the long-continued operation of uniformitarian processes provided a firmer substratum upon which archaeological progress could be created. The discoveries of Hutton, Playfair, Lyell and their ilk in geology, and of Darwin and Wallace in zoology, were fundamental for progress from antiquarianism. It was also the first decades of the nineteenth century which witnessed the birth of modern geographical science, and this was marked in Britain in 1830 by the establishment of the Royal Geographical Society, an institution whose prime concern was exploration. Concurrent with this were a developing British interest in the Middle East and the route to India, a general renewal of concern with the Classical World and ancient civilizations, and a desire to examine the Biblical sites and stories. The journeys of explorers, surveyors and geographers were facilitated by the far-flung tentacles of the East India Company, by the liberation of Greece from 'the usual results of Ottoman bigotry and despotism' (Leake, 1830), and the esatablishment of direct political relations with the Ottoman provinces constituting a unit known as Turkish Arabia (Lloyd, 1980: 10). Dr Arnold of Rugby and Oriel also noted the role of improvements in transport: 'It will be strange if the establishment of steam vessels on the Mediterranean does not within the next ten years do more for the geography of Thucydides than has ever been done yet' (Arnold, 1847: iii).

Thus it was that in a great swathe of country, from Rome in the west to India in the east, scholars, clerics, surveyors, military men and adventurers undertook explorations that were to unravel many of the mysteries of both ancient and modern geography. So, for example, Major Rennell (1800: vii) spent many years 'correcting the geography, ancient and modern, throughout that part of Asia, situated between

India and Europe; in effect the great theatre of ancient history in Asia, as well as of European commerce and communication, in modern times'.

On a more local scale Tod, working in Rajasthan followed up Rennell's work, and while surveying the positions of rivers and cities in connection with the production of a map for the Governor General of India he established the positions and significance of places of antiquarian interest (Tod, 1829). Beaufort (1818: ix), while conducting the hydrographic survey of the southern coast of Asia Minor, had occasion to describe the 'venerable remains of former opulence and grandeur'. The Euphrates Expedition of Chesney in the 1830s set out with its official purpose as being 'to survey the northern part of Syria, to explore the basins of the rivers Euphrates and Tigris, to test the navigability of the former, and to examine in the countries adjacent to these great rivers the markets with which the expedition might be thrown in contact'. However, it also achieved much of archaeological note and among the objects of one of its members, W. Ainsworth (1838), were 'to describe the indices of the Deluge of Scripture' and 'the investigation of the progress of the alluvia of Babylonia, Chaldaea, and Susiana'. Later in the nineteenth century the survey work of the Palestine Exploration Fund (Wilson, 1881) was to lead to major archaeological discoveries, while in Central Asia Sir Aurel Stein's surveys between 1900 and 1915 both filled in some of the blanks on the map and revealed the presence of many important prehistoric sites (Stein, 1923).

Such combinations of survey, exploration, map making and anti-quarianism were to be among the first links between geography and archaeology, and many more studies could be cited (e.g., Hamilton, 1842; Gell, 1846; Williams, 1829; Cramer, 1828, 1832; Rich, 1836). Hamilton was granted the Founder's Model by the Royal Geographical Society in 1844 'for successful and well matured labours upon the physical geography, geology and antiquities of Asia Minor' and the Presidential Addresses of Sir Roderick Murchinson in the 1840s are replete with references to geographers and travellers involved in antiquarian research including Morritt at Troy, Forster in Arabia, Dean Goodenough in the Black Sea environs, and Major Rawlinson near Baghdad. However, perhaps pride of place should be accorded to the Swiss traveller, J. L. Burckhardt (1784–1817), who before he died in a poor quarter of Cairo aged only 32, had penetrated Mecca, discovered the Great Temple of Rameses II at Abu Simbel, and found the long-lost 'rose-red city' of Petra (Sim: 1981).

As the nineteenth century progressed, so did the nature of geography. The relative importance of exploration declined, but the position of academic geography in the universities strengthened. This led to further developments in the relationship between geography and archaeology.

Distribution Maps and the Explanation of Spatial Pattern

The analysis of distribution and locations of phenomena has been a fundamental theme in geography and one which has been central to the links between geography and the study of prehistory. Thus Daniel (1964: 141) has remarked that the 'geographer and the prehistorian meet in the map' and Renfrew (1969: 74) observed that 'in the early years of the present century it provided a whole new outlook in prehistoric research, most obviously exemplified by the use of distribution maps'. In Britain it was probably Crawford (1912) who first adequately appreciated the insights which distribution maps of prehistoric phenomena could provide, for not only did the establishment of distributions have virtue in itself, but Crawford (1922: 257) also claimed that 'its explanation in terms of geographical influences is one of the finest intellectual pleasures that exist'. Crawford was instrumental in the mapping of British archaeological sites at the Ordnance Survey and appreciated at an early date the utility of air photographs as a tool for ensuring the completeness of the distributional coverage.

The establishment of an accurate distribution map 'by its very existence implies the co-ordination of scattered evidences and the establishment of a synthetic relation with their geographical background' (Clark, 1933: 232). Considerable work was expended, especially in the inter-war period, to link the distributional pattern to environmental factors.

The utilization of distribution maps to infer influences caused Fleure and Whitehouse (1916) to argue that prehistoric man in Britain initially lived on hill-tops and only gradually moved down into the valley bottoms, but this approach reached its highest level in the work of Sir Cyril Fox. In his *Personality of Britain* (1938) he combined the distributional ideas of workers like Crawford with the theories of positional geography developed by Mackinder (1902) in his *Britain and the British Seas*, and with the 'personality' concept of the great French regional geographers like Vidal de la Blache (1928). Extending Mackinder's binary classification of Britain into Highland and Lowland, Fox differentiated between the 'imposed' cultures of the Lowlands and the 'absorbed' cultures of the Highlands (see Daniel, 1963 and 1964 for a discussion). On a more local scale the environmental approach was used successfully in his *Archaeology of the Cambridge Region* (Fox, 1923 and 1947), and the whole personality approach has been taken up by other prehistorians, notably by Subbarao in India (Subbarao 1958). The geomorphologists, Wooldridge and Linton (1933), though primarily concerned with establishing the sequence and causes of physical landscape change in the Tertiary and Quaternary – an approach called 'denudation chronology' – were also prepared to try and explain the sequence and controls of human occupance in south-east England. They adopted the distributional approach with regard to the influences of the loam terrains of that region on early man, and stated by way of conclusion that 'it was to plains and low plateaux of a definitive soil constitution as well as to valley floors that Early Man progressively moved' (1933: 310). Their approach followed on from the *Steppenheide-theorie* of Gradmann who attempted to show that the loess had been a potent influence on the distribution and movement of cultures in Europe (see Garnett, 1945 for an early discussion of the validity of Gradmann's model). The role of loess in influencing settlement distributions has been discussed for a long time (Smalley, 1968), and in China Roxby (1938) concluded that it was 'the essential geographical element in the rise of early Chinese civilization'.

Particularly in Europe and in Britain, the distributional approach to patterns in prehistory had strong environmentalist overtones, an approach that was not favoured to the same degree in America where, partly in reaction to the views of Huntington and Semple, there was a strongly entrenched anti-environmentalist school of thought (Willey and Sabloff, 1974: 152).

Environmental Influences on Temporal Patterns

Besides attempting to explain spatial patterns of human activity in terms of environmental influences, the early decades of this century witnessed sundry attempts to see the temporal pattern of cultural changes (whether evolutionary or revolutionary) in terms of natural environmental changes (Lamb, 1968). This was an area of great controversy, but also of immense intellectual fascination.

Within geography, environmental determinism was espoused by many of its leading nineteenth-century practitioners (e.g. Guyot, 1850). Likewise certain historians (e.g. Buckle, 1857) sought to interpret human history in terms of physical 'laws'. A particular theme was the interpretation of different levels of civilization and development in terms of the influence of climatic conditions on human mental attitudes (e.g. Ward, 1909; Taylor, 1937). Areas like the humid tropics, being enervating and relatively constant in their climate from day to day and season to season, were thought to promote backwardness and mental lethargy, whereas zones of mid-latitude cyclonic activity were thought to promote mental activity and adaptability in areas like New England, Western Europe and Japan.

As soon as it became evident that climatic changes had taken place in the Quaternary (see, for example, Geikie, 1874), the possibility existed that the nature and degree of climatic influence might have changed

through time sufficiently to influence the tempo of cultural development. Thus, for example, Huntington and his co-workers interpreted
migration and the decline of cities in Central Asia in terms of
environmental changes and saw dry phases as the driving force of the
Pulse of Asia (1907). There was a widely held belief at this time that in
mid-latitudes and the tropics, the Holocene had witnessed the rigours of
post-glacial progressive desiccation and concomitant hardship for
human societies (Goudie, 1972).

Childe expressed a belief in the link between climatic change and
domestication in the Near East (Childe, 1928, 1952). With the increase
in temperature and postulated drying up of grasslands as the last
glaciation waned, he argued that cultural change was almost inevitable:

Enforced concentration in oases or by the banks of ever more precarious
springs and streams would require an intensified search for means of
nourishment. Animals and men would be herded together around pools and
wadis that were growing increasingly isolated by desert tracts, and such
enforced juxtaposition might almost of itself promote that set of symbiosis
between man and beast that is expressed in the word 'domestication'. (Childe,
1928: 42)

Likewise Clark (1970) postulated that the change from an Upper
Palaeolithic to Mesolithic industry in Europe was a response of man to
the spread of closed forest in place of the herbivore-rich open tundra of
the Late Glacial. New hunting technologies were required. Sauer (1948)
saw the transition period between the Last Glaciation and the warmth
of the Holocene as 'one of maximum opportunity for progressive and
adventurous man . . . it was above all a really favourable time to test
out the possibilities of water-side life'. As sea-level rose, flooding the
continental shelves, rias and other bodies of sheltered water came into
existence. Sea-level changes may also have been important in controlling
migrations from one land mass to another, whether it be across the
Bering Strait (Hopkins, 1967) or across Wallace's Line and the
Australasian seas and archipelagos (Gill, 1965). Other cultural events
that have also been seen in terms of environmental controls include the
rise and fall of the Harappan Civilization, Olympia and Mycenae
(Wheeler, 1968; Huntington, 1910; Carpenter, 1966; Lamb, 1967), the
chequered history of the Pueblo Indians in the USA (Bryan, 1941; Jett,
1964; Griffin, 1967), and the course of human occupation of the inland
delta of the Niger (McIntosh, 1983). Most recently, C. K. Brain (1981a)
has pointed to some of the dramatic temperature reductions that have
been identified for the Cainozoic era and has suggested that they 'could
well have served as stimuli for critical steps in hominoid evolution',
especially through their effects on speciation:

It seems extremely likely that the distributions of certain plants and animals in Africa will have expanded and contracted repeatedly in response to temperature cycles . . . such expansions and contractions will have been topographically intricate with the result that once-continuous distributions will have been fragmented for varying lengths of time. It is precisely in such circumstances of allopatry and small population size that speciation events are likely to occur. (Brain, 1981a: 14)

Although Brain was concerned with hominoid evolution over a long time-scale, it is apparent in some areas, such as southern Africa, that a broad correlation between environmental change, the productivity of environments and human demography is reflected in the archaeological record (Deacon, 1983).

Such ideas of environment influence have always suffered from certain basic problems that have from time-to-time caused major doubts to be expressed about the approach. Apart from the vexed question of free will, four major problems exist:

1 The dating of environmental changes may be inaccurate, creating spurious correlations with cultural changes.
2 Correlation in time of environmental change and cultural change may not imply a simple causal relationship.
3 It is sometimes difficult to identify whether cultural changes have resulted from, or have helped to cause, certain types of environmental change (see Goudie, 1981: chapter 8).
4 There are problems in assessing the nature and degree of past changes in environment (see, for example, the discussions about Late Glacial environments in the USA, by Galloway, 1970; Brakenridge, 1978).

Some authorities have doubted the importance of climatic change itself (see for example, Raikes, 1967), while others doubt that early man was quite so hapless as has sometimes been maintained. Many have reacted against what has been regarded as extreme environmentalism to the extent that undeniably important climatic influences are ignored or dismissed in their analysis. Climatic uniformity (Sauer, 1968) has been preferred to climatic fluctuations (Chappell, 1970b).

Of late, however, there has been something of a resurgence in the inter-disciplinary study of climatic changes and their historical and prehistorical implications (e.g. Brice, 1978; Delano Smith and Parry, 1981; Lamb, 1982; Harding, 1982; Wigley et al., 1981). It has become permissible to think the unthinkable. This return to environmentalist ideas owes much to the increasingly accurate and sophisticated techniques that can be used for establishing chronologies (e.g.thermoluminescence, radiometric dating) and for environmental reconstruction (e.g. oxygen isotope analyses, palynology, scanning electron microscopy, etc.). Such techniques were not available to Huntington and his contemporaries, thereby rendering many of their conclusions premature, hazardous, but exciting.

Although Sauer was ambivalent about the role of climatic change, some of his work was clearly concerned with environmental influence. Especially noted were his attempts to reconstruct the type of environment that might, on *a priori* grounds, have been conducive to the flowering of a particular technical development (say, animal domestication or cultivation) and thereby to predict where such a development might have taken place (Sauer, 1948; 1952; 1956). He championed the importance of areas like south-east Asia as major foci for domestication.

Environmental Reconstruction and Geoarchaeologists

An important part of both the environmental and ecological approaches (*q.v.*) to prehistory has been the attempt to reconstruct the nature of past conditions, especially of soils, sedimentation, geomorphological change, climate and sea-levels during the Quaternary (e.g. Simmons and Tooley, 1981). As Sauer (1956) remarked, 'The age of man is also the Ice Age . . . his span has been cast within a period of high environmental tensions.' In recent years, especially as a result of the study of deep sea cores, loess profiles and lake sedimentation (Goudie, 1983), the degree, frequency and speed of change has been seen to be greater than previously envisaged. The physical geographer, especially the geomorphologist, collaborating with other natural scientists, has played a role in this work, aiding prehistorians on a formal interdisciplinary basis. Such investigations have a lengthy history (e.g. the Pumpelly expeditions of 1904) but have developed greatly with the growth of contextual–functional emphases in prehistoric studies. Contributions by geomorphologists and physical geographers to archaeological projects have included those of Butzer and co-workers in the Near East and Africa (see Butzer, 1972); Allchin and her co-workers of the Oxbridge–Baroda Project in India and Pakistan (Allchin et al., 1971); McBurney and Hey (1955) in Libya; Vita-Finzi (1969a) and collaborators around the Mediterranean basin; Bishop and fellow geologists in East Africa (Bishop and Clark, 1967); Bowler and others (1970) in Australia; Roberts et al. (1979) in Turkey; Caton-Thompson and Gardner in Egypt (1932); Clark (1969) and others at Kalambo Falls; Wright (1968) and collaborators in the Near East; Higgs et al. (1966, 1967) in Greece; Price Williams in Swaziland (Price Williams et al., 1982), and Wendorf and others in Egypt (Wendorf et al., 1979).

The role of geomorphologists has not solely been to reconstruct the past environments of sites that have already been located. By a knowledge of the past location and environment of deposits or environmental resources, it may be possible to predict where undiscovered archaeological sites may occur (see Allchin et al., 1978: vi).

The aim of geomorphologists has involved more than mere climatic reconstruction, for geomorphological changes themselves may be significant controls on human settlement patterns. For example, fluvial, deltaic and marine evolution in the vicinity of Troy (Kraft et al., 1980) mean that the 'events' described in the *Iliad* and *Odyssey* would have occurred in a dramatically different geographic setting to that which we see there today.

One field in which there may be considerable scope for further collaboration is in the prehistory of land bridges and continental shelves:

Recent advances in climatology, oceanography, plate tectonics and estimates of global sea level changes provide a basis for approximate reconstruction of palaeocoastlines and land bridges. The coastal and nearshore conditions at times of low sea level influence human activities in the littoral zone as well as the potential ease of sea crossings over critical straits and channels (Masters and Flemming, 1983: ix)

Palaeogeomorphological techniques may assist in submarine site production (Masters and Flemming, 1983: 622).

However, the collaboration has consisted of far more than geomorphologists assisting archaeologists. Some environment archaeologists, notably Zeuner (1958; 1959), have contributed greatly to geomorphological and Quaternary studies. Archaeological remains and their chronology have been used to assist geomorphologists in a multitude of tasks including the assessment of rates of solution and erosion (Proudfoot, 1965a), the evolution of calcrete (Netterberg, 1969), the ages of tufas (McBurney and Hey, 1955), sequences of erosion and alluviation (Vita-Finzi, 1969a; Bintliff, 1975; Price Williams et al., 1980), swings of sea-level (Flemming, 1969) and the nature and form of slope evolution (Kirkby and Kirkby 1971). The experimental earthwork programme at Overton Down and Morden Bog may have implications for the geomorphologist (see Evans and Limbrey, 1974).

The great advantage of such data from archaeological and historical sources (Hooke and Kain, 1982) is that they give a time dimension to geomorphological process studies of 10^2–10^4 years, whereas most instrumented studies, which have been such a feature of research in the last two decades, tend to cover a time span of only about 1–10^2 years. Sometimes it is important to have this larger time scale to place causes into time perspective. For instance, Vita-Finzi (1969b: 141) says that one of the most important lessons to be learnt from the study of alluvial sequences and associated artefacts is that 'gullying of the kind illustrated in tracts denouncing man's abuse of the soil has operated in times past when noble savages were innocuously picking berries'. Furthermore, the last couple of decades may, for both natural and cultural reasons, have been atypical of conditions over longer-time spans

Renfrew has noted that collaborative work over the last few decades has caused the emergence of a new discipline – Geoarchaeology:

This discipline employs the skills of the geological scientist, using his concern for soils, sediments and landforms to focus these upon the archaeological site, and to investigate the circumstances which governed its location, its formation as a deposit and its subsequent preservation and life history. The new discipline of geoarchaeology is primarily concerned with the context in which archaeological remains are found. And since archaeology, or at least prehistoric archaeology, recovers almost all its basic data by excavation, every archaeological problem starts as a problem in geoarchaeology (Renfrew, 1976: 2).

An indication of the present scope of this approach is given in Davidson and Shackley (1978), and in Hassan (1979), from whose work Table 1 (below) is derived.

Table 1   The main components of Geoarchaeology
(after Hassan, 1979)

The location of sites
Geomorphological analysis of site areas
Regional stratigraphic studies
Sedimentary analysis of deposits
Palaeo-environmental analysis
Technical studies of artefacts
Modelling of the dynamic relationship between human activities and landscape
Conservation and preservation from natural hazards
Dating

Man as an Agent of Change

Man's role in changing the face of the Earth has been a major preoccupation of geographers since the time of Alexander von Humboldt and Marsh (Thomas, 1956). Marsh, a Vermonter, after his journeys in Turkey and elsewhere in the Middle East and the Mediterranean basin, was struck by the landscape changes wrought in the Old World through the clearing of the woodland over many centuries (Marsh, 1864). Although this approach to geography was somewhat eclipsed during the determinist era, it is once again of considerable importance (see Gregory and Walling, 1979; Goudie, 1981; Tivy and O'Hare, 1981).

Early man can no longer be regarded as an impotent agent of change (Sauer, 1956) for numerous studies (Table 2, below) have demonstrated the importance of some of his actions. Special prominence can be given to the use of fire for at least 1.4 million years (Gowlett et al., 1981) and to other means of forest clearance (Darby, 1956; Iversen, 1956). Vegetational changes of significance may have been generated by man, as early as Acheulian times (Sparks and West, 1972: 245), and vegetation types such as savanna, prairie, pampas and maquis owe much to his actions over millennia. The impact of agricultural and/or pastoral activities on rain forest may date back in some areas to the early Holocene (Flenley, 1979). Equally, peat formation and podzolization in Highland Britain (Moore, 1973), the *Tilia* and *Ulmus* declines in the Holocene vegetational sequence (Turner, 1962; Rackham, 1980), the spread of salinization in Mesopotamia four thousand years ago (Jacobsen and Adams, 1958) and the demise of many of the world's greatest mammals in the catastrophe of Pleistocene

Table 2 Select examples of inadvertent environmental change in prehistory brought about by man

Example	Source	Date
Salinization of desert alluvium in Mesopotamia	Jacobsen and Adams (1958)	c. 4000 BP
Peat initiation in Highland UK	Moore (1973)	Mid-Holocene
Soil erosion and valley alluviation in the Mediterranean	Vita-Finzi (1969a)	Late Pleistocene Holocene
Phosphate accumulation and chemical alteration in soils of Amazonia	Smith (1980)	Pre-European settlement
Dust-induced climatic change in India	Bryson and Barreis (1967)	Indus civilization (c. 4000 BP)
Slopewash, corosion, colluviation and phosphorus changes in Maya area. Modification of vegetation by fire.	Deevey et al. (1979)	Mayan
Dune activation in Australia	Hughes and Sullivan (1981)	Late Holocene
Pleistocene overkill	Martin and Wright (1967)	Especially c. 11,000 years ago
Valley sedimentation in UK	Bell (1982)	Since c. 5000 BP

overkill (Martin and Wright, 1967) have been attributed to early man and his hunting or agricultural activities. Thus, the development of some significant characteristics of present-day biogeography, pedology and zoogeography have been initiated by, or result from, the activities of prehistoric man (see Proudfoot, 1956b; Bridges, 1978 for reviews of man's long-term occupance of the soil). Some of these activities may have been inadvertent, while others may have been deliberate (Table 3, below).

Table 3 Examples of deliberate environmental changes wrought by early man

Example	Source	Date
Use of fire in Africa	Gowlett et al. (1981)	>1.4 million years
'Harvesting' of runoff on slopes in the Negev	Evenari et al. (1982)	Nabbatean
Domestication of plants and animals	Reed (1977); Bender (1975); Ucko and Dimblebey, (1969)	Holocene
Control of rivers for water supply in Peru	Park (1983)	Pre-Hispanic
'Mining' of Middle Eastern groundwater by qanāt	Wilkinson (1977)	Pre-Islamic
Agricultural clearance of rain forest	Flenley (1979)	Post-c. 9000 BP
Terracing of slopes in Latin America	Donkin (1979)	Pre-European
Harvesting of crops in Egypt	Wendorf et al. (1979)	Late Palaeolithic

Connected with this role of early man as an agent of ecological change is the modification of whole landscapes – a major concern of historical geographers (e.g. Williams, 1970; Darby 1956; Norton, 1984). Thus, as Daniel (1964: 140) observed, 'the geographer, as he describes his region or chosen area, as he analysis the man-made features of the face of the earth and constructs his geographical context, is constantly coming up against the dead and the decaying ... the geographer then shares the non-functional cultural landscape with the archaeologist and the barrows and banks and ditches of pre-Roman Britain are as much his concern in one way as they are the concern of the prehistorian in another'. Some of the classic French regional monographs include a discussion of how prehistoric events have influenced regional characteristics (see Deffontaines, 1924), and attempts by other European geographers to reconstruct the primitive landscape, whether it be the *Urlandschaft* of Gradmann or the *Altlandschaft* of Jager, have had to depend on archaeological evidence.

System and Locations

During the 1960s many geographers adopted what was widely trumpeted as 'a new geography', and became involved with quantification, systems theory and locational analysis. Furthermore, ecological ideas were widely expanded (see Stoddart, 1967).

Such developments have been reflected in archaeology. For example, Clarke (1972a) identified an 'ecological paradigm' in the 'Post-1960 Explanatory Period' of Willey and Sabloff (1974) and defined it as 'the detailed study of archaeological sites as an integral part of the mutually adjusting environmental and ecological systems in which they were once adaptively networked'. The study of site distributions and locations in a broad ecological context has become important, so that prehistorians have assimilated new advances in spatial and locational analysis from geography at all scales. Renfrew (1969: 75) went so far as to predict that both *Locational Analysis in Human Geography* (Haggett, 1965) and *Models in Geography* (Chorley and Haggett, 1967) 'will become source books in method for an entire generation of archaeologists'. Early arguments between geographers over the validity of some of the new methodology (e.g. Spate, 1960) also occupied prehistorians somewhat later (e.g. Hawkes, 1968; Agrawal, 1970), but in spite of some resistance, the Explanatory Period of archaeology has seen the publication of works which both in terms of titles and origins betray a solid geographical connection. Clarke's *Analytical Archaeology* (1968) has stark affinities with Haggett's *Locational Analysis in Human Geography* (1965), while his *Models in Archaeology* (1972) is overtly modelled on *Models in Geography* (Chorley and Haggett, 1967). Likewise the extraordinarily influential *Explanation in Geography* (Harvey, 1969) had a parallel both in *Explanation in Archaeology* (Watson et al., 1971) and in a paper by Harriss (1971), 'Explanation in Prehistory'.

Given this background, it is not surprising that prehistorians have assimilated many of the new advances. Spatial sampling has been adopted (Mueller, 1974). Wobst (1974) has utilized a simulation approach to boundary conditions for Palaeolithic social systems. Set-theory models have been utilized (King and Moll, 1972). Locational analysis, stemming from Christaller, has been applied to Romano-British settlements (Hodder, 1972), Iron Age settlements (Newcomb, 1968), and Maya settlements in Belize (Green, 1973) and elsewhere (Hammond, 1972). Point-pattern analysis has proved applicable to sites (Washburn, 1974; Pinder et al., 1979), occupation floors and tool distribution (Dacey, 1973; Whallow, 1973; 1974). The 'rank size rule' has been applied to Mayan cities (Adams and Jones, 1981). Higgs and Vita-Finzi (1970: 3) have developed 'site catchment analysis' as 'an independent name for the study of the relationships between technology and those natural resources lying within economic range of individual sites'. Likewise, Jarman (1972: 707) believes that it is possible to view archaeological sites as occupying positions within 'exploitation territories' and to attempt an analysis of the economic possibilities offered by site locations in relation to the available resources. Network analysis has been applied to ancient road systems (Dicks, 1972; cf. Hindle et al., 1972), and Weide and Weide (1973) surmise that, as drainage basins form natural landform units within which one may systematically study the distribution of prehistorical occupational foci, the adoption of the Strahler stream-ordering system would be of use to the prehistorian. Diffusion Theory, stemming from Hägerstrand has been applied to changes in pre-industrial societies (Carlstein, 1983) and trend-surface analysis has been used to identify trends in the diffusion of lowland classic Maya collapse (Bove, 1981).

In view of this explosion of new geographical techniques and methodology in prehistory, it is not perhaps surprising that Clarke (1972) identified as one of the four new archaeological paradigms 'the Geographical Paradigm'. Following the language of Berry (1964) from urban geography, he defined this paradigm as 'the study of sites as patterned systems of features and structures within systems of sites territorially distributed over landscapes in a mutually adjusted way'.

Contextual Archaeology

All the themes that have been discussed so far bring us to a consideration of that approach to archaeology which now most closely integrates geography and the study of prehistory – 'contextual archaeology' (Butzer, 1982: 6 et seq.). Butzer defines its goal as:

... the study of archaeological sites or site networks as part of a human ecosystem. It is within this human ecosystem that earlier communities interacted spatially, economically and socially with the environmental matrices into which they were adaptively interwoven ... Less concerned with artifacts than with sites, contextual archaeology focuses on the multidimensional expression of human decision making within the environment.

He singles out five central themes with geographical antecedents that pervade contextual archaeology:

1 Space (distribution and patterning);
2 Scale (the operation of different processes at different spatial and temporal scales);
3 Complexity (inhomogeneity and uneveness of environments and communities);

4 Interaction (interaction of communities with each other and with the environment); and
5 Equilibrium state (feedback processes involved in readjustments of environments and communities to change).

Once again, however, although geographical concepts and methods dealing with these five themes may contribute to the development of contextual archaeology, there is a prospect that such an approach to archaeology may have repurcussions for geography. To conclude, one can again quote Butzer:

Contextual interpretation of the archaeological and historical records can provide invaluable monitoring experience for the kinds of socio-ecological processes that must be built into probabilistic neo-ecological models. The past is essential not only to understand the present but even more important to evaluate the potential outcome of modern trends. It is here that the contextual approach to the past forms a stimulating and provocative interface with the contemporary problems of a regional development, resource management, sustained productivity and ecological harmony that are becoming central concerns of human geography (Butzer, 1982: 320).

Note

This chapter is an expansion and modification of a paper originally published in 1976 in the *Journal of Historical Geography*, 2, 197–205. The author is indebted to Academic Press for permission to use some of the earlier material.

3 The New Archaeology and Geography

J. M. Wagstaff

The previous chapter described how close relations developed between archaeology and geography, especially in their early days. This chapter starts by looking more closely at the emergence of new thinking in the two disciplines during the 1960s and at the paradigms which resulted. These were similar in that widespread use was made of an hypothetico-deductive approach to enquiry and of statistical analysis. Whilst shared interests in such questions as environmental change and man–land relationships maintained a fruitful interdependence in some quarters, mainstream archaeology and geography drifted further apart in the late 1960s and early 1970s. Part of the explanation must lie in the rather different goals of the two disciplines, but the growing rift can also be attributed to the development of further specialist methodologies, as well as to the emergence of the greater degree of professionalism reflected in the proliferation of undergraduate courses and subject journals. Both disciplines passed through a phase of disillusionment during the late 1970s and early 1980s. The debates on philosophy, epistemology and methodology which have characterized it, though carried out in the virtual isolation of each discipline, have been strikingly similar. In fact, an intellectual convergence can be postulated. It arises fundamentally from the need to work from material evidence and from a shared outlook on the world which has been poor in social theory.

Origins of the New Geography and Archaeology

The new approaches to geographical and archaeological work, which were so striking during the 1960s, developed first in the United States. They were transplanted to fertile ground in Europe, Britain in particular, through widely read publications and personal contacts. The cultural and intellectual environment of the post-war era was conducive to their growth and further diffusion. A mood of optimism swept the Western world in the 1960s, allied to general economic expansion and rising standards of living. Higher education expanded and, with it, the extent of the teaching of archaeology and geography. As the number of practitioners increased, though, the old consensus maintained among small face-to-face groups of scholars began to breakdown and distinct research schools emerged around notable individuals. The trend emphasized the need for non-personal standards of assessing the validity of research (Johnston, 1979: 5–40; Plog, 1982). Science was held in great respect at the time; it had considerable theoretical achievements to its credit before the Second World War, whilst its practical contributions to the allied victory were enormous. Associated with an enthusiasm for science was a belief in the power of statistical analysis and linear modelling, attributable in past to the probabilistic nature of explanation assumed in some scientific fields.

The new geography emerged during the 1950s and 1960s within a consensus which believed that the subject was still fundamentally concerned with areal differentiation (Johnston, 1979: 41–111). It was, nonetheless, characterized by a belief in the certainty of spatial form and morphological laws (Johnston, 1973), as well as a methodology in which hypotheses were explicitly formulated and statistical analysis was *de rigueur*. Although there was a predisposition in favour of these developments because of the natural science orientation of the subject and – in Britain – the working association of physical and human geographers, the new approach emerged unconsciously from two trends which began earlier. The first was the growing importance of systematic studies. In both physical and human geography this led to an increasing interest in techniques of measurement and comparison. Physical geographers became more concerned with processes than human geographers (Embleton and Thornes, 1979), who were interested in the spatial associations of phenomena. The second trend was a mounting dissatisfaction with aspects of the current consensus. The regional tradition of descriptive synthesis and associational and loosely genetic narrative came in for particular attack. Not only did it lack the vigour developed in the more systematic branches of geography, but, despite the vogue for area studies and regional science in the early 1960s, it was also seen as increasingly irrelevant in a phase of overt decolonization and retreat from empire. At the same time, scholars were becoming aware of the sterility of the determinist–possiblist debate over the influence of physical conditions on human affairs and the non-progressive nature of historical geomorphology with its attempts to connect planation surfaces (Bird, 1983; Chorley, Beckinsale and Dunn, 1967–73). Both sides of the discipline came, in effect, to deny the significance of history and, without realizing it, moved close to reaffirming Mackinder's notion (1931) that geography was 'a physiological and anatomical study rather than a study in development'. The philosophical and theoretical underpinnings of all these developments was expounded by Harvey at the end of the late 1960s (Harvey, 1969).

Somewhat later than the geographers, archaeologists during the 1960s began to rethink what they were doing. Greater rigour was called for. Attempts were made to use hypothetico-deductive methods and statistical analysis. Meanwhile – paradoxically – something of an anti-historical bias developed as some scholars began to claim that synochronic analysis was prior to diachronic analysis (Rowlands 1982), which was seen, in any case, as speculative and incapable of proof.

The new thinking grew out of a long period of gestation, stretching back into the 1930s. It emerged from a growing sense of unease about the failure of the synthesizing efforts of the culture–history approach to the remote past which were narrowly based on a somewhat subjective study of artefacts. In any case, the sheer volume of data made the task even more daunting. Another worry was the weak quality of the theorizing about life-styles and society which usually concluded detailed archaeological reports but which were frequently only loosely connected with the data presented. More positive was the realization that the development of Carbon 14 dating in the 1950s removed the need to study artefacts purely for dating purposes. The lifting of this burden offered the opportunity for focusing upon the other types of information which could be extracted from the archaeological record. The potential of this approach raised the question of the most appropriate means for obtaining and exploiting new data (Binford, 1983: 95–7). This, and many of the related problems, were raised in a series of papers by Binford and his students in the 1960s (Dunnell, 1979).

As well as turning to works on statistical method and the philosophy of science to resolve their problems, some of the 'new' archaeologists borrowed extensively from the 'new' geography. In some aspects the development was simply a continuation of the shared tradition outlined by Goudie (1976 and this volume chapter 2), perhaps strengthened by an underlying sympathy with Childe's view that distributional analysis would help to minimize the subjectivity inherent in the classification of artefacts through its ability to generate seemingly coherent patterns (McNain, 1980; 69; Childe, 1951). This seems to be revealed in the importance attached by Clarke to locational analysis as a means of providing an understanding of the variation and interaction between apparently contemporaneous sites (Clarke, 1972a; Johnson, 1977). A related development was the emergence of site-catchment analysis out of a geographer's synthesis of research on rural settlement and land use (Chisholm, 1962), combined with the need to understand archaeological data in terms of the exploitation of territory and resources (Higgs and Vita-Finzi, 1970, 1972; Jarmon, 1972; Jarman et al., 1972). Closely related to site-catchment analysis was the general extension of an ecological approach to archaeological material (Goudie, 1976: 9), especially the increase in the recovery of faunal and floral remains as their potential importance was realised, and the improvement of recovery techniques (Butzer, 1965, 1982).

Disenchantment and Reappraisal

In retrospect, the early 1970s seem like a phase of relative tranquility and consolidation (Cooke and Robson, 1976). Many, if far from all, practising archaeologists and geographers accepted the new methods. Increasingly sophisticated techniques of analysis were devised and there was a movement from simple statistical work into mathematical modelling (Renfrew and Cook, 1979; Wilson and Kirby, 1975). The use of merely verbal description declined and there was a recognition of the importance of clearly formulated objectives and hypotheses, as well as the employment of rigorous methods of research.

At the same time two further developments were apparent. One was the atomization of the two disciplines into sub-disciplines occasioned by the explosion of information and the increase in specialization. Area and period concentration in archaeology was supplemented by the emergence of such fields as bio-archaeology and ethno-archaeology and the elaboration of specialisms in the study of, for example, lithics and ceramics. Geography was already divided in physical and human branches, but these ramified still further. Physical geography spawned various specialisms within the established fields of geomorphology, biogeography and climatology, whilst human geography became more and more sub-divided under such broad headings as economic, historical and social geography.

The second, and possibly related development shared by archaeology and geography was the neglect of central questions in the disciplines. In geography, the problems of recognizing and explaining regional differentiation were evaded (Fisher, 1977; Paterson, 1974), whilst the interplay of physical conditions and human activity became perhaps more of an intellectual embarassment than a challenge (Grossman, 1977; Olwig, 1980). Archaeology, for its part, tended to shy away from explaining socio-economic change and trying to understand, with a long diachronic perspective, what it means to be human (Piggott, 1959; Renfrew, 1980). This neglect was, perhaps, a latent cause of the stirrings of dissatisfaction which the two disciplines began to experience towards the end of the 1970s (Dunnell, 1979; 1980). This discontent, however, had three clear and immediate sources. The earliest was probably a growing awareness of various weaknesses in the use of statistical analysis. Some geographers, for example, began to realize in the early 1970s that the variables which they were trying to compare were not independent, as statistical theory requires. In fact, a degree of autocorrelation is inherent in the spatial quality of geographical data (Cliff and Ord, 1973). This raised the question of the validity of much of the early research in the new geography and the possible further use of simple parametric techniques. Similarly, archaeologists realized that the archaeological record represents not a random distribution, as required by much statistical theory, but a sample biased in uncertain ways by the hazards of preservation, discovery and study (Gifford, 1978). Again, the standing of conclusions derived from an improper application of statistical techniques was questioned. In both disciplines there was a growing awareness that statistical methods simply provide a way of describing masses of data in relatively precise ways and were not themselves any guide to the processes involved in creating patterns. Even then the tendency was to fit data into already-provided templates. Some scholars began to realize that the centrality of probability notions to statistical analysis was itself a barrier to the recovery of the very structures for which they were searching (Atkin, 1981; Gould, 1974).

The second source of discontent was a reappraisal of the hypothetico-decuctive method itself and the positivist outlook which allegedly lay behind its adoption. Whilst some scholars were uneasy about it all along (e.g. Spate, 1960), others simply came to question the appropriateness of natural science methods to disciplines which were increasingly thinking of themselves as social sciences (see below pp. 34–36). Still others were troubled by specific problems. Equifinality was one of these, that is, the generation of apparently similar observed forms by different processes operating along different trajectories through space–time (Harvey, 1967). Another difficulty was that of verifying models of locational behaviour. Although apparent in a number of ways, this arose fundamentally from the assumptions used in the models (e.g., the minimization of effort and the isomorphic quality of space), for they were either untestable or could not be fulfilled under real-world conditions (Webber, 1972; Johnson 1977). Related to this was the problem that hypotheses were frequently tested only within the context from which they arose, whether this was modern Western capitalist society in the case of geography (Brookfield, 1975) or specific cultures in geography (Renfrew, 1982a).

The third source of disquiet was similar. It was the appreciation, in general terms, that the patterns and probabilities revealed by the study of modern situations were not necessarily of diachronic validity, but historically specific. In the particular case of geography, spatial models were also criticized for dealing only with surface phenomena and for being detached from socio-economic theory (Gregory, 1982a). The gravity analogue for interaction and the rank–size rule in urban hierarchies would be cases in point.

Reaction and Further New Developments

Whilst many colleagues in both disciplines continued to work happily with the methods and outlook of the new geography and the new archaeology, as well as within more traditional paradigms, a sense of disquiet continued to grow. During the late 1970s and early 1980s it provoked a number of reactions; both fields witnessed a degree of introversion. A shared manifestation of this was the increased refinement of techniques, no doubt in the belief that better and more reliable data would improve problem-solving. In archaeology, methods of recovery and sampling were considerably improved (Cherry, Gamble and Shennan, 1978), whilst in physical geography better methods of measurement (often instrumented) were devised. Some branches of human geography became extremely adapt at mathematical modelling and numerical analysis. The use of the computer for sorting and analysing large data bases became commonplace and both disciplines were forced to make extensive use of systems analysis. Remote sensing, embracing satellite images and radar scanning (Lyons and Avery, 1977; Lyons and Hitchcock, 1977; Estes and Senger, 1974; Townshend, 1981), offered advances in data gathering, as well as renewed analysis on the *zusammenhang* of phenomena and the importance of a regional scale of resolution. There were subject-specific reactions too.

One of the most notable in archaeology was the reassertion and clarification of some of the trends of the new archaeology which, interestingly, in the present context, has been called *processual* archaeology (Flannery, 1967; Renfrew, 1983b). Binford, one of the founders of the new archaeology, declared in 1977 that the basic problem for the discipline was how to convert the observationally static facts of the archaeological record into statements about dynamic processes. He argued that the necessary clues are 'coded' into the structure of the site, for the material remains uncovered by archaeologists are not only patterned but are the product of patterned behaviour by the members of an extinct society (Binford, 1977; 1983). Accordingly, it is important to learn about the factors which condition how people choose a location, lay it out for their purposes, exploit and maintain it, as well as how one particular site relates to others (Binford, 1983: 145–6). Also important is the need to understand how the archaeological record itself was formed, since the direct products of human behaviour have been transformed by the processes of deposition, decay, erosion and transportation. This overall approach to archaeology differs from an approach which aims at the reconstruction of the archaeological record in behavioural terms and then at explaining the reconstruction. Binford believes that this second approach is seriously flawed in that explanation has no existence independent of the reconstruction. It therefore tends to produce both abstraction and circular argument (Binford, 1981).

Other reactions to the processual approach to archaeology include what Butzer has called 'contextual archaeology' (Butzer, 1978 and 1982; Schoenwetter, 1981) and what is known as 'cognitive archaeology' (Kehoe and Kehoe, 1973; Renfrew, 1982). The scope of contextual archaeology has been outlined in the previous chapter (see pp. 24–25). Here is it sufficient to point out that its main proponent hopes that the approach 'will transcend the traditional preoccupation with artefacts and with sites in isolation, to arrive at a realistic appreciation of the environmental matrix and its potential spatial, economic, and social interactions with the subsistence–settlement system' (Butzer, 1982: 12). Cognitive archaeology is interested in reading the social, intellectual and mental attitudes of past people from the artefacts which they left behind and stresses the importance of ritual and the sacred in the functioning of the cultural system (Flannery, 1982; Renfrew 1983c). Some of the processual archaeologists, however, have doubted whether the material evidence is sufficient to make such attempts worthwhile (Binford, 1977, 1983).

In geography, criticism of the new outlook and approaches was probably most acute in historical geography, a late, sceptical and less than whole-hearted convert (Baker, 1977, 1978, 1979; Baker et al., 1970). In the discipline as a whole, though, four somewhat related reactions can be detected (Johnston, 1979). Perhaps the earliest to emerge was a behavioural viewpoint (Cooke and Robson, 1976; Doornkamp and Warren, 1980). It developed out of the feeling that individuals had been left out by the new geography's 'geometric determinism' (Gregory, 1981a, 1982a), but its formulation was assisted by the increasing awareness amongst geographers of Simon's notions of satisfying behaviour and bounded rationality (1957) which contrasted with the ideas of 'economic man' adopted earlier. The approach concentrates on the 'cognitive understanding which man has of his environment and the way in which this knowledge is stored and organised in the mind' (Green and Haselgrove, 1978). Its devotees argue that spatial behaviour is a function of the image and the image is man's link with his environment (Downs, 1970; Gold, 1980); a concept drawing upon psychological theory.

Related to behavioural geography, is the second reaction to the spatial science and positivist view of the subject. This is humanistic geography (Ley and Samuels, 1978; Ley, 1982). It reasserts the creative dimension of human personality which was repressed in the new geography of the 1960s and, to some extent, resurrects the synthesizing traditions of geographical writing, whilst re-emphasizing the importance of unique events. Although inspiration was drawn from the rediscovery of the work of Paul Vidal de la Blache, who saw man as at the same time both a part of creation and its most active collaborator (Buttimer, 1971; Gregory, 1981a), the roots of humanistic geography probably lie in the renaissance ideals of man, so deeply embedded in the western liberal tradition and preserved by workers in the backward field of cultural geography.

Historical geography was similarly considered a reactionary and unprogressive field during the 1960s by some colleagues (Andrews, 1980; Baker et al., 1969; Bowden, 1970; Koelsch, 1970) but, as well as changing its character to a degree in response to outside criticism and influences, it could not help but preserve a sense of the past. During the late 1970s historical geographers assisted in spreading an awareness of the importance of the historical dimension in understanding present patterns and, through their epistemological debates, revealed the problems involved in recovering the past from the fragmentary surviving evidence (Baker, 1977, 1978, 1979; Doornkamp and Warren, 1980; Norton, 1984).

A final reaction to the spatial-science approach to geography, with its abstract and depersonalized analysis, was the reassertion of 'relevance'. This was embodied in the form of concern for the disadvantaged in society, whether the unemployed in British inner cities or the poor farmers of the Third World. It also involved a growing interest in improving the ways in which resources were evaluated and managed, as well as in the amelioration of risk from physical hazards (Chorley, 1978; Doornkamp and Warren, 1980; Munton and Goudie, 1984). It was marked by a convergence between some aspects of physical and human geography.

Convergence

The firing of intellectual salvoes by intellectual battle groups within the two disciplines has generated a lot of noise, created much smoke and produced some remarkable flashes of light. Occasionally, real inter-change has taken place. However, the inevitable friction of warface and the relative isolation of the main squadrons of the two disciplines have disguised the fact that archaeology and geography are engaged in a similar struggle for understanding. It is exposed by the practical convergence which has taken place within the ambit of contextual archaeology and what might be called historical sedimentology (Bintliff, 1981; Vita-Finzi 1969a; Allchin, Goudie and Hegde 1978; Wagstaff, 1981). The increased attention being given by geography to historical development can only increase it. However, the origins of the intellectual convergence of the two subjects are deeper than a need to borrow expertise from another discipline. They lie in several shared and very basic characteristics which have manifested themselves in recent debates.

Archaeology and human geography have traditionally started from human artefacts, *sesno lato*. Despite some recent trends, they have continued to work with what Renfrew has called 'operational, rather than cognised data – with things as they appear to be to an outsider, rather than as they are to an insider' (Renfrew, 1981; Olsson, 1980: 47e). In archaeology, as in historical geography – and in one sense, geomorphology too – the data are the surviving fragments of a completed record (Heimfrid, 1972), whether these are debris, ruins, account rolls or discontinuous lengths of fluvial terrace. In the mainstream of human geography, research has often started with the man-made elements in the landscape – towns, villages, factories and patterns of rural land use. Strictly speaking, neither discipline observes social facts (dyamics and social interactions), but material facts, and it is from these that inferences are drawn (Binford, 1983: 21). To that extent, archaeology and geography may be better off than the social sciences which are more obviously recognized as such, focusing as they do on the 'unmediated evidence' of buildings, monuments and the structure of the landscape (Mills, 1982). Nevertheless, after the 'revolutions' in both subjects most archaeologists and geographers would now recognize that the description of data and their interpretation are interdependent (Hodder, 1984; Proudfoot, 1981). The two disciplines, in fact, share the problems of how to move not from observable facts, as such, but from the empirical findings to an evaluation of the starting idea (Binford, 1977). In other words, they share, with other academic disciplines, the need to participate in 'a dialogue between concept and evidence, a dialogue conducted by successive hypotheses, on the one hand, and empirical research on the other' (Thompson, 1978: 231). It is also a dialogue which demands from its participants a better understanding of their own interactions with the material world (Binford, 1983: 20), though, as Gregory pointed out, the materiality of social life is weakly developed in the whole of modern humanism (Gregory, 1981a).

From their earliest days both disciplines have shared a natural-science approach to analysis. This is attributable, in part, to the background of some of the early archaeologists and geographers, as well as to the relatively late contact of the disciplines with the other social sciences. However the approach is also due to the robust nature of scientific method and its manifest success in certain fields of enquiry, notably physics. Critics of positivism often take too rigid a view of scientific method and neglect the scientists' constant striving to give meaning to observation and to evaluate how useful these assigned meanings actually are in practice (Binford, 1968; Gregory, 1981a). Admittedly, a tendency developed amongst the followers of the hypothetico-deductive method which seemed to indicate that meaning would automatically be produced by applying the 'correct' method. Such naïvity led to a wholesale ransacking of philosophies of science in search of the 'secret' which gives dependable explanations.

Another characteristic which archaeology and geography have shared is a lack of indigenous social theory, which might conceivably transcend the reliance upon analogues from the natural sciences (Green and Haselgrove, 1978). It was this poverty, as well as an increasing identification with the social sciences, which drove some archaeologists and geographers, somewhat belatedly perhaps, towards Marxism and structuralism. In flirting with Marxism (Quaini, 1982; Spriggs, 1984) both sets of scholars have subscribed, in effect, to the notion that 'modes of production write history in time, social formations write it in space' (Santos, 1977). It may be suggested, though, that a powerful influence attracting them to Marxist forms of explanation has been the material nature of their data. The ideas of historical materialism thus appear helpful to the two disciplines at a fundamental level. Unfortunately, archaeology and geography have followed other disciplines in the inclination of their practitioners to believe that merely manipulating their own propositions to fit a Marxist template somehow provides verification for these ideas, a development which Engels himself deplored as indicative of intellectual laziness (letter to Conrad Schmidt, quoted in Thompson, 1978: 259).

Structuralism has been just as attractive as Marxism in some quarters, but with less rationale in the traditions of the two disciplines. In essence, structuralism is the belief that underlying the surface patterns which are readily observed and described there is a deeper reality – in the present context, socio-economic dynamics of a sort. Currents in this subterranean magma produce the surface patterns. The underlying forces are often not seen, but their configuration, it is suggested, can be inferred from surface clues (Gregory, 1976, 1978b; Gellner, 1982; Kurzweil, 1980). Whilst some have seen structuralism as 'the illusion of this epoch' (Thompson, 1978: 263) and it has been virtually dead in its homeland of France for more than a decade (Kurzwell, 1980: 9–10; New Society, 55, 1981), the basic ideas and vocabulary retain a certain appeal.

In a different vein to the interest in Marxism and structuralism has been the shared inclination to reject the notions of 'uniformitarianism' which have dominated the two disciplines since at least the nineteenth century (Green and Haselgrove, 1978). On the one hand, there is now the realization – perhaps acquired from Marxism – that all human activity takes place in historically and geographically specific contexts which have direct bearing on particular events. On the other hand, questions are being formulated, somewhat belatedly, about the assumption that the ranges of hominoid behaviour (including the structuring of space), artefact variability and areal differentiation over two million years are no greater than those recorded in the tiny sample of recent histories, ethnographies and geographies (Clarke, 1972a). It is now possible to conceive that human nature may have evolved over such a long period of time. Childe's idea that the historical process itself may have been subject to diachronic change (1945, 1949) is worth reconsideration. Meanwhile, physical geographers are beginning to question whether physical processes can always have operated in exactly the same way when the contextual conditions in particular localities were very different from those prevailing today and human interference was minimal (pp. 18–20).

In their struggle for meaning, both archaeology and geography may be at a crossroads where they need to pause and consider how they can develop their own theory and evaluate it, using material or artefactual evidence. The problems they face have been exacerbated by the confusion of tongues arising from the attempts, on the one hand, to justify the continued use of the hypothetico-deductive approach of the natural sciences and, on the other hand, to appropriate explanatory theory from the social sciences. Whilst the epistemological literature has proliferated, it has created only a smokescreen of rhetoric through which the true goals of the disciplines are but dimly discerned. Uncertainty abounds since the advocates of this or that view of the particular discipline have failed to demonstrate its inherent superiority, except in very specific and localized contexts. Methodological plurality may be part of the way forward, as particular methods are applied to specific problems. On the larger scale, though, a reconsideration is due of the role of statistics as the descriptive language of the new archaeology and geography. Whilst mathematics is the only precise and logical language yet developed by man, more radical thought is needed about its application to archaeological and geographical problems. The world is multi-faceted and multi-dimensional, rather than two-dimensional or linear. Patterns are both conditions and consequences, real and perceived. Therefore, topology offers a better way of seeking understanding than purely statistical methods, with Q-analysis and catastrophe-theory also candidates for consideration. But if there are to be any real advances in both archaeology and geography more effort must be given to the development of indigenous theory. Recognition of the common characteristics of the two subjects can only be beneficial in bringing about its development.

4 The Palaeo-ecology of Erosion

J. B. Thornes

Introduction

Hillslope erosion, the main concern of this chapter, has been an area of continuing mutual interest and co-operation between archaeologists, geographers and geologists for at least 50 years. This is primarily because it is a crucial link between erosion and sedimentation in alluvial and colluvial environments, on the one hand, and anthropogenic and climatic change, on the other. It therefore appears to provide a ready means of transforming one into the other from either direction. The actual difficulties in these operations are well documented (e.g. Davidson, 1980). Secondly, where erosion and the related deposition was synchronous and widespread it appears to provide a useful stratigraphic tool for the crude determination of the ages of sites and sediments. Thirdly, it is generally believed that soil erosion both responded to and constrained prehistoric, as well as contemporary, agriculture. Therefore it was, and still is, important in the farming economy. This is true both of direct loss of productivity in the form of eroded nutrients and the indirect loss of land through sheetwash and gullying. Finally, the archaeological evidence provides the geomorphologist with a deeper perspective into soil erosion problems, as they exist today, in terms of spatial and temporal variability of rates of erosion and in terms of fundamental controls.

The broad causal chain for these relationships is shown in figure 1a. Archaeologists and geomorphologists have largely been involved in inferring the inputs, whilst knowing the outputs. Agriculturalists and civil engineers, conversely, attempt to estimate the outputs knowing the inputs. The former tend to adopt a functionalist, qualitative set of arguments and the latter a statistical, instrumental approach. Given the uncertainty as to the relevant inputs and the apparently infinite set of possible outputs, neither approach is likely to provide a definitive breakthrough. In particular, in light of the temporal and spatial

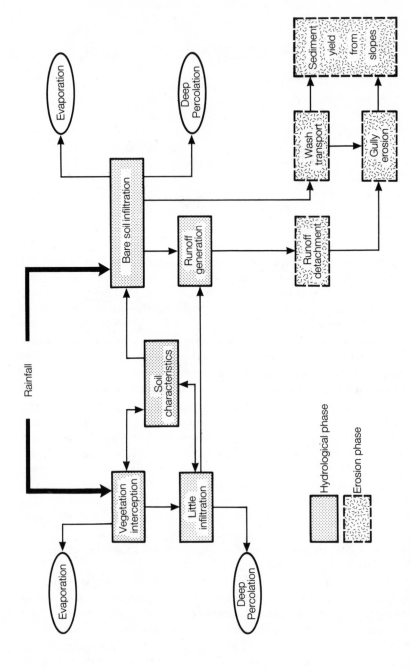

Figure 1a Principal controls of erosion

complexity of erosional and depositional responses in fluvially dominated environments – identified, exemplified and clarified in the works of Schumm (e.g., 1979) – the prospect for inductive and inferential geoarchaeology seems very poor. Furthermore, detailed decomposition of the erosional system (figure 4.1b) reveals a significantly higher level of complexity arising not so much from the increased complexities of the variable web involved as from the implicit non-linearities suggested by the feedback links identified in the diagram. Since 1945 there has been great progress in many of the areas identified in this diagram. The generation of runoff in relation to soil properties is one; the relative role of splash and wash in entrainment is another; and the nature of colluvial processes a third. Much of this progress is summarized, synthesized and carried further in *Soil Erosion* (Kirkby and Morgan, 1980) and need not be repeated here. Rather the purpose of this chapter is to discuss and develop a better understanding of the role of vegetation in the erosional system which, despite some notable exceptions, has been seriously neglected. Not only do archaeologists and geographers stand to benefit greatly from real progress in this area, they are also well disposed to contribute significantly to it, and some already have.

In this chapter I shall be mainly concerned with the reflexive relationship between man and soil erosion as it operates through the vegetative cover. Mechanical and chemical treatment of bare soil through ploughing, tractor-wheeling, fertilizer application, land

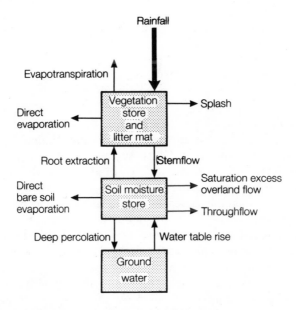

Figure 1b   Detailed decomposition of segment of figure 1a

drainage and even the passage of animals over the bare soil all have important effects on the soil's physical, chemical and hydrological properties, many of which are well documented. Likewise, the effects of artificial crops ranging from trees to pumpkins have all commanded interest. Ironically, however, the effects of natural, modified or regenerating vegetation cover on soil erosion have received a good deal less research, though there has been no lack of speculation. Since these are the major interest of geomorphologists and archaeologists and since they afford a long term perspective on soil erosion which is lacking in crop-oriented studies, they deserve greater attention.

Most arguments concerning historical soil erosion and the (sometimes) resulting sedimentation revolve around the relative roles of man and climate. Moreover, in contextual archaeology the need to establish environmental conditions demands an understanding of the site specific and regional state of the vegetation cover. Three sets of loosely defined causal links are usually implicitly assumed which are here made explicit and form the core of the discussion. They are: (1) more vegetation means less soil erosion; (2) vegetation is controlled by climate in the absence of man; therefore, soil erosion is also controlled by climate under these conditions; and (3) man may reduce, increase or conserve the vegetation and, therefore, influence or control the amount of erosion.

These relations are expressed in their crudest possible form, though it would be easy to cite recent papers in which the level of argument proceeds little beyond what is stated here. There appear to be three important conditions attaching to the development of more precise relationships. First, the level of precision must match the spatial and temporal resolution dictated by the research objectives. On the regional scale, for example, the second proposition may be appropriate, whereas on the site or site-catchment level the effects of climate will be mediated through edaphic control. This idea is well grounded in geomorphology through the elegant paper of Schumm and Lichty (1965) on time, space and causality in geomorphology. Second, the level of precision must be realistically related to the capacity to apply the relationships usefully to the problem at hand, or at least be capable of resolution at several different levels of data availability. In other words, there must be flexibility in the data demand, as well as the spatial and temporal resolution. For example, actual evapotranspiration may be approximated by rough and ready balance models or from species-dependent empirical models or even direct observations. Third, the relationships must be ultimately expressed in such a way as to accommodate the inherent variability of the parameters involved at the temporal and spatial resolution adopted. The trade-off between precision and applicability can only be decided by the problem at hand. In this chapter, then, the discussion will inevitably be conditioned by the author's interest and experience at the catchment scale in semi-arid, especially Mediterranean, environments.

Vegetation and Erosion

In anticipation of a discussion of causal relations between vegetation and erosion, it is worth considering what is meant by 'vegetation'. In the context of soil erosion, it is usually taken to mean the percentage of the surface covered by vegetation when viewed from vertically above. This is not necessarily the compliment of bare area. The measure itself is scale-dependent. As the size of measuring quadrat is increased, the cover value usually stabilizes. It is relatively easily measured in the field, from aerial photographs and from high resolution satellite images. It varies seasonally in seasonally dominated climatic regimes, may show a strong variation through the growth of annuals and may be evolving through time. Its suitability as a measure of vegetation in the context of erosion depends on   (1) its correlation with erosion and deposition at the required scale of resolution; (2) its correlation with other vegetation characteristics which are important in erosion and depo-sitional processes; and   (3) the ease with which it can be estimated from past climatic, palynological or other data. The first two are addressed in the remainder of this section, the third in the next section.

Erosion is ground loss and may be expressed in terms of the average rate of ground lowering (mm yr^{-1}) or sediment yield (kg m^{-2} yr^{-1}). The latter is preferred because it specifically recognizes that lowering is by chemical, as well as physical mechanisms. Chemical removal, though rarely considered in archaeological work, is very important because of the associated loss of nutrients and productivity which follows. Loss of productivity also occurs, of course, from particulate erosion.

That vegetation controls soil erosion is well established, but poorly understood. Hudson (1957) published the results of nine years of experiments in which some plots were covered with mosquito nets and some left bare. On the unprotected plots soil loss was 127 t ha^{-1} yr^{-1} against a value of 1 t ha^{-1} yr^{-1} for the protected plots. Moreover, a plot with full grass cover gave results similar to the mosquito-net plots, suggesting that it is cover, rather than any other plant property, which is responsible for inhibiting erosion. A later experiment by Elwell and Stocking (1976) confirms the role of vegetation cover, at least in relation to extreme events. They cumulated rainfall amounts in the most intense storms and plotted this against soil loss, as shown in figure 2a. This indicates that down to about 70 per cent cover the effect of cover is far less significant than below that level, beyond which soil loss increases dramatically. This important result is now taken to be the general case.

The effects of cover are assumed to be two-fold. It reduces rainfall

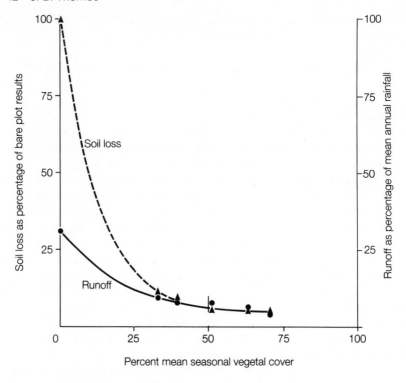

Figure 2   Relationship between soil loss (as a percentage of bare soil values) and runoff, and seasonal plant cover
(based on Elwell and Stocking, 1974)

energy (Elwell, 1981) and reduces runoff by intercepting rainfall, hence increasing the evaporative losses. The first influences soil splash, the second entrainment and transport by wash. Both of these processes have been the subject of intensive research and for the second subject there is a large literature. Not all the results are as intuition might predict, however. Experiments by Moseley (1982), for example, showed that for natural beech forest in New Zealand the kinetic energy of throughfall was actually about 1.5 times that of rainfall in the open during a typical rain event and that splash erosion from falling drops was actually 3.1 times that in the open. Likewise Noble and Morgan (1983) dealing with the single-row crop plant Brussels sprout show that whereas such low plants reduced the kinetic energy reaching the ground, the rate of particle detachment was not reduced. The effects of cover on the energy regime and splash pattern are dependent on height, density and age of crop; however, since cover is related to these it will probably provide a suitable proxy for them. Perhaps more important is the fact that even if canopy covers are generating more rather than less energy, their relevance may be reduced by secondary layers (Brandt, personal communication) or by the litter layer at the forest floor (Wiersum, 1983).

The availability of water at ground level is determined by interception, evaporation and shading effects, which control evaporation losses from beneath the canopy. The first two significantly decrease available moisture for plant growth. For example, at San Dimas, California, for small storms, 50–75 per cent of the gross rainfall was lost, whereas for large storms as little as 3–6 per cent was lost. Of the gross annual rainfall, 43–99mm was lost, depending on the yearly amount. Plant cover in semi-arid lands also tends, through evaporation, to reduce runoff to channels, as shown by the American south-west. The results of observations on Californian watersheds (e.g. Turner, 1985) show that there is a significant difference between forest, shrub and grasslands in the extent of water recovery, illustrating that composition, as well as cover, is important. This is equally true of temperate areas (Gurnell and Gregory, 1985) and, obviously, is important in terms of the impact of human activity which leads to selective cover composition.

At ground level the dominant effects are an increase in surface roughness as a result of stems projecting into the flow and dead plant litter, and the indirect effects of litter on overland flow and infiltration. The former has been studied both theoretically and empirically (as summarized in Thornes 1979); the latter is only poorly understood. Dortignac and Love (1960) showed that variability in infiltration rates was explained (statistically speaking) by the variation in dead surface matter, and our own results in semi-arid Spain confirm this (Lopez-Bermudez et al., 1985). There is often a very indistinct line between litter and soil organic matter, though, whereas the former is highly variable throughout the year in climates ranging from the humid tropics to the deserts, the latter tends to be relatively stable. In studies of infiltration on rangeland soils Tromble, Renard and Thatcher (1974) found that litter was higher under brush, which had a higher crown cover, than under grass and that infiltration rates were correspondingly higher. Although it is widely surmised that roots are important in 'binding the soil together', this effect is poorly understood, if indeed it is important at all. The most likely effect of roots is to increase the organic matter content and the permeability through root death, hence reducing overland flow, on the one hand, and determining the pattern of spatial moisture competition below ground and at the surface, on the other.

Although still imperfectly understood, percentage cover, stem density, surface litter and soil organic matter content are probably the most relevant simple vegetation parameters controlling soil erosion. Unfortunately, even these simple parameters are difficult to model for past natural and man-affected environments. Consequently, it may be more profitable to concentrate efforts on biomass and net primary productivity which are more or less linearly related in forest and woodland for climax and near-climax samples (Whittaker and Marks, 1975). Net production is the amount of organic matter synthesized and accumulated in plant tissue per unit time and is equal to the gross production minus respiration usage. The net production includes growth plus leaves, fruits, flowers and bud scales, branches and roots which are lost to the litter in the course of the year. The sum of net production by all individual plants in a unit area of the surface is net primary productivity. Figure 3a, modified from Whittaker and Marks (1975), shows that for immature (non-climax) vegetation biomass productivity is high. As a stable biomass is reached. the rate of production per unit mass of dry matter becomes steady. The leaf area index (LAI; leaf area/unit ground surface) also correlates roughly with productivity, though in a parabolic fashion. Whittaker and Niering (1974) suggest a two-slope curve with a lower slope (desert and semi-arid communities) of $1m^2/m^{-2}$ for each $190gm/m^{-2}$ yr^{-1} and a less steep slope (about $1m^2m^{-2}$ for 50 $gr/m^2/y$) above a productivity of about 400 $gr/m^2/yr$.

The relationship of litter mass to biomass is more complex because it

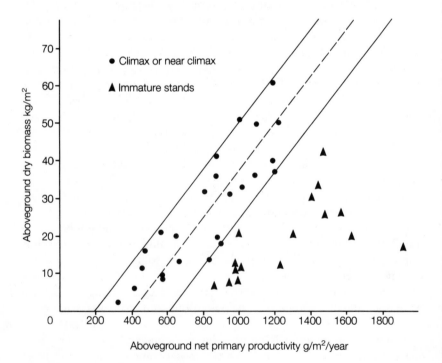

Figure 3a   Productivity–biomass relationship
(modified from Whittaker and Marks, 1975)

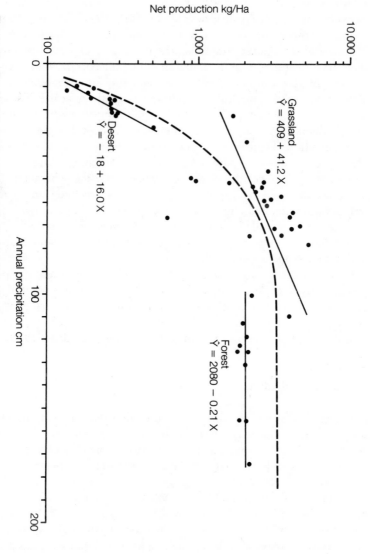

Figure 3b Productivity and evapotranspiration relationships
(based on Lundholm, 1976 after Wagner, 1976)

is determined by the input of dead debris in a manner controlled mainly by the phenology of the plants and by anything that removes dead matter from the plants, such as heavy rain (Rapp and Lossant, 1981) and brousing animals. The mass of above-ground litter often shows marked variations over short distances. Our work on litter–plant cover relations (Francis et al., 1985), reveals a relatively poor correlation between the two in Spanish degraded matorral and the same results are found for other environments (Healey and Swift, 1971).

Soil organic matter amounts are more stable, both spatially and temporarily, and even in degraded matorral the correlation between soil organic matter content, plant cover and moisture content are highly significant at the meso-scale (i.e., archaeological-site scale). The organic matter content is determined by the equilibrium between the inputs of the products of plant litter decomposition and output due to its own decomposition. Typical breakdown rates in tropical forest are 4–5 times greater than in temperate lands through leaching, catabolism and comminution. Since these are controlled by the character of the materials, as well as the leaching (moisture related) and catabolic (temperature related) processes, the rates of breakdown are less climatically controlled than cover or biomass productivity, though Meentmayer (1976) found a linear relation between organic matter loss and actual evapotranspiration.

Despite all these shortcomings, cover, biomass, litter and net primary productivity are clearly interrelated, making net primary productivity and biomass suitable first approximations to vegetation control of soil erosion, and some authors have already used biomass as a variable for representing vegetational resistance to erosion (e.g. Graf, 1979).

Vegetation and Climate

The archaeologist is faced with the dilemma that virtually nowhere in the world can the vegetation be described as natural. Therefore, in considering man's impact on the vegetation some effort has to be made to reconstruct it. In the past, interest has focused on the composition of the vegetation. This is of significance from the point of view of the types of resource material available, the type of shelter provided for man and his prey, because of the sensitivity of certain species to environmental conditions. In all these respects palynology has, on the whole, served both the geographer and the archaeologist well. Equally, it has provided an important vehicle for examining large-scale and large-magnitude shifts in vegetation cover, especially in Quaternary times. In the context of soil erosion it provides a qualitative indication of the time-varying plant cover. A link is needed between composition, in the general sense, and the characteristics which are relevant to erosion. To a first approximation, biomass and net productivity provide this link by virtue of the fact that different plant associations have different, though heavily overlapping, ranges of NPP and biomass. Typical variations of biomass and NPP for the main vegetation types are shown in Table 1, extended from Whittaker and Niering (1975). These data indicate the best approximations that could be made knowing the general cover type. Although there are large variations within each cover type, the differences between the cover types are fairly consistent over a wide range of literature.

Table 1   Typical variations of biomass and net primary productivity

Land-type	Net productivity $g\,m^{-2}\,yr$		Biomass $[(t/ha)]$
	Above ground	Total	
Forest	600–1200	700–1500	200–500
Woodland	150–600	250–600	20–200
Semi-desert	<150	250	4–13
Dry grassland	–	90–170	–
Desert	–	130	2–6

Source: extended from Whittaker and Niering, 1975

Beyond this, where the pollen evidence provides absolute information about types, the assessment of productivity and biomass has to rest on relations established between them and soil moisture (at best) or simple climatic parameters (at worst) for existing cover types. Ultimately, at the site and site-catchment scale, variations will relate to edaphic (especially soil moisture and nutrient) controls, whereas at the regional scale, climatic parameters may suffice. It has to be assumed that in establishing and utilizing these relationships the vegetation character-istics are in some kind of equilibrium with the governing climatic controls. This may imply that they are using water or nutrients or some other resources at an optimum (usually most efficient) level. They are, thus, the outcome of an ecosystem succession in the Odum-Margalef, rather than the Clementsian sense (see the discussion by Macintosh, 1980). In practice, this is difficult to demonstrate and, under some conditions, may be rather doubtful. Nonetheless, it seems to be the best available assumption with the present state of confusion in the succession debate and certainly enables progress beyond the current approaches to palaeo-environmental analysis. Table 2 gives a set of equations relating primary productivity to climatic variables and these do show a reasonable degree of convergence. They indicate that, for dry areas, net primary productivity increases by about $2g\,m^{-2}\,yr^{-1}$ for each millimetre of rainfall and in intermediate grassland about $4g\,m^{-2}\,yr^{-1}$. The latter is close to the figure given by Le Houerou (1981) for

Table 2   Published equations relating primary productivity to actual evapotranspiration (AE, mm yr^{-1}) and precipitation (mm yr^{-1})

Source	Equation
Rosenzweig (1968)	1.66 log AE$-$1.66
Leith and Box (1972)	3000/(1+exp1.315+0.119P)
Leith (1975)	3000/(1$-$exp$-$0.009(AE$-$20))
Walther (1939)	2P
Wagner (1976)	
Desert	1.6P$-$18
Grassland	409+4.12P
Forest	2080$-$0.021P

Mediterranean matorral. There are many limitations to these equations. Each is subject to large errors of estimation, which tend not to be reported in the literature, and some are developed for relatively small ranges of climate and vegetation. Moreover their application in palaeo-environmental studies still requires estimates of past rainfall, or evapotranspiration, or both. They do, however, give us a firmer basis for estimating the likely effects of a change in precipitation on the NPP and biomass, and from these to come closer to the effects of changes on erosion. Such relations implicitly underlie many qualitative and quantitative models of climate and vegetation interactions, such as the well-known Fournier (1961) and Schumm (1965) approaches. By making them explicit, the way is open to considering non-climatic controls as well.

Much more complicated models have been developed for predicting the impact of soil moisture and its related input–output variables on vegetation cover. Most of these (e.g. Specht, 1972; Eagleson, 1978; Floret et al., 1982) are very demanding of parameters and driving variables. As yet palaeoclimatic data are too poor in either quality or quantity to justify attempts to apply these models to studying past changes, and less demanding but physically realistic models based on reasonable assumptions about very basic variables are to be preferred. A feature of recent models is the recognition that seasonality and extreme events are very important. If extreme events occur at times of minimal seasonal vegetation cover, their impact, past and present, is likely to be much more severe. Even in the equations in Table 2, it is recognized by Wagner, Walther and in the data presented by Whittaker and Niering that the dry end of the scale has different productivity relationships (figure 3b), that attunement of vegetation to rainfall is more complex and that the simple 'equilibrium' assumption for vegetation evolution is not adequate (see Zedler, 1982). This is very important for palaeo-environmental impact studies because   (1) the vegetation is here much more sensitive to human activity; and   (2) the smaller seasonal or annual percentage cover means that erosion is more sensitive to litter and soil organic matter variations. Even here, edaphic factors, such as high permeabilities or limiting nutrients, may be very important, especially at the local scale. At the site level topographic controls may be most critical in determining the plant cover. Sorting out the local from the regional components of variation is difficult, even for the period pre-dating human impact, because vegetation and litter exist as a spatial patchwork which is matched by a similar diversity in susceptibility to erosion. Change may be expected to appear in patches as environmental stress increases, and the location of these patches may well determine the pattern of erosional evolution.

Although we have emphasized hillslope reactions, the channels themselves influence and are influenced by vegetation through their effects on soil moisture on the one hand and sediment production on the other. Bull (1979) illustrated the impact of incision in promoting the further growth of gullies by lowering the soil erosion around gully heads and therefore reducing the productivity and the fitness of the vegetation to survive and resist erosion. In wetlands, by contrast, although the propensity to develop saturated overland flow is much greater and hence floodplain discharges relatively higher, the much higher biomass and productivity, coupled with very high litter amounts, means that erosion is much less likely than on adjacent hillslopes.

Vegetation and Man

Given that soil erosion is controlled dominantly by the vegetation cover, significant shifts in the cover, biomass litter amounts and stem density may be expected to invoke changes in hillslope runoff, erosion and sedimentation. The nature and effectiveness of these changes depend on their spatial location, density and timing, so the results are likely to be complex rather than simple. Spatial location is important because it affects the delivery ratio (the percentage of sediment 'escaping' from a catchment) through the nature of possible intervening stores. Density is important because the intensity of change in physical properties is likely to be non-linear with respect to density because of thresholds. The response to two extra sheep in a herd may be quite different for a herd of 20 than for a herd of 200. Timing is important in the sense that a steady state can neither be reached nor maintained if the relaxation time of the system is longer than the mean recurrence time of the disturbances to it.

This last point is well illustrated in the case of fire. Typically, recovery from fire in Mediterranean lands requires about 35 years, after which normal levels of biomass, litter and soil organic matter may be achieved. The probability of fire will continue to increase as dead matter accumulates until ultimately the vegetation is fired again. If fires increase in frequency, for example through purposeful burning for agriculture, there is a progressive degradation of the cover to low cover density pyrophytes such as *Cistus*. This sequence is thought to produce the *tomillares* of Mediterranean Spain composed of species such as *Genista, Cistus* and *Thymus* with covers typically of 60–70 per cent (figure 4).

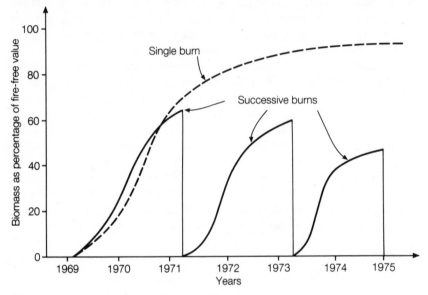

Figure 4   Typical Mediterranean fire-recovery cycle

The huge literature on man's impact on vegetation in the Mediterranean alone would require several volumes for review, but three elements can be highlighted in relation to the theme of this chapter – impact, recovery and modelling. A large number of empirical observations directly and indirectly relate erosion to human impact on the vegetation cover. These mainly come from catchment experiments, usually from catchments ranging from a few square kilometres to a few hundred square kilometres in size. A good example is the study by Hibbert, Davis and Scholl (1974) of chaparral conversion. In this investigation, in Arizona, three catchments had their shrub covers virtually obliterated by chemical and mechanical treatment and burning in order to increase runoff by reduction of evapotranspiration. Taken together, the results showed as increase in runoff and sediment output. The total sediment yield in the first three years was 25 times higher than in the preceding 13 years, partially as a result of the increased soil water repellency after burning. Two particular results bear further reflection. The first is that only by great effort was it possible to keep the catchment clear of vegetation. As thinning of bushes progresses, the remaining plants obtained more water and could grow. This means that unless over 50 per cent of the shrubs are removed, there is no change in runoff. Secondly, in the catchment allowed to recover naturally, water and sediment yield had reverted to normal after only three years. This example illustrates that work is required to maintain an area in a vegetation-free condition, even at the semi-arid margin (c. 600mm yr^{-1} rainfall). The same is true in the tropics but to a much greater degree, despite the infertility of the soils.

The second set of studies is concerned with the actual pathway and rate of recovery after change. The initial capacity for regeneration of biomass is assumed in most palaeo-environmental studies to be more or less negligible. The literature has tended to emphasize secondary succession towards a new climax, accompanied by higher sediment yield. Neither need be the case. In fire, in grazing and in light ploughing the main effect is often a temporary reduction in biomass. Conversely, where there is a progressive change of cover without a major reduction in biomass, catastrophic erosion may not occur. Zedler's (1982) investigation of post-fire changes in Californian chaparral schrub indicates that there fire results in a small mortality and a large reduction in biomass. The effect of fire was to re-establish the cover at higher densities than before the fire. There was also a clear spatial bias in the recovery pattern induced by soil moisture gradients.

The third group of topics relates to modelling human impact in 'total ecosystem' studies, such as those carried out in the International Biological Programme (Goodall and Perry, 1981). These studies seek to evaluate the effects of future management strategies, such as differential stocking rates, alternate versus continuous grazing, differential rainfall or natural changes, as in rainfall variations. To the extent that they are successful, they are of direct interest to palaeo-environmental reconstruction. An example is the work of Wilkin and Norton (1974). This model attempts to predict the course of the foragable biomass of different dry rangeland species. Again, it is assumed that without stocking each plant species will be at equilibrium, the different species jointly constituting the climax vegetation for the site. The productivity of each species is adjusted to average annual grazing and temperature, and grazing utilization is based on the herbivore population present, so that the total amount used is proportional to the length of the grazing season. This is distributed among different forage types. Similar models have been obtained for sheep grazing, again involving production–consumption functions for each of the major species present (Seligman, Tadmor, Noy-Meir and Dovrat, 1971). Although these models are relatively untried and over-complex for the type of data available to prehistorians, they are of direct relevance to the prehistoric grazing problem. Further discussion of some of the typical models for arid and semi-arid grazing situations is given in Goodall (1982).

At the site-catchment scale the patterns of spatial utilization are again very significant in determining the incidence of erosion. Point-centred grazing, usually water based, has quite different effects to extensive or nomadic patterns. The herding pattern described by Baskin for mixed goat and sheep herds (figure 5, Baskin, 1974) is similar to that found in eastern Andalucia, for example. These circuits are dominantly controlled by the pattern of land holdings and, unlike the *mesta* regime elsewhere in Spain, are largely confined to the poorest pastures, augmented by stubble grazing after the fresh spring growth has disappeared. Le Houerou (1981), estimates an average sheep density in the Mediterranean of about 2.2 sheep-equivalent/ha, requiring approximately 2000 kg ha^{-1}yr^{-1} of dry-matter intake. In terms of net annual productivity of areal phytomass, this is in the middle of the semi-arid range, and for maquis and garrigue represents a rainfall of about 500 mm yr^{-1}. However, assuming that only about half of this production is palatable, to sustain such a density requires about 4000 kg ha^{-1} yr^{-1} and, therefore, a precipitation of about 1000 mm. These figures, however crude, indicate that stocking densities of about 2 sheep/ha are easily capable of depressing cover below 70 per cent. Large areas of the Mediterranean drylands have been stripped bare, especially since sheep and goats (which have a capacity for ingesting much more woody

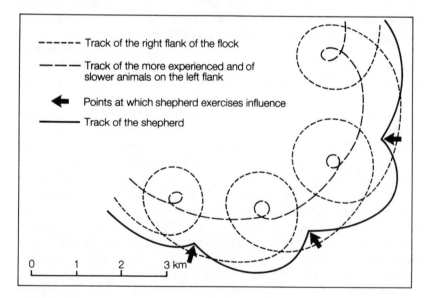

Figure 5   Patterns of movement under hard grazing
(based on Baskin, 1974)

material) are often herded together. The local effects seem to act as triggers to basically unstable situations, whether this is induced by human activities, as in the *arroyo* initiation in California, or by slight climatic variations, as suggested for southern Arizona (Cooke and Reeves, 1976).

The impact of animals is not, of course, restricted to biomass consumption. Organic waste production and consequent soil fertilization are important in redistributing organic matter more widely and improving soil nutrient status and infiltration rates. By contrast, heavy stocking results in soil compaction and decreased infiltration rates which, in turn, increase runoff. Grazing is also one of only a few ways in which prehistoric communities affected the vegetation cover, though it is probably one of the least difficult to grasp. Firewood collection, wood for construction and later for shipbuilding, cultivation in its many and complex forms and channelization, terrace and berm construction, have all had direct or indirect effects.

Interactions

In the simple causal chain, adopted in the Introduction to this chapter, it was assumed that biomass and net productivity come into equilibrium with soil moisture, which in turn is controlled by rainfall and evapotranspiration. Man is then viewed as a predator on the vegetation, reducing the cover below a critical level and hence initiating erosion. It is suggested, as a first approximation, that the percentage bare soil be estimated from the reduction in biomass, and that conventional erosion models then be applied to the bare areas. Some of these models are discussed in Morgan (1981). An improved, though more data-demanding procedure, suggested by Carson and Kirkby (1972) and developed by Kirkby (1976), is to estimate water lost by storage and evaporation and hence not available to runoff, and then use the computed annual runoff for estimating soil erosion. This procedure was used by Gilman and Thornes (1985) to estimate erosion around Argaric sites in south-east Spain. It requries, as do most models, an estimate of actual evapotranspiration, which in palaeo-environmental reconstructions requires some guesswork about past climates. This model, like Eagleson's (1978), assumes a moisture controlled equilibrium vegetation cover. However crude the application of these approaches to prehistoric situations, they do offer a line of attack to this very complex problem. At the same time, further exploration is required in at least two areas.

The first of these is to continue to improve our knowledge of the erosion–vegetation interaction. Relatively little seems to be known about the spatial competition for moisture by plants at the hillslope scale and its relation to runoff generation and erosion. Whereas most erosion models currently assume a uniform runoff on hillslopes of average length, under even very sparse vegetation, runoff lengths are rarely more than a few metres and anastomozing, rather than planar. There appears to be an important feedback in which the flows between plants, concentrated by the plants themselves, recharge the root zones of the plants. This is one of the many mechanisms whereby plant growth may take on a logistic (S-shaped) growth curve through time, for example after disturbance. There is also potentially a logistic growth in the erosional yield, constrained usually by a limit to available transporting power but ultimately by the lack of soil. The competetive interaction by erosion and vegetation for water might lead to stable erosion–vegetation equilibria at below the climax level, as suggested by Le Houerou (1981), Noy Meir and Seligman (1979) and others, and modelled conceptually by Thornes (1985). The general isoclines for a simple competitive model with logistic growth in both variables are indicated in figure 6. Very often, at least in the drylands, the starting points are these erosional 'sub-climaxes', rather than the full vegetation cover usually assumed and implicit in our earlier discussion. The all-or-none approach to vegetation cover is clearly inadequate.

The second area for improvement is our knowledge of the quantitative effects of predation by man and his animals on the natural vegetation. Some of these effects are well known for commercial

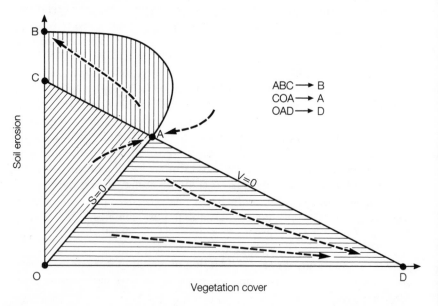

Figure 6   Isoclines for a simple competitive model of logistically growing vegetation and soil erosion
(based on Thornes, 1985)

stocking in semi-arid grasslands. By contrast, studies of pre-technic man as a gatherer, grazer and cultivator in relation to vegetation impact are largely qualitative and directed mainly to the anthropological roles which such activities played. There is still scope for a considerable investment of research here which could have direct relevance to contemporary problems.

In this chapter it has been possible only to sketch rather superficially a fresh approach to the issues of erosion and colluviation in relation to vegetation cover and its modification by man. In geomorphology, the last decade was the decade of hydro-geomorphology. The next decade is likely to be dominated by concern for the role of biological processes in geomorphology. This promises to provide important new lines of enquiry for archaeologists and geographers alike.

5 Geography and Prehistoric Subsistence

R. W. Dennell

The main aim of this chapter is to look at the ways in which geographers can contribute to studies of prehistoric subsistence. This apparently simple objective is greatly complicated by the diversity of each field of study. A geographer's interest in landscapes, for example, can be expressed in a variety of ways – through geomorphology, sedimentology, pedology, hydrology and the other ingredients of physical geography; or through human geography, with its analyses of settlement patterns, market and communication networks, demographic trends and so on. All these are directly relevant to archaeologists interested in prehistoric subsistence, but their field of study is equally diverse. At one end of the chronological spectrum, it deals with our earliest tool-using proto-human ancestors of some two million years ago; at the other, with the hunter–gatherers of southern Africa, Australia and the Americas that remained prehistoric until they came into contact with people of European origin within roughly the last century. In subsistence terms, prehistoric societies can be hunter–gatherers (capable of sub-division in numerous ways), horticulturalists and agriculturalists. By later prehistoric times, in Europe and parts of the Americas and Africa, many of these agricultural societies were 'complex' in terms of their social organization, settlement patterns, concerns with warfare, trade, exchange, rank and status.

This diversity of interest in both disciplines has two consequences that beg comment. The first is that, within each, unity is often more apparent than real. Within prehistoric archaeology, for example, it is often the case that a prehistorian interested in the subsistence of one area, period or type of society will have stronger academic links with colleagues in other disciplines than with many of his own colleagues: the same occurs amongst geographers. Secondly, although the links between geographers and prehistorians tend to be many and diverse, it is still possible to recognize some major arteries. These major arteries are especially important in that they considerably influence the way the research proceeds, and cannot be understood without some reference to the way that prehistoric studies have been, and are, structured. The main structure is long established, arising largely from the way that prehistoric archaeology began and developed in Europe in the last century. Amongst European and Near Eastern prehistorians, there is a basic division between Palaeolithic and Neolithic studies. In northern Europe, the Mesolithic was added to the Palaeolithic, very much as an afterthought, as both were primarily users of chipped stone artefacts, were hunter–gatherers and thought to be genetically related, unlike the Neolithic, which was believed to represent immigrant farming communities who used, amongst other things, pottery and polished stone. This divide is still an important one, particularly at the level of university teaching, even though the division between the late Mesolithic and early Neolithic has become so indistinct in many areas, as to become more or less arbitrary.

This division has two consequences. The first is that specialists in the Palaeolithic/Mesolithic are primarily concerned with hunter–gatherers, whereas students of the Neolithic and later periods deal mainly with agriculturalists: this dichotomy has obvious effects upon their contacts with researchers in areas outside Europe. The second, and more relevant here, is that Palaeolithic/Mesolithic archaeology has been primarily *site-orientated*, for the simple fact that landscapes have changed dramatically over the last few thousand years, and consequently the vast majority of Palaeolithic and Mesolithic sites have been either destroyed or buried. Northern Spain is an excellent case in point. This area is fairly rich in late Magdalenian sites that data to the end of the last glaciation, and so far some 34 or so have been discovered. However, as Foley (1981: 161–2) points out, the actual number of settlements likely to have been created during this period may well have been over 50,000. By contrast, prehistorians studying Neolithic and later periods usually do so in landscapes which still retain many features from earlier periods and include a sufficient number of sites to enable settlement patterns to be a primary target for study. Because of this, the main geographical stimulus to Palaeolithic archaeology has tended to come from its 'physical' side, since that can contribute most to the analysis of the contents of sites; conversely, 'human' geographers, with their expertise in the analysis of settlement patterns, have been more evident in studies of agricultural, Neolithic (or later) landscapes.

In recent years, another important division has tended to arise in the way that subsistence-orientated prehistorians conduct their research. This is between on-site and off-site archaeology: the former are primarily concerned with analyses of the contents of sites, whether zoological, botanical, artefactual or whatever, and the latter with the distribution of sites across landscapes. Each has generated a great deal of innovative research in the last few years, and developed its own links

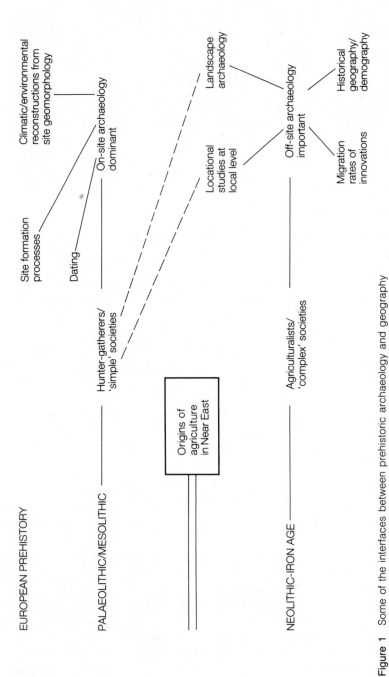

Figure 1 Some of the interfaces between prehistoric archaeology and geography

Although this presents a highly simplified account of how the two disciplines have interacted in recent years, the figure indicates how the classic divide between the Palaeolithic–Mesolithic and later periods still heavily influences the type of collaboration that occurs.

with disciplines such as geography. As with the traditional division between Palaeolithic/Mesolithic and Neolithic/Iron Age, it has been physical geographers who have contributed most to on-site archaeology, and landscape/human geographers to the study of off-site data. Thus, it is not uncommon to find that major developments in the analysis of hunter–gatherer sites have dealt with on-site data, and been helped by physical geographers before being transferred to later, agricultural sites; or that methods for analysing settlement distributions across landscapes have begun in Neolithic or later contexts, been aided by human geographers and then been applied to earlier, hunter–gatherer examples. There are, of course, some important exceptions to this generalization, but it seems sufficiently valid to serve as the basis for exploring the relationship between these two diverse fields of enquiry. Figure 1 provides a summary of these links.

On-side Archaeology, Prehistoric Hunter–Gatherer Subsistence and Physical Geography

The last ten years or so has seen a fundamental revolution in the way that archaeological sites are studied and this has already necessitated a considerable amount of rethinking about many aspects of prehistoric subsistence. Although examples can be taken from almost any period, the most influential have concerned African early hominid sites, between 1.5 and 2.5 million years old. The debates over these form a useful starting point, since they highlight many methodological issues, including the relationship between archaeologists and other researchers, including geographers.

Until a few years ago, prehistorians tended to regard Palaeolithic sites along the lines indicated in figure 2. That is to say, they took as their starting point the type of sites created by contemporary hunter–gatherers in places such as Australia, North America or Africa that had been reported (usually in a very cursory manner) by ethnographers in the eighteenth and nineteenth centuries. When investigating prehistoric sites that seemed similar, they (not naturally) assumed that they had been formed in the same way. Thus, Mesolithic shell-middens in Denmark were seen as essentially the same as those recently used in southern Africa; concentrations of smashed bone. Palaeolithic stone tools and architectural traces such as post-holes and hearths were assumed to represent the same type of camp as used by modern hunters in, for example, Africa or North America. The essential point here is that the association of shell or animal remains with stone tools (and occasionally with architectural traces) was seen as *causal*: that is to say, it was thought that they were found together *because* human activities

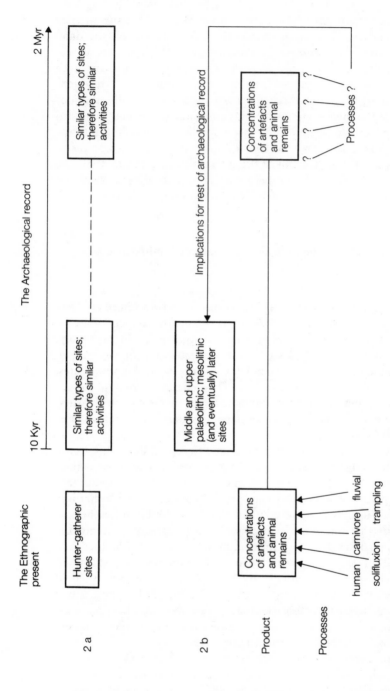

Figure 2 Changes in the way that prehistoric hunter-gatherer sites are investigated

In 2a, the emphasis is upon the end result of the processes that could have formed a site, and human activities are seen as the primary causal ones. In 2b, the emphasis has shifted to looking at the processes behind the product, and human agencies are seen as only one of many that might have been responsible. Also indicated is the point that recent archaeological work on this problem has so far concentrated upon sites more than 1.5 million years old; the resulting lessons have yet to be applied to younger sites.

had resulted in bones being smashed and stone tools discarded at the same time.

This approach had some important methodological consequences. In particular, it ensured that interpretations of the *contents* of hunter–gatherer sites were the domain of the archaeologist and that the role of other disciplines was very much as a service industry. Thus, zoologists would be required to identify the species of animals associated with stone artefacts, and physical geographers to provide palaeo-environmental reconstructions and a chronological framework, but it was primarily the archaeologist who attempted to elucidate the meaning of the site.

In the 1960s, archaeologists working in East Africa at localities such as Olduvai and Koobi Fora began to find sites more than 1.5 million years old that seemed to be undisturbed, and which contained the same kind of concentrations of smashed bone and stone tools as found on later Palaeolithic sites. Again, not surprisingly, these were interpreted in the same way, and so claims were soon made for 'kill sites' where animals had been killed and butchered, and 'living sites' where food obtained elsewhere was shared within a group. A notable consequence of these claims was that hunting, the use of home bases, food sharing and, perhaps, the nuclear family and sexual division of labour (the males hunting and the females gathering and child-rearing) were seen as among our earliest 'human' characteristics (see e.g. Isaac, 1978). In a real sense, this approach ensured that the behaviour of the Kalahari bushmen was foisted upon their Pliocene ancestors; all that was lacking, perhaps, was the camp fire, the bow and arrow and the transistor radio.

Both the outcome of this approach, and the approach itself, were challenged by two major sets of work. The first took place in southern Africa on the bone accumulations at Makapansgat, a site probably 2.5–3.0 million years old, that had produced thousands of ungulate bones, as well as some hominid remains, investigated from the 1930s onwards (see Day, 1977). The main discoverer of these, Raymond Dart, was very much struck by the types of bone preserved and their fracturing patterns. There were, for example, far more lower jaws than upper ones; the distal parts of limb bones were far commoner than the proximal ends, and so on. His argument (Dart, 1957) was that hominids had hunted their prey and, having eaten the meat, then selected those parts of the skeleton that could be used as tools. Thus, mandibles would have made effective saws, split limb bones could have been used as daggers and clubs, and tails even used as whips. It was from this assemblage that the cumbersome term 'osteodontokeratic' (bone–tooth–horn) industry was coined.

Among the researchers who began to have doubts about Dart's conclusions was Brain, who began a series of seemingly unrelated experiments in the late 1960s that have become classics of their kind.

What he did was to monitor the ways that dogs scavenged goat carcasses in modern Hottentot villages. From these observations, he realized that dog scavenging produced almost exactly the same type of faunal assemblage as found at Makapansgat (Brain, 1969). After a long series of similar experiments on other carnivores (Brain, 1981b), he concluded that most of the animal remains – including the hominids – were the result of leopard predation. On his argument, the remains had become part of the cave deposit because the cave had a large open chimney, at the top of which would have grown trees (as today), where leopards would have taken their prey for eating and then dropped parts of their meal into the cave, either inadvertently or after they had finished. Thus, by concentrating upon the *processes* that led to the formation of an archaeological site, he transformed the status of the hominids at Makapansgat from tool-using, carnivorous hunters, to the more modest level of being merely the occasional prey of another predator.

This research created a major inconsistency between Brain's own research and the conclusions being drawn at the time from open-air early-man sites in East Africa, where most investigators were arguing that hunting and food sharing were in evidence at around the same time that the leopards of Makapansgat were casually discarding pieces of hominids down cave chimneys. Probably the strongest impetus for change in the explanation of these sites has come from Binford, whose attempts at trying to understand Palaeolithic sites led him to observe the type of faunal assemblages produced in Navajo villages and Eskimo camps (see Binford, 1983 and associated references). The principal lesson drawn from these observations was that one needs to understand the *processes* behind the *product*: that many processes can be (and usually were) responsible for the formation of Palaolithic sites, that the association of smashed bone and stone tools can be *casual*, not *causal*, even though it might look at first sight like the type of hunter–gatherer debris observable today. In particular, Binford argued that many of the patterns observable in East African sites could have been produced through what he called 'fluvial jumbling', especially as many of these sites are by, or in, former stream channels (see e.g. Binford, 1977).

These criticisms undoubtedly encouraged the attempts of excavators such as Isaac to understand more fully the processes that led to the formation of these early hominid sites. As a consequence, many of the claims for 'kill' or 'living' sites have been (or are being) discarded. One example is the HAS (Hippo–Artefact Site) at Koobi Fora, initially seen (Isaac, 1978) as the result of a group of hominids stripping the meat off a (perhaps already dead) hippopotamus and discarding a few tools in the process. Current observation tends more to the view that this association is fortuitous, and that the site represents material swept into a shallow depression through stream action. Similarly, closer inspection has cast considerable doubt on the identification of the so-called living sites (see Isaac, 1983 and related papers).

Two methodological developments arising out of these debates are worth noting. The first is that archaeologists have tried hard in the last few years to develop ways of seeing if there was a causal relationship between the animal remains and stone tools in these early sites. The most promising of these at present lies in examining bone material for cutmarks made by hominids, as opposed to tooth marks left by other carnivores. At many of these sites both are present, but in a few instances where the marks are superimposed, it is sometimes possible to establish whether hominids scavenged from carnivores, or vice versa. For example, Bunn (1981) and Potts and Shipman (1981) have shown that at least some of the animals represented at Olduvai and Koobi Fora were modified by hominids before being scavenged by other animals (see also Gamble, 1981). The second, and more widely relevant, trend has been to involve other disciplines much more closely than before in the analysis of the contents of these sites. Geomorphologists, sedimentologists and pedologists, as well as others, are much more crucial than before in elucidating how stone and bone became associated with each other (see e.g. Behrensmeyer and Hill, 1979; Shipman, 1981). This shift to using other disciplines as integral rather than ancillary aids has created a subdiscipline of early-man studies that is usually grouped under the general heading of *taphonomy* (from the Greek, *taphos*, meaning burial).

This revolution in the way archaeologists approach early-man sites is currently proceeding in two directions. The first is that the lessons so learned are being applied to the rest of the Palaeolithic record, with often considerable effect. One example (out of many that could be chosen) are the elephant hunters of the Middle Pleistocene. These claims (e.g. Leakey, 1981: 118) were based largely upon the twin sites of Torralba and Ambrona in Spain, where the remains of elephants were found associated with Acheulean tools (including cleavers and hand-axes) in the vicinity of a former river channel (Butzer, 1965; Freeman and Butzer, 1966). Although explained initially as the debris left after groups of hominids (*H. erectus*) had ambushed and butchered herds of mammoths on their summer migration, it now seems likely that most of the artefactual and faunal material was swept into the channel independently of each other, and there is no firm evidence that the elephants did not die of natural causes (see Binford, 1981). Another example is the so-called 'bear cult' of Neanderthal man (see e.g., Abel, 1935; Szafranski, 1960). This somewhat bizarre claim arose from the presence of Mousterian artefacts in caves containing often thousands of bear remains. Although these were once interpreted as places which Neanderthals had regarded as some kind of shrine occupied by their totem, it now seems more reasonable to suppose that these caves were primarily winter denning areas for bear, but sometimes frequented by Neanderthals in the summer (Jequier, 1975). A third and final Palaeolithic example concerns the presence of man in Britain in the glacial maximum (18 kyr bp). Carbon 14 dates of animal bone in cave deposits containing stone artefacts can be interpreted as evidence for man in Britain at this time providing one assumes a causal relationship between the artefacts and animal remains. However, it is more likely that the animals were killed by hyaena, and, if one regards only those dates taken from hearths, there is no clear evidence for a human presence in Britain until the deglaciation was under way after 13500 b.p. (Jacobi, 1980).

It is inevitable that the next few years will see the application of these lessons both to the Palaeolithic/Mesolithic record, and to later periods. In the course of this reappraisal, many statements about prehistoric subsistence based on a direct, causal relationship between artefacts and animal remains will be discarded. One may also confidently expect physical geographers and other kinds of environmental archaeologists to be much more closely involved in explanations of site contents than before. There is no reason why, for example, Brain's observations on how Hottentot dogs scavange goats are not directly applicable to the interpretation of faunal data from an Iron Age or, for that matter, medieval village; nor is there any reason why geographers should not become involved in sorting out whether 'activity areas' in late-prehistoric sites are such, or the product of other, natural, agencies.

The second trend one may expect is that this type of work will link up with similar but isolated lines of enquiry that began with the investigation of agricultural sites. Much of this work could now be regarded as 'taphonomic' but was not at this time, as the term (although coined in 1940) did not come into widespread usage until the mid 1970s. Examples are Schiffer's (1972) analysis of the cultural and non-cultural factors (C- and N-transforms) that affect the type and distribution of material within an archaeological site; Meadow's (1975) discussion of how patterns of refuse discard affected the type of faunal assemblage produced from different parts of Hajji Firuz, a Neolithic site in Iran; and the author's work on the factors affecting the preservation of carbonized plant remains in archaeological contexts (Dennell, 1972, 1976; see also Hillman, 1973, 1981). In a real sense, therefore, physical geographers can look forward to making a very considerable contribution to explanations of the contents of archaeological sites, regardless of period or location.

Off-site Archaeology, Agricultural Subsistence and Human Geography

When sufficient field work has been undertaken to show the probable original distribution of sites in a region, and where the landscape itself can be reconstructed with some confidence, landscape archaeology can come into its own, and it is here that human geographers have contributed a great deal to the study of prehistoric subsistence. This contribution can take a number of forms. One is to see why certain areas were preferred for settlement and others avoided; another is to examine the particular factors underlying the choice of location of individual settlements. Other questions of general significance concern determining whether or not a site was occupied year-round, or only seasonally; if the former, whether some of its inhabitants utilized seasonal sites (as with modern transhumance), and if the latter, where the occupants spent the rest of their time. Colonization is another general issue that figures largely in many discussions of subsistence, particularly where it involves agriculturalists occupying either vacant territories or land already occupied by hunter–gatherers. Finally, the origin(s) of agriculture is one of those topics that is a major preoccupation of prehistorians interested in subsistence, and also one that has fascinated geographers for a long time.

   The starting point of all these kinds of enquiry is the distribution of prehistoric sites across a landscape. It is often the practice in these kinds of study to distinguish between large- and small-scale enquiries. However, this is problematic, as the prehistorians' and geographers' use of scale do not always coincide. Geographers tend to emphasize the spatial aspects of scale: thus, a large-scale investigation might involve an area the size of Britain, or even Europe, and a small-scale investigation an area the size of a small river-system. To a prehistorian, however, scale is often seen in demographic terms. Thus, a small-scale study might involve establishing the annual territory of a single group. In some cases, the areas involved may be extremely large. For example, some Near Eastern pastoralists migrate up to 800km between their winter and summer pasture (Spooner, 1972), and the Nunamiut Eskimo range over an area larger than France (see Binford, 1979: 272). Conversely, a large-scale study might involve numerous communities, but occupying a fairly small area. Because of this possible source of confusion, it is perhaps better to select the main contributions that human geographers can make to studies of prehistoric subsistance without specific reference to the size of area involved.

Site distributions, ecozones and subsistence

At an early stage in prehistoric archaeology, prehistorians and geographers realized that there was a considerable amount of valuable information in the distribution of sites in areas that were well mapped and which had been thoroughly surveyed for sites. An early and classic examples was Fox's (1932) *Personality of Britain*, which attempted to show how environmental factors determined the different patterns of cultural development in prehistoric England. Usually, studies of this kind have had more modest objectives and confined themselves to explaining why sites of a particular subsistence base are found in some areas but not others. Two criteria are usually applied to evaluate this kind of study. The first is one of *elegance*: in other words, what is the smallest number of key variables that will explain the distribution of the highest proportion of the sites under consideration? The second is that of *testability* – the extent to which subsequent fieldwork confirms or invalidates the initial hypotheses. Two examples, both of early agricultural communities, can be discussed to show the value and dangers of this type of study.

The Linienbandkeramik (LBK) of Central Europe   At the end of the fifth millenium BC a large number of farming sites were established for the first time over much of Central Europe, within a broad band between Czechoslovakia and the edge of the North European Plain. Their inhabitants used a distinctive type of hand-made pottery, reared livestock, grew cereals and pulses, and lived in large wooden long houses, up to 40 m long and 6 m wide (see Milisauskas, 1978; Tringham, 1971). Although many of the excavated sites contain several of these houses and give the impression of very large communities, it seems likely that they contained perhaps only 40–60 people at any one time, and simply rebuilt their houses nearby when required (Hammond, 1981). The consensus of opinion is that the inhabitants of these settlements were colonists who originated from the north Balkans and displaced the indigenous late-Mesolithic hunter–gatherer groups, who disappear from the archaeological record shortly after.

As has long been noticed, many of these sites are on loess (see figure 3). This was initially explained in a number of ways. One was that these areas of loess were only lightly wooded and thus the land was easily cleared for cultivation. Another was that the loess 'corridor' of Central Europe provided scope for people who relied upon slash-and-burn cultivation to colonize a large area swiftly; this explanation was also supposed to account for the rate at which settlements were apparently founded and then abandoned over a large area. It should be added that there is no reason now to suppose that these people practised slash-and-burn cultivation; indeed, the botanical evidence suggests that permanent fields and hedgerows were integral parts of the landscape in even the earliest of these settlements (Willerding, 1980).

Whilst many of these settlements are on loess, others are not; moreover, there are large area of loess in Central and Eastern Europe that were never settled by LBK communities. These anomalies have thus encouraged others to examine the significance of other facts, such as soil texture and drainage, incidence of frost, seasonal patterns of temperature and rainfall, and so on. A good example of this approach is by

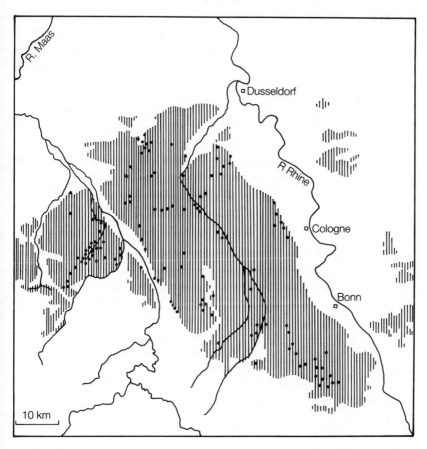

Figure 3 Distribution of Linear Pottery sites between the Rhine and Maas rivers, north-west Germany. Vertical hatching shows loess soils

(After Champion et al., 1984.)

Sielmann (1971) who showed that a variety of factors were probably of importance in Central Germany, including soil texture, winter and summer temperatures, frost and snow. Similar work of a high standard has also been done in Poland by Kruk (1980) and by Milisauskas (1979).

Agricultural origins in the Near East: from Fertile Crescent to non-centre One question that has particularly fascinated geographers, prehistorians and many other types of researcher is that of agricultural origins in the Near East. Geographical involvement in this problem has been particularly strong in two ways. The first has been in trying to establish whether climatic and environmental change – especially at the end of the last glaciation – can be cited as a primary cause for the early development of agriculture in this region. The second, and more relevant here in the context of spatial analysis, has been to ascertain what type of conditions were particularly suitable for early agriculture.

The history of this latter quest raises some interesting issues that can be discussed after a brief résumé of its main landmarks. 'Modern' thinking on where agriculture first developed can be set at Breasted's (1916) famous notion of the 'Fertile Crescent': that perennial water would have been the most critical variable and thus agriculture would have begun along the main river valleys of the Nile, Tigris and Euphrates and, perhaps, the intermediate strip of coastal Palestine. Support for this view, he claimed, also came from the point that the oldest known cities were found in these areas. Excavations between 1918–39 of large urban sites in these regions occasionally found, at the base of deep surroundings, very scant evidence of the type of community postulated by Breasted; to that extent, his hypothesis seemed validated.

Refutation came with Braidwood's famous fieldwork campaigns in the Zagros mountains of Iraq and Iran in the 1950s and 1960s and later in south-eastern Turkey. He was initially attracted to these areas because they received sufficient rainfall for dry farming, would have contained the ancestors of domestic cereals, sheep/goat and cattle; and (more importantly perhaps for an archaeologist) sites were smaller and thus easier to excavate – there was no need to remove several metres of proto-historic and historic strata before reaching the early-Neolithic levels. It was, thus, his excavations at Asiab, Karim Shahir and, most importantly, Jarmo (Braidwood and Howe, 1960) that led him to argue that agriculture developed first in what he called the 'hilly flanks of the Fertile Crescent'. Discoveries, at about the same time, of similarly early and probably (in part, at least) agricultural settlements in Palestine, such as Jericho, 'Ain Mallaha, did not seem to disrupt this view to any great extent.

Just as Breasted's views were invalidated by subsequent fieldwork, so Braidwood's concepts had to yield to the results of later discoveries. In the 1960s, Mellaart found evidence of equally ancient agriculture in western Turkey at sites such as Can Hasan, Hacılar and the slightly later one of Çatal Hüyük (Mellaart, 1965), all of which were in a region supposedly totally devoid of Neolithic settlement through some undetermined climatic reason (see Lloyd, 1956: 53). At about the same time, the earliest farming sites in northern Greece were also shown to be of comparable antiquity to Jarmo. Thus, the originally compact notion of the 'hilly flanks of the Fertile Crescent' had to be enlarged to include areas as far west as the Aegean.

In the 1960s, Butzer attempted to show which areas were suitable for early agricultural settlement by mapping the distribution of such sites against different ecozones, based primarily on soil type and natural vegetation (see figure 4). Even though there was a wide variety in the type of locations, from the Dead Sea Valley to the highlands of Western Iran, this analysis suggested that, in most cases, the most favourable conditions were in the Mixed Oak Forest belt; exceptions such as Jericho could be explained by the presence there of a large spring in an otherwise arid landscape. This analysis suggested that it was still possible to envisage a 'centre' from which agriculture gradually moved outwards. Whether the discovery of an early farming site like Mehrgargh in Pakistan (Jarrige and Meadow, 1980) means that one can still usefully consider a 'centre' for an area that now stretched from the Aegean to the Indus remains to be seen.

This example makes two points by comparison with the success of the LBK example. The first is that this type of ecozonal analysis has to have a secure data base if it is to be more than a rough *ad hoc* exercise. In the case of *bandkeramik* settlement, this is reasonably the case: it is

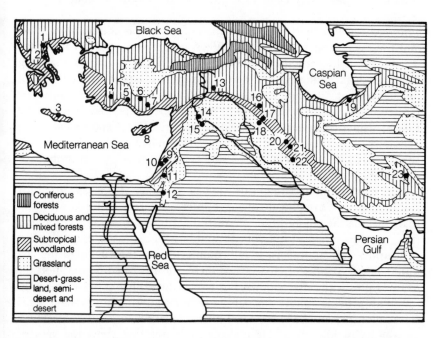

Figure 4 Natural post-glacial vegetation of the Near East and location of early farming sites (c. 9000–5500 BC)
(Based on Butzer, 1964.)

1 Nea Nikomedia, 2 Sesklo, 3 Knossos, 4 Hacılar, 5 Suberde, 6 Çatal Hüyük, 7 Can Hasan, 8 Khirokitia, 9 Ain Mallaha, 10 Mt. Carmel caves, 11 Jericho, 12 Beidha, 13 Cayönü, 14 Mureybit, 15 Abu Hureyra, 16 Shanidar/Zawi Chemi, 17 Karim Shahir, 18 Jarmo, 19 Hotu cave, 20 Asiab, 21 Sarab, 22 Ali Kosh, 23 Kerman

highly unlikely, for example, that any will be found in Spain, Britain, or Greece. By contrast, so much of the Near East (and adjacent areas, such as Soviet Central Asia and the Indian subcontinent) remain unexplored that the distribution of early farming sites is still highly uncertain. The second point is that both prehistorians and geographers need to have a clear notion of what is being discussed in the context of early agriculture. Braidwood's 'village–farming community', for example, is a multiple concept, as he himself (Braidwood, 1973) came to recognize: it compromises year round settlement, a type of social organization based on household production and an agricultural subsistence base. There is no reason why all three need have developed at the same time; indeed, if one accepts some of the evidence from late Pleistocene sites in the Near East (Noy and Higgs, 1973; Jacobsen, 1976) and the Aegean, it is possible that agriculture began long before the appearance of sites such as Jarmo and Jericho. In other words, ecozonal analysis might so far have thrown more light on where a social transformation occurred, than on one involving changes in the type of resources being used.

Colonization   In the last two examples, space was the main variable and time was held as a constant. When geographers and prehistorians discuss the colonization of an area, the main aim is one of analysing trends both through time and across space. This type of study is one of the benefits of ^{14}C dating, since that allows reliable isochrones to be plotted. This in turn enables one to explore the factors that affected the rate at which colonization proceeded, its direction(s) and extent. Two examples, both concerning agricultural colonization, can be used to show the merits and dangers of this type of study in the context of prehistoric subsistence.

The first, and more straightforward, is where an area is colonized for the first time. Examples involving hunter–gatherers and a continental scale include the colonization of Australia after 40 thousand years, and the Americas after ?25,000bp. A similarly large scale example, but concerning agriculturalists, is the colonization of the Pacific in the last 4,000 years. At present, analysis of these are frustrated by the shortage of early sites with reliable dates, but will in due course prove rewarding.

Islands provide a more amenable case for analysing how vacant areas were colonized and have attracted much attention from biogeographers as well as prehistorians. From the latter's point of view, the area of useable land relative to the total area of land and sea is usually small; secondly, on the assumption that good anchorages and landing places were key variables, archaeological survey in those parts of islands usually yield early sites that can be dated. A good example of this kind of study is Cherry's (1981) study of the colonization of the Mediterranean islands. Here, he considered such variables as size of island, distance from other islands and the mainland, and the height of each island. This example, based heavily on analyses of the larger scale of the Pacific, showed neatly how the process of colonization was slower in the West than East Mediterranean, and how an initial swift settling of the large islands was followed by a long period of stasis, during which smaller but accessible islands were not occupied.

A more ambitious and controversial example is that by Ammerman and Cavali-Sforza (1971), this time on the agricultural colonization of Europe after 6000BC. What they attempted was to utilize the results of ^{14}C dating to show how the rate of agricultural expansion across Europe varied, in much the same way as geographers have studied trend surfaces. Their study entailed several features, some more reliable than others. On the positive side, their study showed the rapid advance of Neolithic features through south-eastern and Central Europe, and a slower, later progression through northern Europe, the British Isles and Scandinavia (see figure 5). More controversial are two aspects of the way that the archaeological data were treated. First, as Barker (1975) pointed out, it is by no means clear that the study monitors the spread of agriculture: in many cases there is no evidence that domestic crops or animals were used at a site and sometimes all that has been dated is the first appearance of pottery. Whilst this sometimes first appears along with domestic resources, it often does not; in some cases (as in Denmark) pottery was used long before agriculture appeared, but elsewhere the earliest pottery may have been obtained through exchange. The second criticism concerns whether colonization was actually involved over the whole of Europe, as opposed to any other process that could result in the adoption of agriculture in areas where the resources were not locally available. One possibility is, for example, that hunter–gatherers acquired them from adjacent farming communities and developed them of their own accord, as this author has argued for Britain and western Russia (Dennell, 1983, 1985). These criticisms underline a general methodological point made earlier: that the archaeological record is the product of several processes and these have to be understood before the end result can be explained. In this example it is more than likely that prehistorians – especially in the last century – were unduly influenced in how they regarded the spread of agriculture across their own continent in prehistory by the way Europeans colonized much of the hunter–gatherer areas of Australia, Southern Africa and North America in recent times.

Seasonality   One especially important aspect of studies of prehistoric subsistence is whether occupation sites were lived in all year round or not. This issue impinges on many discussions, especially those about intensification: that is to say, whether hunter–gatherers or agricul-turalists adopted more intensive means of obtaining and/or increasing their food supply by sacrificing mobility for permanence. One example

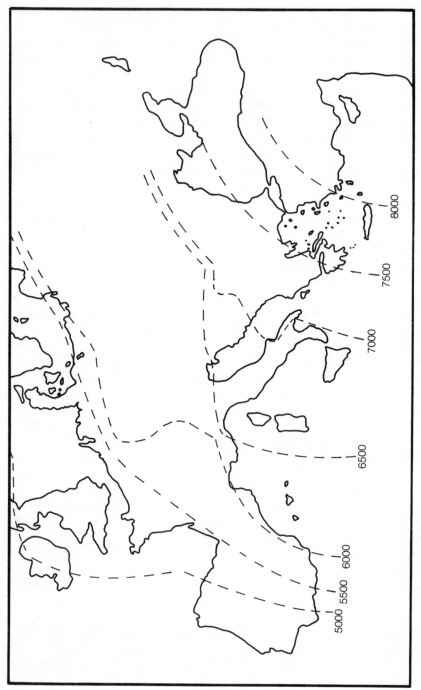

Figure 5   The spread of early farming sites in Europe in years BP

might be hunter–gatherers who developed food-storage techniques to enable them to stay year round in a place instead of following their staple animal resource; another might involve highland regions being used through the year by agriculturalists instead of during the summer only, on a transhumant bases. This issue of seasonality is also an important one where there are two types of stone industries in adjacent regions – do these represent the products of two 'peoples', or are they seasonally-varied tool-kits of only one?

There are two main ways of establishing whether a site was used seasonally or year round. The first is to see if the contents of sites include seasonal indicators, such as the remains of migratory birds or fish, or different kinds of plant; or of vermin that require a year-round supply of refuse. The second is to consider the *location* of the site in relation to the distribution of the key resources throughout the year. One influential example was provided by Higgs et al. (1967). They argued that the two Palaeolithic cave sites of Asprochaliko and Kastritsa in western Greece were the winter and summer bases respectively of one group who followed red deer (their staple resource) between their winter and summer pasture. (It remains to be seen if current re-evaluation of this work will confirm the hypothesis, Bailey et al., 1983a.) This example cloned innumerable others in discussions of late glacial Italy, Spain, France and Germany – almost anywhere, in fact, where prehistoric sites were found in highland as well as lowland areas.

Two points need to be made about this type of analysis. The first was made earlier – that the contents of sites need to be examined to show that they were the product of human occupation and not of other agencies. The second is that even if this is the case, further evidence besides the location of a site is needed to confirm its seasonal usage. This at present is difficult: it is far easier to obtain evidence for summer occupation than for the winter, so that an absence of winter indicators does not necessarily mean that people were absent. At present, the most precise seasonal indicators are probably the growth rings on shell fish (e.g. Bailey et al., 1983b), but this technique is obviously fairly limited in its application.

Site-catchment analysis Last, but certainly not least in this résumé of the ways in which geographers have contributed to the study of subsistence through landscape archaeology, is the technique of site-catchment analysis. This technique grew out of a methodological problem that is one of the most intractable in studies of prehistoric subsistence, namely that of sample comparability. That is to say, if a site has been properly excavated, the specialists concerned should produce detailed reports of the relative importance of each animal resource, or plant food, or (in midden sites) of each type of shellfish.

The problem for the excavator is to decide whether the bulk of the diet was from plant or animal foods. One way of circumventing these problems is to look at the local surroundings – or catchment area – of a site, to see what type of resources were probably available and in which proportion each could have been produced.

When site-catchment analysis was first formulated, Higgs and Vita-Finzi (1970) made unashamed use of two sources, one geographical, the other ethnographic. Chisholm (1968) noted that in many subsistence agricultural communities, land more than 5 km from the farmstead was often not cultivated because the costs of doing so outweighed the benefits obtained. Similarly, Lee (1968) observed that the !Kung bushmen of the Kalahari rarely collected plant foods more than 10 km from their camps, for the same reason. Thus, Higgs and Vita-Finzi suggested that these distances could be used to delineate the areas exploited by prehistoric farmers and hunter–gatherers respectively; to overcome the effect of topography upon linear distance, they also suggested that these radii should be converted into time-distances, of a one- and two-hour walk respectively. In their initial use of this technique, they were concerned with establishing whether cereal crops could have been the main source of food for the inhabitants of Nahal Oren, a late-Pleistocene and early-Holocene site in coastal Palestine that many had suggested was a very early example of an agricultural community. They subsequently concluded that there was so little agricultural land nearby that, however conspicuous mortars, grinding stones and sickles might be in the contents of the site, gazelle and, later, sheep/goats, must have provided most of the inhabitants' food.

Since this initial use, site-catchment analyses have been conducted all over the world, at first by Higgs' graduate students (and in some cases, by their students) and later by American archaeologists (see e.g. Flannery, 1976; Findlow and Ericson, 1980). It has also attracted considerable criticism, some of which is worth noting here. One is a methodological problem, that landscapes change, and so one has to be sure that the resources being mapped would have existed when the site was occupied. For example, in the Mahidasht area of western Iran, over 10 m of alluvium has been deposited in the last 1,000 years, seriously reducing the height of earlier sites (and doubtless burying others) (Brookes et al., 1982). A second general criticism is that this technique makes no allowance for the social landscape in which settlements were located, and decisions over where best to locate a site are not necessarily determined solely by the procurement of staple meat and plant foods. A third point is that the technique is applicable only to those hunter–gatherers who are foragers and thus habitually obtained their food from their immediate surroundings. In the case of logistic hunters, who 'target' specific resources that are then cached and used later far from their main camp, catchment analysis is singularly inappropriate (see Dennell, 1980). Finally, it is once again necessary to establish from the contents of sites that occupation sites are being considered, and not other kinds.

These criticisms notwithstanding, the technique was and is important in encouraging an interest in the local surroundings of a site as a source of potentially useful data. Providing it is used critically, and applied either to forager hunter–gatherers, or to agriculturalists who operated in landscapes that have not changed substantially, it can be useful in providing a set of propositions about the subsistence of a prehistoric site that can then be tested through excavation and associated work.

Conclusion

Prehistoric subsistence is a fascinating topic in two ways. The first is that it provides a wide range of vantage points from which to examine most aspects of the prehistoric record, irrespective of area or period, or even type of data. Secondly, it also affords an equally wide variety of windows through which the relationships between prehistory and other disciplines can be viewed. In some cases, the views can be fairly mundane and much the same from year to year; in others, they can be rich, varied and constantly changing. Geography falls into this latter category on account of the diversity and long involvement with studying the ways that landscapes have developed and been used. Because of this interest, it is safe to predict that geographers will continue to contribute greatly to the study of many facets of prehistoric subsistence over the next decade. Almost as safe is the prediction that this involvement will continue in the same way as now. Sometimes it will be direct and will involve geographers working closely with archaeologists, as happened for example, when catchment analysis was originally formulated. At other times (and increasingly commonly in prehistoric studies), archaeologists will adopt geographical techniques and concepts and use them with, perhaps, the occasional alteration to suit slightly different needs: the application of island biography to island archaeology is one example cited in this article, and other similar instances will doubtless occur. Taphonomy offers perhaps an example of a third type of collaboration; in this case, the initial stimulus came from a sifferent discipline (palaeontology) and was then modified for use by physical geographers and palaeolithic archaeologists.

What is much harder to predict is where the most innovative developments are likely to occur between geographers and economic prehistorians. This is partly because the importance of prehistoric subsistence within prehistoric studies generally is a recent phenomenon and one that was very much a part of the new archaeology that followed in the wake of the new geography in the 1960s. Perhaps like many of the *nouveau riche*, those studying prehistoric subsistence have tried hard to establish a long pedigree for their field as proof of their new-found respectability. This should not conceal the fact that economic prehistory, palaeo-economy, or whatever else one calls the study of prehistoric subsistence, is still a fledgeling discipline and, as such, is still uncertain as to how to interface with other facets of prehistoric archaeology – most notably with the studies of the social environment of prehistoric groups (see Dennell, 1983: chapter 1). Geographers have, perhaps, the most advice to offer on this topic and it is here that the most fruitful collaboration can be expected in the future.

6 Landscape Archaeology

B. K. Roberts

Landscape

The term 'landscape' is surprisingly difficult to define. W. G. Hoskins in his introduction to K. J. Allison's *The East Riding of Yorkshire* (1976) touched upon a key distinction: between 'scenery', to which we can all react aesthetically, and 'landscape', scenery examined with a trained eye. He emphasized, quoting Constable, that 'We see nothing until we truely understand it'. Earlier geographical writing stressed the distinction between the physical or natural landscape and the cultural or man-made landscape (Haggett, Cliff and Frey, 1977: 6–7), and while contemporary work is now blurring this distinction, for man's influence permeates the natural world far more deeply than could be imagined even two decades ago (Evans, Limbrey and Cleere, 1975; Limbrey and Evans, 1978), the contrast is useful. The elements making up the cultural landscapes of western Europe – buildings, enclosure boundaries, road and path networks, field shapes and superficial land-use – normally reflect closely the last two hundred or so years of documentable development. Indeed, much of the visible, perceptual cultural landscape of the region has undoubtedly been generated since the mid-eighteenth century.

However, this is not the whole story. Select from this scene just one relatively simple element – the hedgerow. In many parts of Midland England, hawthorn hedges established during the eighteenth century enclosure movement can still be seen, cutting across ridged fields whose surfaces reflect, at the latest, eighteenth-century ploughing (Roberts in Sawyer, 1976; 3030; Beresford, 1979: 38, 135). However, some hedgerows actually follow the curve of the former reversed-S plough-lands, surviving as fossils even when these latter are wholly destroyed (Beresford, 1979: 133). In this way, an eighteenth-century hedge line may reflect a furlong structure which was a feature of the landscape four hundred or more years earlier. Some hedge lines are dominant, so that other hedges tend to join to them because they follow the line of a former high headland bank, where two furlongs met and the ploughs were rested, cleaned of mud (eventually raising the headland above the field proper) and then turned (Taylor, 1975: 84–6, 109–11; Hall, 1982: 6). A proportion of these headlands can follow the course of Romano-British or even prehistoric boundaries (Ford in Sawyer, 1976: 292–4), while dominant hedge lines will reflect the presence of parish or township boundaries, and an increasing body of evidence suggests that these may be of great antiquity (Bonney in P. J. Fowler, 1972: 168–86; Sprat, 1982: 160). Thus, an eighteenth-century hedgerow, itself now incorporating nineteenth-century trees, twentieth-century barbed wire and, sometimes, a Victorian bedstead, may reflect a boundary line two thousand or more years old. The term *antecedent* can be applied to such older landscape elements which control the course or character of later impositions, while the term *successor* can be applied to these latter.

Nevertheless, there is more to a hedgerow than its physical existence as a boundary, for, as Max Hooper has shown, there is an approximately linear relationship between its age in centuries and the number of shrub and tree species of which it is constituted (NCSS, 1971; Pollard, Hooper and Moore, 1974). In this way, it has proved possible to demonstrate in regions of old enclosure the presence of hedgerows which may have actually survived *as hedgerows* for over a thousand years, where woodland survivors such as the bluebell and wild garlic can still persist in the ground flora. Even without excavation, the hedgerow constitutes historical evidence. It can, as a physical object, be examined and assessed in the light of present knowledge, and indeed 'explained' without recourse to either excavation or documents. This is the foundation of landscape archaeology, a study technique whose foundations are found in field archaeology (Crawford, 1953; Bradford, 1957; Phillips et al., 1963; E. Fowler, 1972), but which has been developed and expanded by historians (notably W. G. Hoskins and M. W. Beresford), and geographers (Harry Thorpe, C. C. Taylor, M. Aston, C. J. Bond and T. Rowley). Indeed, there is now a journal, *Landscape History*, which was launched in 1979 as a 'forum for those interested in a multidisciplinary approach to the study of the landscape and its evolution, and of the interrelationship of man and his environment'. If a distinction does exist between landscape archaeology and landscape history it is a fine one and in a recent review article the archaeologist David Austin identified the existence of a 'loosely structured but definable interdisciplinary group of scholars interested in the landscape history of Britain' which includes 'not just archaeologists and historical geographers, but also, for example, social and economic historians, architectural and local historians, toponymists and palynologists' (Austin, 1985: 201). While the ultimate roots of all this work undoubtedly lie in Meitzen's great study of 1895, there is no doubt that in Britain W. G. Hoskins and Maurice Beresford (the latter working in close collaboration with J. K. St Joseph and John Hurst), have had the most profound impact upon the practical study of landscape evolution: thus Hoskins' *Making of the English Landscape* (1955) and Beresford and St Joseph's *Medieval England: An Aerial Survey* (1979) can now be seen as seminal, stimulating work by many scholars (St Joseph, 1977; Frere and St Joseph, 1983; Newton, 1972; Millman, 1975; Mitchell, 1976; Parry and Slater, 1980; Cantor, 1982, to name but a few).

All studies of the past, in fact, draw their evidence from three fundamental sources – documents, archaeology and the landscape. Documentary materials have long been the mainstay of historical investigations, giving as they do a synchronous view of past situations. They do not, of course, necessarily reveal the true course of events, for even where there is no deliberate intention to deceive, the presence of bias, imperfect information, credulity or simple human error mean that the historian is always presented with the task of winnowing the grains of truth from the total harvest of written sources for each century (for example, Finberg, 1964; Chibnall, 1955; Hallam, 1965; Harvey, 1965; Ravensdale, 1974; Howell, 1983, to cite studies by historians with a landscape content). Archaeology, in contrast, focuses initially upon material remains and traditionally has dealt with tools, weapons, buildings, fortifications, burials and sites where the ceremonial seems to have been the dominant motivation (Renfrew, 1974; Megaw and Simpson, 1979; Cunliffe, 1974; Burgess, 1980). Once a site is excavated it must be interpreted and this has led archaeologists towards the construction of models which allow a particular site to be placed in a broader context. These points will be considered in more detail below, but any archaeological excavation may be thought of as the micro-dissection of a small piece of landscape, and so the study of landscape represents a third key to the past. Landscapes, which may de defined as the assemblages of real-world features – natural, semi-natural and wholly artificial – give character and diversity to the earth's surface and form the physical framework within which human societies exist. They are closely linked to all aspects of human life, for not only are there practical economic bonds – the majority of human beings which have ever existed were hunter–gatherers or peasant farmers – there are also powerful social, religious and psychological bonds. This is a timely reminder that landscapes contain figures. At first these appear as mere shadows, the wielders of the stone axes and the firebrands, but as documents become available even the impact of individuals can be defined and assessed – for example, Launcelot Brown and Thomas Telford.

Two essential conclusions derive from this discussion: first, the content of landscape is both variable in date and extremely complex in character; second, landscape studies fall within the scope of several disciplines and, to be successful, demand the integration of many types of evidence. The essential theme of this volume concerns the interface between geography and archaeology, but in the discussion which follows the role of an older discipline, history, cannot be ignored.

The Geographical Dimension

No treatment of landscape studies can ignore the substantial geographical literature upon this subject, and in an important summary of key philosophical themes of geographical enquiry Clarence J. Glacken argued that 'in the history of western thought men have persistently asked three questions concerning the habitable earth and their relationship to it. Is the earth which is obviously a fit environment for man and other organic life a purposefully made creation? Have its climates, its relief, the configuration of its continents influenced the moral and social nature of individuals and have they had an influence in moulding the character and nature of human culture? In his long tenure of the earth, in what manner has man changed it from its hypothetical pristine condition? (Glacken, 1967: vii). Ultimately, these questions derive from those conscious senses succinctly defined by de Chardin (1959: 37–8), human awareness of spatial immensity and temporal depth, of number perception, proportion and scale, of quality or novelty, of movement concealed within extreme slowness, and, overall, the possibility of structural unity concealed within extreme diversity. Of course, all scholars, even within a single discipline such as geography, would ask different questions of a given landscape; on the other hand, all would tend to be concerned with the balance between stability and change. Baker (1972: 16–17), citing Berkhofer, reminded geographers of a checklist of 'questions to ask when endeavouring to measure change', namely, when did the sequence of events start, what followed what, why did it happen in that sequence, why did it occur when it did and why did not something else occur, and how long did the entire sequence take? To these, Baker notes, the geographer must add the occasional 'where?'!

Although they may phrase them differently, archaeologists are also concerned with the substance of these questions. To bring this argument to a focus: each generation inherits a landscape, much as an individual or a family might inherit a house; each generation uses that property, changing it, adapting it to new needs, new demands, so passing it through a filter of use. Thus, the inherited landscape, the inherited house, will contain a mixture of features, some of them relatively old, some relatively new, and by adding some completely new elements and changing or wholly destroying inherited elements, each generation bequeaths the present to the future. Both landscape archaeology and landscape history are concerned with understanding the development of this complex palimpsest and in defining and understanding the generative forces at work. Thus, once the lineaments of a landscape have been described, questions emerge, at first random, but then increasingly formalized as study proceeds and evidence and hypotheses accumulate. As long ago as 1941, Carl Sauer described this process when he wrote 'the historical geographer must ... be a regional specialist for he must not only know the region as it appears today; he must know its lineaments so well that he can find in it traces of the past, and he must know its qualities so well that he can see it as it was under past conditions. One might say he needs the ability to see the land with the eyes of its former inhabitants, from the standpoint of their needs and capacities. This is about the most difficult task in human geography' (Leighly, 1963: 362). Few archaeologists or landscape historians, particularly fieldworkers, would disagree with these sentiments.

In 1971 Hugh Prince produced a summary of the approaches to historical geography which contained a section dealing with the 'morphogenesis of the cultural landscape'. This rather inelegant term derives from the title of the published papers of the Vadstena Conference of 1960 (Helmfrid, 1961) and describes the retrogressive analysis of the forms and patterns visible in the present landscape and earlier map sources, with the objective of tracing their antecedents. The German roots of this method were amply clear and even in 1961, Uhlig, in the face of English scepticism, was stressing two points: first, the forms of settlements and fields are the objects of observation and classification, but this is no narrow aim, for they reveal facts and raise questions to supplement those derived from documents; second, morphological studies undoubtedly bring together forms, superficially similar, from widely separated time periods, but this is not to ignore chronology, for the survival of what can be seen to be older forms in distinctive regional environments must, for the geographer, raise many questions. His analysis (in Helmfrid, 1961: 306–79) of the diagram of the 'different possibilities of open-fields' makes it clear that he was well aware of both their diverse chronological contexts and the diverse socio-economic forces generating them. When this preliminary study is set alongside the Thirsk–Titow debate concerning the origins of open, common, sub-divided fields (Thirsk, 1964; Titow, 1965), the more recent attempt at an analysis of the principle functional components of British field systems by Bruce Campbell (Rowley, 1981: 112–29) and Bob Dodgshon's arguments concerning the impact of tenure and land law (1980), it is then possible to glimpse the framework of more rigorous understanding of the causes of the observable spatial and temporal variations in field systems.

The importance of this Vadstena volume, bringing to English scholars some of the results of continental work was considerable, and this was paralleled in the urban field by the work of Conzen (Whitehand, 1981). Geographers such as Harry Thorpe (in Small, 1965: 85–111), June Sheppard (1966, 1974, 1976), Brian Roberts (1972) and Mary Harvey (1980, 1982, 1983, 1984) have all drawn ideas from these Germanic/ Scandinavian roots. Other parallel traditions existed, well-exemplified by the work of Alan Harris (1961) which, although clearly influenced by the ideas of H. C. Darby (in Finberg, 1962: 127–56; Darby, 1973), was nonetheless distinctively landscape orientated. Other studies, from Cambridge by J. B. Mitchell (1954), C. T. Smith (1967), Oxford by J. M. Houston (1963) and F. V. Emery (1969) and Leeds (Eyre and Jones, 1966; Jones in Finberg, 1972) have made important formative geographical contributions to the study of cultural landscapes.

In sharp contrast, a recent and remarkably comprehensive review by the American, William Norton, affords only limited space to landscape-based studies (Norton, 1984: 123–6, 142–5). Significantly, neither the word 'landscape' nor the term 'morphogenesis' appear in the index! This is in spite of the volume of work generated by historical geographers and others in related fields since 1961. Nevertheless, all overviews are selective, and that by Norton reflects his interest in geography's recent energetic attempts to build a theoretical base. However, he does define very clearly a methodological dilemma which permeates morphogenetic analysis: forms and processes are circularly causal; processes produce forms which then affect subsequent processes (1984: 25–6). Morphogenetic analysis has always tended to build from forms to processes, but modern geography, now much influenced by social theory, at the moment prefers to build from hypothesized processes (perhaps stochastically generated) towards possible forms. Nevertheless, a survey of the literature from Britain and Europe – both, significantly, regions with old landscapes – demonstrates clearly that morphogenetic analysis is part of the historical geographer's tool-kit and that the evidence derived from this source is a vital supplement to that derived from documents and excavations.

The Content of Landscapes: the Limitations of Surface Evidence

Much work in historical geography has been concerned with the description and explanation of the visible content of landscapes, including regional contrasts (Harris, 1961), settlement patterns, both rural and industrial (Jones, 1969; Roberts, 1982a, 1982b), field systems (Baker and Butlin, 1973), village forms (Sheppard, 1966, etc.; Harvey 1980, etc.), building styles (Meirion-Jones, 1971), and the character of frontiers (Parry, 1978). This has involved work undertaken at many scales. Nevertheless, the contribution by scholars in other disciplines – Beresford's work on deserted villages, where a mixture of geographers, historians and archaeologists were also involved (Beresford and Hurst, 1971), Barley (1961) and Brunskill (1971) on vernacular architecture, Rackham (1976) on woodlands, and place-name scholars on settlement distributions (Cameron, 1965; Fellows Jenson, 1972, 1978; Gelling, 1978) – emphasizes the multidisciplinary approach to landscape elements. Many of these are, of course, highly specialist studies (Taylor and Taylor (1985) on Anglo-Saxon churches for instance).

The economic historian, Joan Thirsk, in her map of sixteenth-century farming regions in England created a distribution of paramount importance to all scholars concerned with landscape evolution. She herself saw her map as 'very tentative', stressing that the 'boundaries between the regions are the most tentative of all, and will certainly require amendment in the light of more detailed local investigation' (Thirsk, 1967, 4). However, her map is particularly important because it frames the context for all other studies. Indeed, it is so fundamental that there is an urgent need both for a discussion of the criteria upon which it was based and for the production of a revised version. In effect, it defines 'landscape' regions and is relevant to both geographers and archaeologists (see Baker and Harley, 1973: 66). Unfortunately, no national map was attempted in the context of Baker and Butlin's *Studies of Field Systems in the British Isles*, although it is often easier to undertake such a task at a more primitive stage of knowledge (Gray, 1915) than in a more sophisticated context, where the definition of significant criteria is more of a problem. In spite of the volume of work, there are still surprising gaps: the *Atlas of the Industrial Revolution* currently in progress (edited by Jack Langton) may do for that period what Hill's atlas did for Anglo-Saxon England (1981), a study which, depite problems, is sound nourishment for the imagination. To give one practical example: to contribute to the *Atlas of the Industrial Revolution* in the time available, the author had to build around Harry Thorpe's 1964 map of rural settlement, and the task of creating a sound overview map of nineteenth-century rural settlement types in Britain, one fundamental basis for the study of earlier regional contrasts, has yet to be undertaken!

Nevertheless, visible landscapes are like icebergs: only a small proportion of their real substance lies above the surface. As was shown in the discussion concerning hedgerows, the distinction between a 'living' or a 'fossil' feature is never easy, and while, to the practised eye, many landscapes do show traces of former activity, these are not ubiquitous. To take one case, earthworks: growing up in the Midlands of England the author accepted these as normal landscape features, but travel throughout many areas of northern Europe quickly shows that some landscapes are richer in visible remains than others. Deserted village sites in the Midlands, often on clays, are disappointing comparied with the remarkable survivals in the Yorkshire Wolds, where the individual buildings of farmsteads may be traced. In the north of England the clear survival of regular row plans as whole depopulated visible earthworks provided one measure of their relative age, even before excavation or the use of documents. In part, these contrasts are undoubtedly a reflection of local geological conditions, but nonetheless England is 'earthwork rich' compared with many parts of northern Europe and Scandinavia. In Denmark, surface traces of Celtic fields or ridge and furrow are few (Newcomb, 1971), and in Sweden, while surface remains, house sites and stone enclosure boundaries do survive in marginal woodland zones, earthworks seem to be almost wholly absent from regions such as Öland and Uppland, where villages predominate.

Of course, there may be more earthworks than have so far been noted, for, as Beresford's work demonstrated, many deserted villages actually mapped by mid-nineteenth century surveyors were simply overlooked by scholars! The presence and absence of visible remains pose questions concerning the impact of subsequent land-use upon field remains, and it is a truism that today's soil marks were yesterday's earthworks and will be tomorrow's crop marks, a progression reflecting the gradual destruction of upstanding features by the plough. Work by both archaeologists and geographers (Fowler, 1972, 1975; Benson and Miles, 1974) have revealed, during the last two or three decades, hitherto unimagined quantities of sites in regions as contrasting as the claylands of Northumberland, the Fenlands, the river terraces of the great English rivers, and in the upland fringes of the Pennines, Wales and the South West. This is not merely a British phenomenon; the picture which is emerging is one of landscapes being reorganized, not once or twice, but again and again, during the six thousand or so years between the start of the Neolithic period and the present day.

A number of repurcussions flow from these observations. First, man has influenced the landscape very thoroughly indeed, and a succession of superimposed crop marks must raise questions concerning soil evolution, as well as the development of society and economy. Second, the impact of these discoveries upon our assessments of earlier population levels is profound and estimates of later prehistoric levels are now at least as high as the lower estimates for the medieval period (Fowler in Limbrey and Evans, 1978: 1–12; Dodgshon and Butlin, 1978: 87–89). Thirdly, the extent to which the visible elements of the landscape can be used to undertake morphological analysis must be questioned, for what is visible can only be the final stages in an immensely long sequence of development. Finally, the conclusions which can be legitimately drawn from the visible landscape, concerning for example the siting of settlements or the evolution of field systems, must always be tempered by a knowledge that they may be wholly conditioned by unseen antecedent structures. In such a context, assumptions about the existence of an even passable data base must always be questioned. Furthermore, while Taylor's recognition of 'zones of survival' and 'zones of destruction' (in Ucko et al., 1972: 109–13) undoubtedly contains some truth, the occurrence of survival, adaptation or destruction must reflect not only upland/lowland contrasts, but also centuries of local land-use, the presence or absence of estates, as well as local soil qualities and current farming practices. Furthermore, any landscape will incorporate virtually unascertainable balances between stability and change, 'continuity and cataclysm' (to borrow from Finberg, 1964: 1–20), set within a temporal context spanning several thousand years. An increasing awareness of this daunting complexity presents challenges for the archaeologist, the geographer and the historian; a balance must be achieved between the beguiling detail of description based upon the tangible evidence, and models designed to lead towards an understanding of the generative processes likely to be involved. These must be inferred from indirect evidence, for, in the memorable words of Alan Baker, 'dead men do not answer questionnaires'.

In practical terms, landscape studies fall into three distinct categories. First are those where direct documentary evidence exists in the form of maps, a context in which archaeological investigation is rarely used. Broadly, this involves only the last three hundred or so years, for while earlier maps are known, it was only during the second half of the seventeenth century that detailed estate maps were produced in any numbers. Second, there are those situations where some documentary evidence exists, but as this is rarely directly related to landscape features much information about landscape must be culled from survivals and excavations, and document/landscape linkages must be inferred. This phase extends from perhaps the middle-Saxon period (AD 650–850) to the seventeenth century and may, of course, be further sub-divided on the basis of the quantity and quality of documentation, but our perception of the period is filtered through a knowledge of the temporal divisions recognized by generations of historians. Finally, there are those periods for which fragmentary landscape survivals and excavation provide the main body of evidence. The later Iron Age and the Roman period are, of course, illuminated by some vital contemporary, or near contemporary, written sources, but the earlier millenia of prehistory constitute a dark well, plumbed only by a succession of accidental, causal or scientifically engineered discoveries.

Each of these categories presents very different problems for landscape analysis and we have here a logical basis for differentiation: the first category is indisputably concerned with landscape archaeology, while the last is indisputably landscape history. The second emerges as

debatable land, a sort of marchland between the interest of archaeologists and historical geographers, where skirmishing is made more
complex because of the existence of an indigenous tribe – the
historians!

The Archaeological Contribution

The last quarter century has seen fundamental changes in the volume
and nature of archaeological evidence in Britain (Roberts in Dodgshon
and Butlin, 1978). The systematic application of the technique of air
photography (St Joseph, 1977), linked to an appreciation of the degree
to which site survival reflects passage though a complex filter of land
use in subsequent centuries, has led to a 'quantative revolution' in
archaeology (Taylor in Fowler, 1975: 107–20). This was undoubtedly
coupled with an increased awareness that large numbers of sites *could*
survive (a barrier comparable to the four minute mile!), which
stimulated increased field work (Hayfield, 1980). The process of
discovery, as many recent publications attest, continues unabated. The
theme of this chapter, landscape archaeology, fortunately allows a
selective treatment of the very large body of literature now available.
Thus, the archaeologist of the mid-1980s brings a range of refined
excavating skills, new technologies, new resources and, in some
measure, new questions to bear upon the material substance of an
individual site. For the present purpose these may be summarized as an
increased awareness of the physical contents, for in addition to the
remains of buildings, boundaries, enclosures, pottery and other goods,
sites are now seen to have the potential to reveal in their accumulated
layers evidence for vegetation and soil conditions, local climate, and
even social relations and territorial linkages. Of course, sites differ
enormously in character, but 'home bases' of any period accumulated
deposits which, if noted and recorded, can throw light upon a
remarkable range of human activities, and the concept of 'site-
catchment analysis' (Higgs and Vita-Finzi, 1972) encapsulates an
important way of thinking. The gathering and interpretation of much of
this evidence now falls into the field of 'scientific' archaeology
(Brothwell and Higgs, 1969) and 'environmental' archaeology, making
possible the reconstruction of the details of such human activities as
'eating, ailing, living, moving and dying' (Shackley, 1985, chapter
heads).
   Three interrelated developments may be isolated for particular
comment, before drawing the discussion towards a concluding assessment of the limitations of landscape archaeology. First, excavation is
central to the discipline of archaeology, and, at the core of all site
interpretation, lies the concept of stratigraphy. Many new attitudes are

drawn together in Edward C. Harris's book *Principles of Archaeological Stratigraphy* (1979). His succinct discussion moves from the more conventional examination of sections, to a consideration of stratigraphy in plan (i.e. layers have a horizontal extension and create complex sets of transgressions), the importance of interfaces (where erosion rather than deposition took place – the geological concept of an unconformity is a sound example of this), and finally presents a system of rigorous recording procedures using a diagrammatic matrix. This is not a theoretical study; it has now been applied on many sites, and is of proven value in the unimaginably complex context of urban archaeology. Barker's study of *Techniques of Archaeological Excavation* (1977) places the Harris matrix in a broader context and treats the difficult question of how far excavations can be problem orientated or must simply seek to detect 'what is the whole sequence of events on this site from the beginnings of human activity to the present day?' (Barker, 1977: 41). This debate divides archaeologists, although in terms of landscape archaeology the author has no doubt that the latter approach is the correct one. This conclusion does not necessarily exclude planning excavations within the context of a broader policy involving sampling, either of total landscapes, or of sites thought, before excavation, to belong to one specific period. Such techniques, together with the use of aids such as Munsell soil colour charts, are helping to objectivize the inevitable subjectiveness of excavation, while computer recording techniques will eventually wholly transform the nature of the whole site record available to later scholars (Powlesland, 1983a).

The second development, particularly during the last two decades, has been an emphasis upon environmental archaeology as a context within which to assess sites, and there is no doubt that this has been tremendously productive (Simmons and Tooley, 1981; Butzer, 1982). However, in a recent study Bradley points out that, while economic patterns are amenable to archaeological analysis, 'the emphasis on "man–land relations" reveals a basic environmental determinism' (Bradley, 1984: 2)! In practice, economic and social conditions cannot be separated and economic processes must be seen in terms of social relations. His book, *The Social Foundations of Prehistoric Britain: Themes and Variations in the Archaeology of Power*, is an attempt to establish a series of interpretative models. Of course, the roots of these developments lie outside archaeology and geography (see the Introduction and chapter 3, above), but the pressures to adopt this way of thinking in archaeology do, in part, derive from those contexts where both archaeological and documentary evidence are available, particularly where the latter is not super-abundant. Thus, Klavs Randsborg's *The Viking Age in Denmark* (1980) begins with an analysis of the state and the socio-political sphere, drawing upon limited documentation (even including the cryptic evidence of runestones), before assessing the material remains, while Richard Hodges in *Dark Age Economics* (1982) pushes the evidence a little further.

A third development takes account of two vital contact zones. The first, where the land meets man, involved soil quality; while the second, where man meets the land, is represented by the ever-changing landownership mosaic. Land usage, a function of the two, radically affects the survival or destruction of archaeological materials. These, embracing in effect the entire land surface, bring the argument back to landscape archaeology. Much recent work is concisely described and adequately documented in *The Past Under the Plough* (Hinchcliffe and Schadla-Hall, 1980), while an increasing awareness of the massive complexities of sub-surface cultural landscapes is gradually pressuring archaeologists towards area stripping on a very large scale, seeing these as samples of 'sites' which may involve areas of a hundred kilometres or more (Powlesland, 1983b; 1984). This brings archaeology to a consideration of those 'assemblages of real world features, natural, semi-natural and wholly cultural, which give character and diversity to the earth's surface' (ibid.), all of which can now be seen to contain immense distances of time (de Chardin, 1959: 38).

To conclude this section: Archaeology has been drawing upon the evidence of distribution maps for many years (Crawford, 1921). In spite of their undoubted limitations, often demonstrably imperfect data, bias resulting from varied immensities of work, and tendency to assume, without excavation, that similar forms are indeed the same (for example, moated sites (Aberg, 1978: 2) and deserted villages (Beresford and Hurst, 1971: 66) such maps serve to generate questions which eventually allow more refined distributions to be created which are based upon more rigorous criteria. Crude as the first versions may be, they allow elements of spatial differentiation, at first only dimly discerned, to be identified and tested. They can also create contexts within which the presence of socio-political factors can be assessed. For example, the distribution of moated sites demands explanations which include the overall distribution of wealth and social conditions, as well as physical conditions (Le Patourel and Roberts in Aberg, 1978: 46–55). As Austin (1985: 208) stressed, with the medieval period in mind, 'the archaeologist needs to use all the material he recovers from excavations to examine a range of hypotheses generated within social, economic and agrarian history as well as historical geography'.

The Limitations of Morphological Evidence

It is possible to identify six principal areas of criticism concerning the morphological analysis of landscapes: (1) the dating of the elements is, in the absence of excavation or documentary evidence, always difficult and sometimes impossible to achieve; (2) excavation will normally reveal that what is visible at the land surface is only an eroded portion of the final phase of a site before agriculture, be this arable or pasture, took over; (3) the classification, typology and comparison of landscape elements often leads to simplistic inferences and unwarranted associations; (4) the relationship between morphology and documentation is difficult to establish with any certainty, and there is a lack of rigor in methodology and presentation; (5) morphology provides no evidence concerning the real processes which generate the similar or diverse forms; and (6) there is the constant danger of the creation of simplistic reductionist models whose relationship to reality is questionable.

All of these undoubtedly contain elements of truth, and all of them interlock with each other, but as both geographers and archaeologists will continue to be faced with the problems of describing, dissecting, analysing and explaining the evolution of complex landscapes, we cannot escape the challenges they represent. The questions raised will be examined in the context of claims that the plans of some villages, visible on the ground and on earlier maps, do have a tangible contribution to make to an understanding of medieval conditions, and a useful point of origin for discussion is the present author's paper of 1972 concerning Durham villages. There it was suggested that 'the basic plan type originated before 1200 and that traces of twelfth-century property boundaries . . . sometimes survive' (Roberts, 1972: 54). While these arguments, and others presented elsewhere (papers by Sheppard and M. Harvey; see also Roberts and Glasscock, 1983), will not be reiterated, this topic forms a convenient focus for a more general discussion of criticisms levelled at the technique of morphogenetic analysis.

The establishment of both relative and absolute chronologies is fundamental to all studies of the past. Writing in 1978, Roberts (in Green et al., 1978: 301–5), suggested that four separate but inter-locking chronologies are involved. The first is absolute chronology, normally so unattainable as to be virtually theoretical. The remaining relative chronologies involve three principle elements: hierarchical – that suggested by place names, where important places tend to appear in the records first; fiscal and tenurial – for the rents, renders and services attached to a place can often be designated old, newer and most recent; and finally the chronology of key elements of the visible landscape – for example, village plans or the number of fields in a given system. Even in the best possible circumstances, the relationship between these chronologies will never be clear-cut: within even a limited region the complexities can be almost unimaginable. While place names have much to tell us (Cameron, 1965; Fellows Jensen, 1972, 1978; Gelling, 1978), the information they provide about settlement and settlement patterns must be treated with considerable

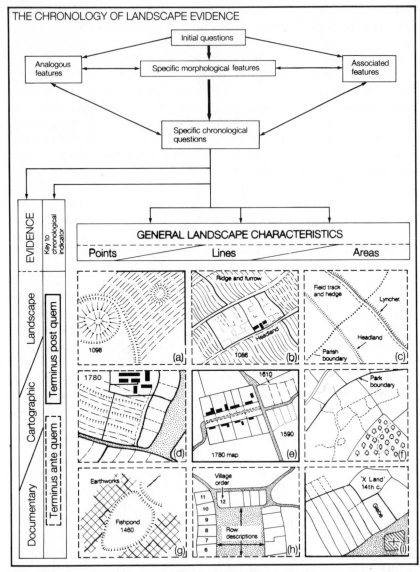

THE CHRONOLOGY OF LANDSCAPE EVIDENCE

Initial questions

Analogous features

Specific morphological features

Associated features

Specific chronological questions

EVIDENCE

Key to chronological indicator

GENERAL LANDSCAPE CHARACTERISTICS

Points   Lines   Areas

Landscape

Terminus post quem

Ridge and furrow

Field track and hedge

Lynchet

Headland

1098   1086   Parish boundary   Headland

(a)   (b)   (c)

Cartographic

Terminus ante quem

1780   1610   Park boundary

1590

(d)   1780 map   (e)   (f)

Documentary

Earthworks   Village order   'X Land' 14th c.

Fishpond 1460   Row descriptions   Glebe

(g)   (h)   (i)

Figure 1   1 An unbounded network system where exchange in the region is direct and no division of labour exists; 2   a bounded hierarchical system where exchange in the region may be controlled by some central authority, but where the production and distribution of commodities is low; 3 a solar central-place system where an administered market exists in the region, maintaining a low level of commodity production and distribution, and an equally low level of social stratification; 4   a dendritic central-place system in which a monopolistic market (gateway community) occurs on the edge of the region to control prestige goods exchange and the production of limited commodities for external distribution; 5   Two variants of central-place systems in which interlocking competitive markets generate a high level of production and distribution in a well-regulated socio-economic system.

caution, not least because they are clearly often territory names as well as place names (Sawyer, 1976: 1–7; see also Sørensen in Sawyer, 1978: 1–33), and field evidence for village-shifts begs many questions (Taylor, 1983: 116–17).

In practice, much dating in landscape history must use archaeological dating procedures, employing superimposition, together with limited documentation or excavation, to establish the *terminus post quem*, the date after which a given feature must have been constructed, and the *terminus ante quem*, the date before which it was established. This assumes that a relative date, 'feature X lies over feature Y', can be unambiguously established (see figure 1), or that a sufficiently close correlation between the landscape and a document can be achieved to warrant postulating a linkage. The limitations of this method derive not from the intrinsic procedure, for archaeological chronologies are constructed upon similar foundations, but upon the scale of application and the tendency to date by unsupported association (Austin, 1985: 205). There are, of course, questions of scale here: Sheppard's analyses of Yorkshire villages embraced a large region and a very large sample, while Roberts relied on the use of a *terminus ante quem* derived from documentation which, admittedly, related only to a very few villages. Nevertheless, much of the debate is one of emphasis, for even in 1972 a note of caution was entered: 'the Harrying of the North . . . was but one episode . . . but such devastations were a permanent feature of life in the north until the borders became quiet', and it was recognized that village planning may have extended over several centuries (Roberts, 1972: 54). To see the repetitious regularity of northern village-plans as the result of one prime cause would be simplistic, but we are left with a fundamental question: throughout the whole of the north of England village plans are found which are variations upon the same basic idea; they are less prevalent elsewhere (Roberts, 1979). In *some* cases documentation and even excavation (Roberts, citing Austin, in Sawyer, 1976: 310–11), suggest the plans originated before 1300, before 1200 and possibly before 1130. How can this be explained? What social and economic forces could generate these plans? Over what period of time? The essential point is that these questions were generated by landscape survivals and, while there is indeed evidence for post-medieval structural revisions (Roberts 1978: 250–1; 1982a: 17), there is also an impressive body of documentary evidence to imply that, in many villages, key elements of the visible plans did have medieval roots. There is a close parallel with deserted villages, where later work has refined Beresford's chronology (Dyer, 1982). The different is that before 1300, before 1200, and still less before 1100, there can never be the volume of supporting documentation Beresford was able to produce.

The types of chronological statements which can be made using the evidence from the landscape, maps and other documents are summarized in figure 1. It emphasizes the importance of relative dating, but cannot show the key problem, that of establishing chronological limits – a date before, say, 1086, could either be AD 1085 or 1085 BC. Taking the case of the village which appears to be laid out over ridge and furrow, yet is a 'new village', documented in 1086 (based on Newton Bromswold): Even if the ultimate age is not debated further, its presence, before 1086, must raise questions not immediately derivable from any other category of evidence (Hall, 1974; VCH Np. 1: 311; VCH Np. 4: 27–8). In this situation, comparison with other known examples and the relationships between spatially associated landscape elements becomes of vital importance. What is quite clear from these examples is that both morphological relationships, and typological sequences derived from such evidence, must be anchored to the evidence of excavation or documentary material in order to move beyond a very general relative chronology. On the other hand, given sufficient cases, research time and a measure of critical assessment arrived at through debate, there is no reason why generally approved chronological appraisals of many landscape features should not emerge. This is, after all, a normal procedure in archaeology.

Excavation, to pursue the second theme, normally reveals the intricate details of a very small landscape sample. There is no doubt that what appears at the surface is very limited, as the work at Wharram Percy has revealed (Hurst, 1984), and even under favourable conditions morphological analysis is no substitute for excavation. It is, nevertheless, an important complementary technique, providing that its inherent limitations are appreciated. Given the current expense of excavation and the fact that only a limited number of sites can be made available for the archaeologist, then the analysis of surface remains, surviving either as isolated features or integrated within the living landscape, represents an essential non-destructive extension of research (Rodwell, 1981: 140). Even when dealing with a site composed purely of earthworks and soil or crop marks it is, with accumulating experience, now often possible to attempt a measure of interpretation (Rahtz in Hooke, 1985: 211–12) and even to postulate phases of development or the presence of antecedent structures (Taylor in Limbrey and Evans, 1978: 132). When these relict features are integrated into the framework of a living settlement, the possibilities for hypothesis construction and even interpretation are enormously enhanced.

The third and fourth criticims of the morphological approach must be considered together. It cannot be disputed that the construction of classifications and typologies can lead to associating temporally disparate features which are superficially the same, but this criticism seems to be often based upon the assumption that classification is the objective of the excercise! Classification is a necessary way of reducing to order the diversity of the real world. It is a means of sharpening observations, for it forces questions concerning the characteristics which are used as a basis for the logical groupings: if two settlements are found to be 'almost identical' and separated by a thousand years of time and 500 miles of space, then this must raise questions concerning the differing socio-economic forces which generated them. The fact that two slopes may appear to be of the same angle but generated by different processes does not, at the stage of initial observation and recording, obviate the need for a geomorphologist to measure the slope angles. In the context of a complex situation, initial hypotheses are often simplistic, but they are susceptible to elaboration providing – and only providing – this is generally perceived to be a worthwhile exercise. There is no question that the 'correlation' of morphological evidence and documentary material is difficult, but, pointing no specific fingers, exactly the same problems exist in the interpretation of those pollen diagrams which extend into historic time, while it is often easier, in a historical context, to interpret a limited range of documents than a fuller set which demonstrate more complexities and inconsistences. Questions of scale permeate the linkages which can be made between landscapes and documents: work by Bond (1973, 1979), at first attempting a general correlation between the records of monastic estates and their landscape content, but moving towards the systematic identification of specific features, provides a technique which is closely tied to a defined context and which opens a door to further analysis of numerous studies by historians in which the written records are viewed almost in a vacuum.

The point about rigour in presentation is an important one. This view was very sharply expressed by the historian Britnell (1982), with some justice, if little understanding. This delicate question can be illustrated with reference to the work of two historians. Let it be said that in neither case is criticism implied: the examples, derived from the work of two scholars with a strong interest in landscape, both using very good source materials, are cited merely to stress the problems.

For medieval Cuxham, Paul Harvey (1965) produced a 'conjectural plan' of the village in the early fourteenth century: he talks of the evidence and even produces a careful appendix in support, but ultimately he could not document all the steps in his argument and his careful statement, commenting upon a list of tenants, that 'it seems reasonable to suppose that this corresponds to the order of the tenements along the village street', represents a critical link we must take on trust. Cecily Howell, in an even more detailed account of Kibworth Harcourt (1983), actually attempted to document each toft, but a careful reading shows that each step of the reasoning is not documented and that assumptions, or perhaps even 'imaginative leaps' are made. The author suggests that there is a general problem here: the publication format (so often failing to separate problems and questions), the data accumulated and the concluding hypothesis or explanation, has in this field (to mix metaphors) been a sea-anchor for many years. Data, which may be susceptible to alternative interpretations, are very difficult to use when embedded in descriptions, explanations, hypotheses and footnotes. In this way, tentative and even suspect conclusions find their way into more general arguments. Archaeologists, who must systematically destroy their evidence, have faced the problem of 'how to publish' for years (Grinsell et al., 1966), and a satisfactory solution may only have appeared with the advent of microfiche and the computer.

Turning to the two final areas of criticism: Austin (1985) questions the ability of studies based upon morphology to reveal anything of the processes which generated the observed forms and patterns. The observation of morphology and the explanation of the process, are indeed 'two separate actions' (Austin, 1985), and the only context in which the neutral, mute evidence of landscape can reveal anything of the reality, as opposed to the generality, of process is in the context of a particular study, where questions are asked, observations made, data accumulated, and reasoning and critical judgement applied. A deserted village is indisputably evidence of the process of depopulation and a geometrically regular plan is evidence of the process of deliberate planning, but to explain both demands much more than simple inference. Until we turn to the broader context, be this the work of Beresford or Lockhart (in Parry and Slater, 1980: 249–70), we cannot see further, for the morphology – as *evidence* – is too limited. Furthermore, it must be stressed that classification is a *tool*, not an objective: it is but one way of using a category of evidence – the features of the landscape.

That scholars interested in morphology have made unwarranted 'assumptive leaps' cannot be disputed, but few would argue that visible morphologies can be explained purely in their own terms, without recourse to a consideration of the nature of the societies and economies with which they are associated. However, Austin raised serious questions when he noted 'to my mind . . . typology which places a street village inhabited entirely by half virgate bondholders in the same class as one formed entirely by freeholders' tofts is missing the point: they are essentially not the same type of community' (Austin, 1985). In this he is both wrong and right: if the two plans are almost identical then they undoubtedly do belong to the same morphological group, but that the two communities inhabiting them are indeed tenurially different can hardly be disputed, unless an act of collective enfranchisement had taken place! There is, however, a point not to be missed. While England, regular two-row plans may indeed (sometimes) be inhabited by bondsmen and are, perhaps (to make an assumption), explicable in terms of lordship and planning, in Sweden essentially the same plans are the living places of tenants who are not normally considered to be subservient to a superior lord. In the circumstances postulated, if deliberate planning can indeed be proven, then the existence of identical or similar plans, of broadly the same date but present in differing social, economic and geographical contexts, raises a host of important questions concerning territorial and political organizations, and the varied factors which generated, sustained, and diffused the planning processes.

The final criticism – that many explanations of given sites are too simplistic, that there are insufficient alternative hypotheses and that more complex models incorporating social and economic components are needed – is not a barrier to future development. Models, in particular, have much in common with classification: they are easily created, but few prove to have wide acceptance or lasting value. Will the models presented by Rahtz concerning the work-strategies at Wharram Percy or Roberts dealing with the temporal development of rural settlement forms and patterns (in Hooke, 1985: figure 15.1, 15.3 and 2.7), prove to be more than ephemeral? Both, one may suspect, were primarily designed as aids to communicating complex ideas, but models and landscapes have one thing in common – both must suffer the acid test of time!

The strands followed in this discussion, drawn from three major disciplines, will probably never be woven into a single coherent whole. Indeed, the author believes strongly that while landscapes provide data and pose questions, they do not in themselves form a separate field of study. They provide sources for evidence which can be brought to bear upon problems formulated within the cores or at the edges and interfaces of established disciplines such as archaeology, geography and history, and, of course, many others. However, given the fact that landscape studies will continue, there is a clear need for the characteristics of the technique to be more clearly enunciated. The word 'characteristics' is carefully chosen: what is done? how is it done? what are the advantages? what are the limitations? If they can be agreed, the answers, above all else, will provide an important bridge between the varied traditions of scholarship which find a shared interest, if not always shared objectives, in the study of the landscapes wrought by human societies.

7 Industry: Landscape and Location

E. G. Grant

Industry, as one of the principal economic activities of mankind, is of interest to both geographers and archaeologists. A considerable literature has been created covering the economics of industry, the growth of industry, the location of industry, industrial buildings and processes, and the products of industry. There is, however, considerable divergence in the approaches of geographers and archaeologists to industry.

Within the discipline of human geography, industrial geographers have been largely preoccupied with analysing the location of industry, while historical geographers have concentrated on the development of the space economy, particularly during the last 200 years. Archaeologists have had a long interest in industry, including stone tool manufacture, metallurgy, pottery manufacture and building construction, with the emphasis very much on the materials, technology and artefacts of industry rather than on industrial organization or the relationships of industry and society.

Industrial archaeology, in theory, brings the methodology and techniques of archaeology to the study of the material remains of industry, particularly those of the capitalist (i.e. factory-based) mode of production. However, few industrial archaeologists have approached the subject via a formal training in archaeology; most have been recruited from industrial history or the history of technology. The result is that geographers, traditional archaeologists and industrial archae-ologists have approached the analysis of industry from very different viewpoints and this is responsible for an almost complete lack of integration between them. The purpose of this chapter is to review recent research in these areas in order to make practitioners who approach the subject from different viewpoints aware of each others' interests, assumptions, concepts and methods. Eventually this approach may create agreement on what might be investigated and suggest how some kind of integration may emerge from the several approaches.

Geographical Perspectives on the Location of Industry: an Emerging Diversity of Approaches

Geographical studies of industrial location have encompassed important theoretical developments in the last twenty-five years. Until then, formal models of industrial location (often referred to as 'classical' and 'neo-classical' approaches) were based on how the individual firm responded to such economic factors as transport, labour and access to the market. The classical approach was based on a large number of small, single-product firms with labour- and energy-intensive systems of production and spatially constrained locational requirements. Twentieth-century changes in the structure, technology and scale of industry encouraged some neo-classical industrial location theorists to modify these models of location in order to try to accommodate such changes.

Other locational analysts, however, have largely abandoned the classical and neo-classical theories by approaching the subject from completely different viewpoints and theoretical positions, The principal argument is that it is not only the locational factors that change and require examining; rather, the firms themselves have completely changed, as has the wider economic and social system. Before the location of industry can be analysed, the industrial environment – encompassing world market conditions, the state of the national economy, government attitudes to industry, the labour supply, and so on – has to be understood.

Two differing lines of thought have emerged from this rethinking. The behavioural approach to industrial location argues that it is not possible to have one model to explain all the variety of locational behaviour that exists within industry. Instead, a whole range of explanations for firms' behaviour in space has been put forward, with particular emphasis on how large multiplant and multinational firms organize their activities between different locations – that is, their internal geography.

In contrast, structural approaches to industrial location focus their attention on how a firm's use of space is determined within the wider economic and social structure(s) within which it operates. Marxist analysis has become a popular method of approach for the structural school because of its emphasis on the development of production under capitalism. It provides a link between spatial and non-spatial behaviour by relating locational trends and the behaviour of individual firms to changes within the system as a whole.

These different approaches to industrial location are not necessarily exclusive, nor is any one approach more correct than another. They were formulated for different reasons and each affords a different type of explanation to the locational problem. Their relevance and applicability to historical industrial patterns is what interests us here and, in order to assess that, a fuller description of these approaches is necessary.

Classical location theory

The beginnings of classical location theory are generally attributed to the German economist Alfred Weber. Weber's (1909) analysis was largely limited to manufacturing industry for which he made several basic assumptions. His attention was confined to single product, single-plant firms operating in a perfect market with the aim of minimizing costs. Weber highlighted three main factors that influenced industrial location: he first identified the point where minimum transport costs with respect to material and market costs would operate; he then added labour costs and the local factor of agglomerative or deglomerative forces as factors that might cause firms to deviate from the minimum transport cost location in the interest of lower overall costs. Although himself an economist, Weber demonstrated this model with a physical analogy whereby a triangle of forces acting on a body (this is, the firm) came to equilibrium, for example, where the locational pulls of materials and markets balanced each other.

Weber's model has been continually criticized since he first promulgated it, particularly in terms of its *a priori* assumptions, its simplistic nature and its neglect of demand. It is often argued that profit maximization would be a more acceptable rationale than cost minimization, while Weber's primary emphasis on transport costs and his assumptions about perfect competition are frequent objects of attack (Smith, 1981). Weber's initial contribution to the field of industrial location was followed by several other neo-classical models within the same framework, emanating from economists and regional scientists including Palander, Hoover, Lösch, Greenhurt and Isard (Smith, 1981). Although some geographers embraced location theory from an early date, it was not until the analytical and quantitative 'revolution' in geography in the 1960s that geographers began to make significant contributions to industrial-location theory, and then mainly as neo-classical modifications to existing theory. The chapter by Hamilton in Chorley and Haggett's *Models in Geography* (1967) is still largely dependent on the classical economists. David Smith, one of the principal proponents of industrial-location theory from within human geography has, however, contributed a theoretical framework for geographical studies of industrial location (Smith, 1966, 1971, 1981). Smith defends Weber and has adapted Weber's model to overcome some of its simplicities, showing how it can be modified to provide a more general variable-cost theory, and at the same time be integrated with demand factors via the concepts of the revenue surface and the spatial margins to production.

However, the principal objection to classical location theory remains – that it is divorced from the real world; reality never matches up to the ideal situation. Even when applied to nineteenth-century industries, when firms were smaller, less diversified and the stage of economic development less advanced, there is still considerable deviation from the ideal. Some see this as acceptable and exercise their arguments in trying to explain the deviation. Massey (Open University, 1977) regards this as an unacceptable splitting of the firm into two parts – that which accords with the *a priori* model and that which does not – which is an impossible situation because the firm as a whole is unique.

The neo-classicists are aware of this situation and Smith suggests a dramatic widening of the philosophy:

While some traditional models (including that of Weber) remain helpful for the solution of specific practical problems, the development of more general spatial models of the entire production – distribution – consumption process seems now to be a more constructive route to take. To focus attention on individual components of this process, thus missing its essential unity, is a classic case of failing to see the wood for the trees (Smith, 1979: 54–5).

He seems to have in mind here not only the general equilibrium economic systems models of central-place theory or of Löschian landscapes, but also models that incorporate non-economic factors into the explanation of location. However, as Gregory (1981b) (in a welcome reappraisal of Weber) has pointed out, Weber himself was aware that location theory had to be set in a wider and more complex social, cultural and economic framework.

Behavioural approaches to industrial location

Behavioural approaches to industrial location are largely concerned with how certain attributes of a firm – organization, ownership, size, decision-making procedures, and so on – influence the spatial behaviour of the firm (Keeble, 1977). Carr (1983) in a review and critique of behavioural industrial-location theory sees it as trying to understand not only the internal relationships between firm organization, performance and growth, but also the relationship between the firm and its local or regional social and economic environment.

Hamilton (1974) identified two main areas of behavioural locational analysis: (1) location decision making and linkage patterns; and (2) spatial variations in firm organization and development. A major interest within the latter is the spatial behaviour and organization of large, multiplant multinational enterprises. Keeble (1977), with concepts derived from both the neo-classical and behavioural schools, has used aggregated empirical data to categorize locational trends. By means of a location-preference matrix, he charts a fundamental shift in Western industrialists' spatial preferences. Until the 1950s industrialists tended to show a locational bias towards large metropolitan areas at the centre of the national space economy. Since then the preference has been for locating in smaller settlements, often in peripheral areas. This may be partly explained in behavioural terms as it 'Reflects, in part at least, the increasing significance of non-economic residential amenity considerations in modern location decisions' (Keeble, 1978). However, more traditional neo-classical explanations can also be sought, because costs can be cheaper in peripheral areas, particularly labour costs (Moore and Rhodes, 1984).

This trend (which has been identified in Britain, France, Germany, U.S.A., etc.) repeats a much earlier but similar trend. In the fifteenth to seventeenth centuries, industry (particularly the wool industry) displayed a shift down the urban hierarchy towards more rural areas. This historical phenomenon has traditionally been explained in classical location terms – cheaper and more adaptable labour, fewer guild restrictions, plus the presence of raw materials and water power (Thirsk, 1961). A more behavioural explanation based on considerations of the size, ownership and decision-making processes of the industrial units would provide a very different perspective.

Spatial variations in firm organization and development have encouraged the study of the 'geography of enterprise'. First proposed by McNee (1960), the geography of enterprise is concerned with how firms organize their activities over space rather than looking at 'industry' in an abstract or aggregated manner. Although initially formulated to create a more humanistic approach to industry it has become closely identified with 'the study of the influence of the policies and structures of multiproduct, multiplant enterprises on changes in industrial location and on processes of regional economic development' (Hayter and Watts, 1983: 157). Walker and Storper, however, dismiss the geography of enterprise, along with the rest of the behavioural approach, because of 'excessive attention to the internal conditions of the corporation and to strictly technical explanations for organisational change' (Walker and Storper, 1981: 489).

Massey (Open University, 1977: 16) believes that the behavioural approach shares the same problems at the classical approach in trying to bridge the gap between theory and reality. The behavioural approach cannot, in the end, cope with reality because of the enormous number of individual factors it brings to the analysis and which it tries to categorize into types and describe as models. Though the behavioural approach to industrial location has certain merits, particularly in appreciating that firms do have individual personalities, behaviour still has to be explained and not just described, and explanation can only come about from an understanding of the larger forces of structural and social change.

Systems approach to industrial location

The interest in systems theory ideas that arose in geography generally in the 1960s encouraged a systems approach to industrial location, particularly as expressed by McNee (1974), but also in a rather looser sense by Hamilton and Linge (1979), as well as Rees, Hewings and Stafford (1981). The basis of the systems approach is that industry does not operate in isolation but as part of a wider and more complex system in which the individual components behave in particular ways as a result of interactions between themselves and with the environment beyond. In other words, when applied to industry, changes in any one industry or any one member (i.e. firm) affects all the other elements of the system.

Storper and Walker (1979) criticize the systems approach because of 'misspecification of the economy as an industrial system, focus on technical change as the main process at work; limited conception of economic structure in terms of linkages and relegation of the system'. Storper (1981) concedes that the systems approach emerged because of the complexity of social organization similar, in fact, to the structural approach, but he criticizes the systems attachment to the product cycle rather than capital accumulation, labelling it further as 'technological determinism' (Storper, 1981: 34). Hamilton and Linge (1983: 7) respond to this by seeing the systems approach as wide enough to encompass all modes of explanation. They see a kind of hierarchy of perspectives with the neo-classical approach 'nesting' within the behavioural approach, in turn nesting in the structuralist framework. However, a lot more research into real locational situations is required before it is possible to say if these three approaches to industrial location do relate to each other in the way suggested.

Structural approaches to industrial location

Dissatisfaction with some of the previously described theories has led Massey (1973, 1979) to raise important questions about the purpose and direction of industrial location research. She argues that the separate existence of industrial-location theory is open to question:

In different ways, many of the classical theories of industrial location have proceeded as though the object of study were an abstract firm – that is one without effective structural relationships with the rest of the economy . . . The immediate question is . . . the presumed separation of spatial behaviour from the economic system as a whole. In fact, of course, the two are intimately related at all levels. (Massey, 1979: 57)

Massey largely dismisses neo-classical theory because of its over-dependence on an idealist model of the individual firm which is abstracted from the particularities of history and geography:

The whole concept of an ahistorical formal model of human behaviour is a misapprehension. Forms of behaviour are themselves produced, not given. They result from particular historical conditions and from position within the total system at any point in time. Different forms of economic system, and different structural positions within any one such system will produce different forms of behaviour ... The approach should be to define the structure of an actual situation in time and space to some quintessential core of similarity. (Massey, 1979: 60–1).

Massey (1979: 70) suggests that one way to solve the problem posed by both the neo-classical and behavioural explanations of industrial location theory is 'to interpret behaviour as the product of the overall structure of the system in which the individual firm is set and of its place within that structure'. She further argues that industrial-location theory is unable to explain spatial behaviour because the causes lie beyond the realm of spatial analysis. Spatial behaviour cannot be divorced from the totality of non-spatial economic behaviour, and it is crucial to understand the operative structural economic processes which underlie spatial phenomena. These processes may well be non-spatial, but the aim is to try to identify those which are spatially significant. Any question about location must be historically specific:

It is the search for eternal – and thus philosophically *a priori* – statements about behaviour which has produced the theoretical difficulties and inconsistences which ... constitute a fundamental criticism of industrial-location theory. We cannot as industrial-location theory persists in trying to do, normalize for history. (Massey, 1979: 72)

Massey's approach has not gone without criticism. Wood (1980), although accepting the limitations of autonomous industrial-location theory, believes that structural analysis also leaves questions unresolved because of its historically specific (or retrospective) emphasis. In studies of contemporary change it is not always possible to identify the processes of change that are operating, so that it is usually necessary to start with the firms themselves. This, however, should not be a problem for investigations of past industrial location. With the benefit of hindsight it may be easier to identify the structural economic processes and how they shaped economic space. Nevertheless, as will be discussed later, most historical studies of industry have still largely focused their attention on individual firms.

Industrial location in a Marxist perspective

There is some debate whether a Marxist perspective in geography falls within or outside a structuralist approach. Johnston (1983a: 111) distinguishes between 'structure as construct' and 'structure as process' and argues that the latter, which identifies dialectics not only within the infrastructure, but also between the infrastructure and the super-structure, can successfully embrace most interpretations of Marx. A Marxist approach tries to relate the patterns of the superstructure to processes operating within the infrastructure. Despite what many geographers and archaeologists have attempted to do, the patterns cannot be relied upon to identify wholly the processes that created them. Furthermore, the processes only make sense within theoretical and ideological frameworks; space and time are not 'independent variables' – they are part of the ideological structure. Marxist analysis is thus different from the positivist approach of creating a model as a generalization about reality to provide the theory, because it is the Marxist analysis itself which provides the theory, i.e. a particular way of looking at the structure of the system.

The introduction of Marxist thought to industrial-location theory has been fruitful in stimulating new thinking, particularly the need to consider the processes that create industrial economies (Taylor, 1984: 264). Walker and Storper examine the central position of capital in relation to industrial location, based squarely on Marxist theory. Their main thesis is that the 'geography of industry unfolds principally as a consequence of the dynamics of accumulation, rather than as a result of the static allocation of activities to their best location with respect to the distribution of markets, labour and materials' (Walker and Storper, 1981: 481). Instead of the siting decision being given paramount consideration (as in neo-classical theory), Walker and Storper put forward the earlier investment decision as the initial and crucial step. This is not very different from that which a behavioural analysis of the location decision making process would do, but, instead of conceptualizing this step in management's own terms, Walker and Storper conceptualize it in terms of the circuit of capital. For them, the location problem arises as soon as the investment capital takes the form of production capital, as production involves a stock of fixed assets that is essentially immobile; thus, the conditions of location are part of the process of investment. Because investment changes through time (as new investment and changes in production, technology and organization of existing investment) the 'key to understanding the present day patterns of location, then, lies in the historical causes of changing investment patterns and the evolution of industry' (Walker and Storper, 1981: 486).

Massey and Meegan (1979) adopted a Marxist perspective within a 'macro-structural' approach to just such production and organizational changes in their analysis of the electrical engineering and electronics industry. That, and similar studies, shows a strong temporal correlation between location change and fundamental changes in technology (requirements for production) and organization (forms in which capital appears), but one cannot assume that one can generalize from these specific contexts to explain the location of other industries. Walker and Storper further refine this view:

The gist of the Marxist model of capitalist reproduction is that capitalism creates a restless drive to expand, to develop the forces of production, and generally to rearrange the social structure of accumulation. Because of this, it is forever altering the basis for the industrial space-economy, regardless of the initial distribution of factor supplied ... old products obsolete processes and uncompetitive plants and firms disappear, rolling up the carpet from behind, as it were ... In the long run restructuring simply means *industrial evolution*. (Walker and Storper, 1981: 489)

Walker and Storper also stress the central importance of labour, as capital accumulation is only possible if the structural requirement that labour demand and labour supply come together is fulfilled (Walker and Storper, 1981: 485). The key connection in the production system is that between capital and labour, which have a relationship of depedence–antagonism; managing labour is a major preoccupation of the firm (and one source of conflict), as well as locational change. Storper and Walker (1983) build on this by relating the theory of labour to the theory of location, to identify the geographic distinctiveness of labour, and to show how a structural model of employment and job creation can be created.

Applying Industrial-Location Theory

From the above discussion it can be seen that studies of industrial location have moved on since the classical ideas of Weber. Archaeologists are usually well aware of the ideas of Weber and Christaller and, in general, are willing to adopt spatial theories (e.g. Hodder and Orton, 1976). However, since industry is an area neglected by archaeologists, there have been few attempts to apply classical location theory to archaeological studies of industry. The theoretical developments outlined above demonstrate the much wider range of concepts available for studying industrial location, a diversity that reflects the wide range of theory now being discussed within geography as a whole. Johnston (1983b) sees post-1945 Anglo-American geography as characterized by three philosophies, each with a separate theoretical base: positivism, humanism and structural philosophies. The above theories of industrial location can at least be partly accommodated within these wider philosophical approaches.

Historical geography and industry

Although location theory and, more narrowly, industrial location, have been subjects for some considerable debate, studies of industrial location within historical geography have received considerably less attention. In a survey of current historico-geographical research, Baker (1977) reported that only about 5 per cent of research topics were on industrial themes, despite the fact that two-thirds of historical geographers were researching into the eighteenth and nineteenth centuries.

Repeating the exercise using the data compiled by Whyte (1984) shows industrial topics to be slightly less – under 4 per cent of the total. Furthermore, most research in industrial historical geography has been conducted within positivist and idealist frameworks. A recent article from the *Journal of Historical Geography* illustrates this. Gittens (1982) in his 'Soapmaking in Britain: a study in industrial location' abstracts his article as follows:

The geographical location of manufacturing industry depends on the balance of advantage of proximity to market, access to raw materials especially when there is marked weight loss in manufacture, a suitable labour supply, efficient transportation and a cheap and reliable supply of energy. These factors are exemplified in the location of soap manufacture in Britain in the mid-nineteenth century.

Gittens's account certainly informs about a somewhat neglected industry, but his concern with location in purely neo-classical concepts leaves the impression of an industry dominated by supplies of tallow and soda.
• An important attempt at applying industrial-location theory within historical geography is Langton's (1979) study of coalmining in south-west Lancashire. Langton discusses the merits of Weber's least-cost approach and Lösch's market-area approach, concluding that though each is suited to analysing certain empirical situations 'neither theory can accomodate both spatially variable costs and spatially variable demand. Even when the industry concerned is as economically uncomplicated as mining, and given full data on all relevant variables, no theory exists which will allow the ascertainment of the optimum location pattern of the industry' (Langton, 1979: 6). He further argues that explanations are impossible because the situation is so complex,

but he still has a role for this kind of normative theory as it at least provides for an ordered description of the processes of change.

Langton develops the argument further by linking location theory with systems theory to produce what he terms a model of a Löschian mining system. Despite the detailed structuring of such a model, Langton concludes that Lösch's theory is inoperable, and that 'it simply demonstrates that under certain conditions an equilibrium location pattern is possible' (Langton, 1979: 1). However, by discussing the theory the main elements of the system, at least, are identified and can be considered, though Langton believes that the lack of causal analysis in historical geography is inevitable, given the difficulties over data and the theoretical problems in recreating the past. Langton's approach is essentially a traditional one and in many respects represents the acme of the positivist approach in historical geography of the 1960s and 1970s. Nevertheless, it is a polished piece of work, based on impeccable scholarship.

In a series of articles Alan Baker (1972, 1977, 1978, 1979, 1982) has charted the progress of historico-geographical thought and practice over the last fifteen years. By 1979, Baker was discerning a 'new beginning' in historical geography that was pointing the subject in an exciting, though for many historical geographers unfamiliar, direction. The principal change has been towards a more humanistic historical geography, with theories of human agency closely borrowed from social theory. In looking to where historical geography had been, Baker (1979) writes:

Much historical geography has been focused upon *landscapes* transformed by man rather than upon *man* as agent of landscape change, upon artefacts rather than upon ideas, upon actions rather than attitudes, upon external forms rather than internal processes. In short, much historical geography is open to many of the criticisms which have come to be levelled against the geographical fraternity of spatial analysts.

Baker reiterates a line he has taken many times: 'the nature of that human struggle to control and structure time and space – the process underlying the form – should be of paramount concern rather than descriptions of temporal or spatial organization'. He also stresses the fundamental need for historical geographers to adopt an ideological approach to their research, as time and space are structured by ideologies.

Baker recommends Marxian humanism as an ideological fount for historical geographers, first because historical change, social conflict and social justice are central to Marxian viewpoints, and second, because by so doing, historical geography and human geography will converge to the benefit of both. In his 'On ideology and historical geography' (1982) he considers historical geography to be failing without recourse to ideology and concepts and methods developed in other disciplines. Social and economic history have successfully embraced new perspectives, much of it derived from the Marxian and structuralist writings of social theorists generally (Iggers, 1975). If historical geography is to be seen as a social science, it must embrace theoretical development in the social sciences generally, as both archaeology and history have already successfully done.

Turning to the historical study of industrialization, Baker (1982: 237) identifies two traditions of scholarship. Clapham, Ashton and Hartwell viewed industry from a materialistic and bourgeois viewpoint as opposed to the humanistic standpoint of the Hammonds, Hobsbawn and E. P. Thompson who saw industrialization as costing more in human misery than was gained in material terms. Baker considers that H. C. Darby had considerable influence in promulgating the bourgeois, materialistic view of history within historical geography. Baker does not deny that both groups can produce 'legitimate histories', but he feels 'the time is long overdue for historical geographers to consider seriously Marxist methods of historical analysis and to ask to what extent it would be a constructive step to move towards a Marxian humanism'.

Derek Gregory is one historical geographer who has eschewed historical geography's traditional concern with patterns rather than processes and places rather than people. In *Regional Transformation and Industrial Revolution* (1982b), Gregory breaks with these traditions, basing his ideas instead upon the application of social theory in explaining the transformation of the West Riding woollen industry and particularly the change from the domestic to the factory system between 1780 and (roughly) 1840. Gregory's basic argument is that the local changes in society and experience were part of a much broader process of changing economy, politics and ideology. Gregory has consistently advanced a critique against positivist explanation in geography (e.g. Gregory, 1978a, 1978b, 1981a, 1982b) and has played an important role in presenting and interpreting social theory for human geographers. Human agency and the role of the individual are central to his ideas, and he frequently contrasts the positivist versus humanist debate in such opposing terms as the neo-positivist's 'spatial organization of society' and the humanist's 'social organization of space' (Gregory, 1981a: 3).

Gregory (1981a) cites the volume of essays *Humanistic Geography: Prospects and Problems*, edited by Ley and Samuels (1978), as an important contribution to the resurgence of humanism in geography but goes beyond the type of humanism developed by Ley and Samuels and puts forward the idea of Marxian humanism which, he argues, should clarify 'the relationships between human agency and structural transformation which ought to lie at the very heart of any properly human geography . . . geography must restore human beings to their worlds in such a way that they can take part in the collective transformation of their own human geographies; and without an adequate understanding of history, there can surely be no genuine embrace of creativity, contingency and change' (Gregory 1981a: 4).

Gregory outlines four models of historical change seen in terms of the relationships between society and the individual: reification, voluntarism, dialectical reproduction and structuration. He strongly favours structuration as a model for explaining social change because it offers an integration of both humanist and structuralist perspectives. Gregory draws heavily on Giddens's formulation of structuralism – 'that in the reproduction of social *life* (through systems of interaction) actors routinely draw upon interpretive schemes, resources and norms which are made available by existing structures of signification, domination and legitimation and that in doing so they thus immediately and necessarily reconstitute those *structures*' (Gregory, 1981a: 8–10). By so integrating humanist and structuralist perspectives, the materialist base of society (the infrastructure) retain its significance, while still recognizing the importance of human agency (Johnston, 1983b: 196). In *Regional Transformation and Industrial Revolution* (Gregory (1982b) links two main themes: the progressive transformation of labour as it was absorbed into the factory system; and the 'progressive transformation of the political and cultural process' particularly in how Parliament responded to the crises created by popular protest and unrest over the changing situation. Gregory argues that the way he has disentangled these two strands is based on the theory of structuration: 'as the new structures of domination came to be instantiated in both the capitalist economy and the capitalist state, so the structures of signification and legitimation were compromised and challenged in social practice' (Gregory, 1982b: 260).

Gregory's discussion of the various struggles and conflicts that were manifested in the economy, politics and within ideology contributes to the 'totality' within which the woollen industry was transformed. Although Gregory rarely uses the concepts of location or landscape in their everyday meanings, the changing landscapes of woollen production in Yorkshire in the nineteenth century are a reflection of the dialectics of the mode of production. Cosgrove (1984) extends this concept with the idea that culture mediates between overarching material forces and spatial patterns. Landscape is one expression of the relationship between culture and economic and social structures:

Within the apparently seamless habit of any social formation the economy conceived as the production of material goods, and culture conceived as the production of symbols and meaning, coexist and continually reproduce social relations through the action of living human beings. Economy and culture, structural necessities and human actions, interpenetrate and relate dialectically, each structucturing the other as it is structured by the other'. (Cosgrove, 1984: 56)

All cultural landscapes are symbolic landscapes and so industrial landscapes are symbols of the capitalist mode of industrial production. Cosgrove (1984: 63–4) perceives a dual significance of land during the period of transformation to industrial capital: on the one hand land was seen as having purely newly acquired exchange value, while, on the other, the use value and status value of bourgeois land was still important enough to be replicated by the nouveau riche. However, historical geographers have investigated the symbolic landscapes of status land (e.g. landscape gardens or Palladian planning) rather more thoroughly than they have studied the symbolic landscapes of industrial capitalism.

Archaeology and Industry

The archaeological study of industry has progressed along rather narrower pathways than has the geographical study of history. Prehistoric and historic archaeologists have examined industry more as a component of cultural development than as an area of interest in its own right, while industrial archaeologists have almost wholly restricted their investigations to the landscapes and material remains of the Industrial Revolution. Much social theory has been taken on board by archaeologists, particularly structural and Marxist theory, but it has so far had little impact on archaeological studies of industry, despite the latter being an obvious candidate for such theoretical applications.

Industrial archaeology

In the last twenty-five years industrial archaeology has developed rapidly as an area of interest, but it has had limited impact on either academic archaeology or geography. Most practising industrial archaeologists were not initially trained as archaeologists and this determines the four categories into which they essentially fall: (1) social and economic historians occupying teaching posts within higher education; (2) museum curators or others associated with museums; (3) writers and popularists on the subject; and (4) amateur and often highly motivated and skilled technicians who individually, or as members of groups and societies, do much of the 'dirty work' of the subject.

Industrial archaeology first emerged as a subject in Britain in the 1950s, when economic, social and technological historians realized that many of the buildings and machinery of the Industrial Revolution were being swept away by the great swathe of post-war re-development that reached its peak in the 1960s and early 1970s. The choice of the name industrial archaeology was almost fortuitous, the point of it being to distinguish the study from industrial history which, being based on documentary sources, was perceived as something different. Like any emerging discipline, much early industrial archaeology was concerned with discovery, recording and classification, work often done under rescue conditions when buildings were about to be demolished. However, a quarter of a century later, after a vast amount of data collection by dedicated recorders, the subject has hardly developed from a conceptual standpoint. Butt and Donnachie (1979) see industrial archaeology as 'essentially a field study concerned with elucidating industrial history. First and foremost it involves the location, surveying and recording of the sites and structures of industrial activity.' Butt and Donachie (both of whom are economic historians) believe that the industrial archaeologist 'is not usually so dependent upon careful excavation and stratigraphy as his colleagues in other branches of archaeology'. Thus, it is hardly surprising that industrial archaeology has been largely ignored by traditional archaeologists, with the result that it occupies an academic no-man's land on the margins of archaeology, historical geography, social and economic history and the history of technology.

Industrial archaeology has failed as an academic subject because its amateur participants are happy to keep it as an enthusiasm or hobby, while its professional proponents are usually already part of another mainstream academic subject. Buchanan (1982: 22) saw 'the need to relate industrial archaeological evidence to existing interpretations of economic growth and social transformation and, indeed, to use such evidence to modify the interpretations'. However, Walter Minchinton, in a survey of the subject for a special issue of *World Archaeology* in 1983, was still putting forward the rather weak definition that industrial archaeology 'is concerned with the discovery, listing, recording, and where appropriate, the preservation of the physical remains of past economic and social activity'.

Industrial archaeology cannot make independent intellectual progress simply as the handmaiden of industrial history and historical geography (though that is not to say that its contribution to those subjects is unimportant). By examining the physical remains of industry – nearly all the remains examined have dated from the period of the Industrial Revolution – these branches of history and geography have been strengthened and enlarged by the infusion of new data. David Smith's progress to becoming a neo-classical industrial-location geographer was via the historical geography of the East Midland's hosiery industry (Smith, 1963). Smith also examined the industrial landscape of the area and his book *The Industrial Archaeology of the East Midlands* (Smith, 1965) is now regarded as one of the more informative and academically rigorous volumes on industrial archaeology that were published in the great outburst of print in the 1960s.

Throughout Britain, the spatial and temporal frontiers of social and economic history have shifted as a result of data collected by industrial archaeologists. Hitherto unrecorded coalmines in Shropshire, fulling mills in Gloucestershire and granite quarries in Scotland have added dots on maps and lengthened tables and lists. The history of technology is, in some respects, better understood but made more complex from closer examinations of the remains of machinery.

Not all historians are agreed that industrial archaeology has provided much of importance. Riden, writing in *Antiquity* for 1973, and thus presumably for an archaeological readership, baldly states that 'the task of the industrial archaeologist is to provide raw material for the economic and social historian of the eighteenth and nineteenth centuries'. However, he goes on to argue that industrial archaeologists are failing in that task, mainly because of the mediocrity of their output, much of it being superficial local history. He argues that archaeology has a progressively diminishing contribution to make to knowledge the closer one approaches the present. He considers that post-medieval archaeology, covering the early modern period up to the eighteenth century, does have something to offer the historian, but 'any nineteenth-century historian will prefer to use written evidence rather than archaeology to establish a particular fact and can usually find the necessary documents. There are vast areas of nineteenth-century economic history to which archaeology can contribute nothing more than dustjacket illustrations' (Riden, 1973: 213). Riden does admit that the study of nineteenth-century working-class housing is an area where the techniques of the industrial archaeologist (combined with documentary research) can produce meaningful results to such questions as 'whether miners in South Wales lived in better houses than their counterparts in Durham; whether railway companies gave station-masters more comfortable homes than coalowners gave pit managers'. It is rather naïve of Riden to admit this aspect of industrialization and ignore the rest. If relevant questions can be asked of industrial housing, surely similar archaeological questions can be raised about the size and organization of factories and whether different owners allocated the same working space, tools and machinery to workers in similar jobs.

Despite Riden's welcome strictures about higher standards in industrial archaeology (and by that he simply means better recording), he still perceives industrial archaeology as a tool of history. This 'handmaiden' approach is found in regard to all branches of archaeology from the prehistoric onwards; prehistorians, classical scholars and medieval historians are all happy to accept the data recovered by archaeologists, but few would argue that the only role of prehistoric, classical, medieval, post-medieval, urban, social, and so on, archaeology is to service other disciplines. Industrial archaeology is apparently relegated to this role because industrial historians requiring information on the material remains of industry have done the fieldwork themselves.

Excavation is justified where the remains are wholly and/or partly buried but, as White (1977) emphasizes, the excavation techniques used by industrial archaeologists are comparable with Victorian pick-and-shovel clearing out of the 'rubbish' in and around ruined monasteries. There is a great tendency on industrial sites to follow brick walls or stone footings and floors often ignoring associated timber structures surviving only as post holes or slots, some of which may be the remains of the earliest phases of the buildings. Similarly, stratified occupation levels are given scant treatment, often destroyed in the search for samples of the product (such as pottery) or waste materials (such as iron slags). White's (1977) strictures on the need for excavating industrial sites to the highest professional standards, published in the *Industrial Archaeological Review*, have had some impact and articles are now appearing that acknowledge the role of excavation in the projects described (e.g. Rees, 1980; Bennett, Jones and Vyner, 1980; Fairburn, 1980).

The Archaeological Study of Industry

Although traditional archaeologists have largely ignored its archaeology, the study of industry before the Industrial Revolution has been pursued by archaeologists for some time, even if the volume of output is not large. The great question, of course, it what do we define as 'industry'? It we use a very broad definition that includes craft industries such as the manufacture of stone and wooden tools, baskets and pottery containers and simple uses of metal, then a large part of the literature of archaeology could be reclassified as industrial archaeology. Even a more restricted definition that includes one or more of: (1) the concept of ownership of raw materials; (2) control of industrial processes; and (3) organization of labour, still leaves a large field of study. There is a growing literature on ancient and classical industry, most of it based on archaeological sources, such as Tylecote (1962) on *Metallurgy in Archaeology* and Shepherd (1980) on *Prehistoric Mining and Allied Industries*. This literature cannot be ignored by archaeologists, and I would submit that such work must be considered as industrial archaeology.

Mainstream archaeologists are also turning to the serious study of quarries and lithic production systems, as exemplified in the volume edited by Ericson and Purdy (1984) and in another theme-issue of *World Archaeology* (vol. 16 (2), October 1984). Ericson (1984) laments the relative lack of previous work on quarrying and lithic production systems but, building on his earlier work on exchange systems, he proposes methods for the reconstruction of lithic production, particularly by looking at regional production systems. One may not consider that the simple modification of a lithic resource to make stone tools qualifies as 'industry', but at certain positions in time and space it certainly did. Ericson also discusses such concepts as the regional lithic resource base, procurement strategies, social distance between knappers and consumers, labour investment and modes of transport. The whole question of quarry access is crucial; if access is open and individuals and small groups of people can freely obtain raw material when they want it, this can be considered pre-industrial. But once production becomes more organized and the quarry has a defined ownership or limited access to certain groups of people, then it can be considered that one is dealing with an industrial production system.

Ethnographic data can help to raise additional questions about the more distant past. Clarke (1935) in an article in *Antiquity* described the contemporary flint-knapping industry at Brandon in Suffolk, where immense quantities of gunflints were produced. He examined the source and mining of the raw material, production methods and tools used, and he showed that flint knapping was reserved to a certain few families living in the village of Brandon. This early study in ethnographic industrial archaeology has largely been forgotten, but the questions Clarke raises could be just as applicable to an industrial archaeological study of the nearby neolithic flint mines at Grimes Graves.

There is also a growing interest in Romano-British and medieval industry, and some work of a high standard is appearing. Tim Darvill and Alan McWhirr have produced a series of papers on the manufacture of brick and tile in Roman Britain (Darvill and McWhirr, 1982, 1984; McWhirr, 1979). Starting with an analysis of the brick and tile works supplying Cirencester, they have analysed the product (particularly through makers' stamps), the scale of manufacturing enterprises, the sources of demand and how it was distributed. By extending their study to the whole of the British Isles, they have been able to put forward models of economic organization of brick and tile production, part of which was based on ethnographic data from eighteenth- and nineteenth-century Britain (Darvill and McWhirr, 1984). There can be no denying that this important innovative work is industrial archaeology.

The Council for British Archaeology Research Report, *Medieval Industry* (Crossley, 1981), resulted from a pioneer conference that brought together a large number of archaeologists and historians, though the individual papers usually reflect the main subject discipline of the author. Although not recognized as industrial archaeology as such (the term is hardly used in the report), the papers by Crossley, Rahtz, Moorhouse and Drury are based on archaeological sources and the latter two papers on the medieval pottery and brick and tile industries respectively show considerable promise for geographers in the broader analyses of material remains in terms of their centres of production, distribution and consumption.

The growing recognition of the role of industry is apparent from the increased appearance of papers on this topic in *World Archaeology*, including a theme number specifically devoted to industrial archaeology. In fact, *World Archaeology* is a pioneer journal here in showing a willingness to publish articles on industrial archaeology of all periods. The theme volume, for example, included such diverse topics as the Pennsylvania Railway ore dock at Cleveland, Ohio (Miller, 1983) and the casting of farm implements and similar tools in ancient China (Rostoker et al., 1983). *World Archaeology* also published an important paper by Rowlands (1971) on the archaeological interpretation of prehistoric metalworking. Rowlands questions the role of the smith in the European Bronze Age, particularly Childe's idea that smiths and miners constituted distinct crafts or castes. By using ethnographic data from modern, small-scale societies, Rowlands shows that the role of the smith can be highly variable and that no particular status can be automatically assigned to him. Building on the variation of role, status and output of smiths, Rowlands also questions chronological or cultural groupings on the basis of small quantities of metalwork. So-called 'founders' hordes of of scrap and 'merchants' hordes of typologically similar objects may have simpler explanations than middlemen acting as traders or scrap collectors.

There is, thus, considerably more scope for industrial archaeology practised within the theory and method of mainstream archaeology than has hitherto been realized. Using the above definition of industry, that is, the appearance of organized production techniques on a scale greater than a craft, then industrial archaeology can be pushed well back into prehistory. Specialized industry is one of the great discontinuities of human cultural history, comparable with the invention of farming. If the term 'Industrial Revolution' was not so firmly identified with the period of steam-power technology of the eighteenth and nineteenth centuries, then it could be a candidate for adding to the neolithic and urban revolutions of later prehistory. Childe, in coining the term 'neolithic revolution', may well have preferred 'agricultural revolution', but as that term is also closely associated with certain technical advances applied to farming in the post-medieval period, then the neolithic revolution has stuck as the term for the first emergence of farming.

Though Childe laid great emphasis on industry in his various writings (e.g. Childe, 1930, 1936), he considered the emergence of technology and organized industry as part of his second or urban revolution. We may take a similar view and see industry as just one aspect of the emergence of complex society, but the importance of industry in the formulative period of prehistory from the fourth millenium cannot be denied. The discovery and mining of metalliferous ores, the smelting, alloying, casting and forging of metals, the use of the potters' wheel, the organized production of pottery, bricks and tiles, the manufacture of coloured and clear glass, and the construction of irrigation systems, monumental architecture, ships and wheeled transport, must be considered as no less than a revolution in industry and technology. It does not matter that this is not conventionally labelled the Industrial Revolution. What does matter is that, for five or six thousand years, organized industry has been of major importance in the emergence and continuance of civilization. In this long time-scale, the Industrial Revolution can be seen as one phase in industrial culture associated with industrial capitalism – manufacture by machines in factories, the application of steam and electrical power, and the creation of a numerically large, disciplined and highly specialized working class.

The archaeology of the Industrial Revolution is thus a part of the archaeology of industry generally. The fact that economic historians and historical geographers are also interested in the period of the Industrial Revolution, and have adopted the techniques of field survey and excavation to investigate the material remains of the Industrial Revolution, is no reason for archaeologists to look down their noses at this area of work. Even though industrial archaeologists (such as Raistrick, 1972) often argue that there is no early time-limit to their study, few industrial archaeologists have worked on sites dated earlier than the sixteenth or seventeenth centuries, an exception being the excavation of Chingley Furnace in the Weald (Crossley, 1975). Crossley's report is published as a Royal Archaeological Institute monograph, and it is interesting to see that when industrial archaeologists actually used traditional excavation methods the reports appeared in the mainstream archaeological literature.

However, the archaeology of industry implies considerably more than the application of field and laboratory techniques. The archaeologist of industry must look at the material remains of industry from the broader perspective of archaeological theory and method. Theoretical positions in archaeology change through time, but recent developments in archaeological theory are particularly important for studying industry. Archaeologists are now framing complex questions about social organization, power and ideology. It is time that major questions on industry as part of human culture were also being asked. The exploitation of the environment for raw materials to be transformed into material goods, and the creation of industrial society and industrial landscapes are undeniably important themes in the emergence and maintenance of civilization.

Archaeology and Social Theory

Theoretical developments in archaeology over the last few years have paralleled, to some extent, those in geography. Both subjects have had to face an intellectual crisis caused by the questioning of the relevance of positivism and both subjects have raided social theory for concepts and theoretical frameworks. Tilley has exmined systems theory and structural Marxism as possible frameworks for explaining and under-standing socio-cultural change. He argues that systems theory has so far proved inadequate because it tends to neglect internal conflicts and tensions within a social system, but structural Marxism offers a useful alternative framework for explanation. Archaeologists are trying more and more to apply structural-Marxist integrations of the 'human characteristics of mind, meaning, intention, motivation and choice . . . within the broad constraints of environmental and cognitive parameters' (Tilley, 1981: 382). Most of this application is to prehistory, and the definitions and phraseology of structural Marxism have to be reformulated to deal with socieites and modes of production outside Marx's original consideration.

In a later paper, Tilley (1982) seeks an understanding of the nature of social formations and their internal changes through 'dialectical', rather than traditional structuralism, dialectical because it sees a constant play-off between the structures and individuals and groups and the social formations. Like Gregory, Tilley embraces Giddens's theory of structuration whereby human actions result from structures and, in turn, structures are instantly reformed by the agency of individuals. He briefly discusses social contradictions in relation to the capitalist mode of production, where the contradictions between the dominant and dominated classes is usually much more obvious. Although the conflict between capital and labour has been considered at some length by social theorists and social and economic historians, it has not been fully pursued by archaeologists. This is not, perhaps, very surprising since the majority of archaeologists are interested in pre-capitalist modes of production. However, industrial archaeology, despite being concerned with the material culture of the capitalist mode of production and its strong links with industrial history, has, curiously, neglected this aspect of social theory. Indeed, industrial archaeology has neglected almost all theory in some kind of mistaken belief that it could approach the material remains of industrial society with no particular methodological or explanatory framework.

The diversity of approaches possible within Marxism has been outlined by Spriggs (1984), but at the same time the views of many Marxist anthropologists and archaeologists can be brought together within 'a unified human and social science in history. In this sense "Marxist anthropology" or "Marxist archaeology" are self-contra-dictory terms' (Spriggs, 1984: 3). Knowledge is socially based and historically dependent. It is therefore impossible to achieve absolute certainty. We can only question the past within the ideological frameworks of the present and there are no absolute and final answers.

The more questions we ask, the more answers we may be able to put forward. There is tremendous scope for interchange of ideas between geographers, archaeologists, anthropologists and historians in this area, but there is little evidence so far that this is happening in a meaningful way. Certainly Gregory (1978, 1982) has interpreted much social theory for geographers, and Gregory's work is frequently quoted by archaeologists. So far little that has been written by archaeologists has appeared in the work of geographers. One would certainly expect some common ground between historical industrial geographers like Gregory and industrial archaeologists, but this area has failed miserably.

If archaeology is considered to be a social science, then archaeologists examining industry must formulate their investigations from social theory generally. A great deal of social theory – whether functionalist, idealist, structuralist or Marxist – has been examined by archaeologists and geographers, but very little attempt has been made to apply this to the material remains of industry. Factories, coalmines, blast furnaces and railway lines may appear rather banal forms of evidence for archaeologists, but they are not only the physical creations of mankind, but also the places where the economies of complex society and the conflict between capital and labour have met and been played out. The industrial economy is embedded in society; it cannot be separated from social development.

This is particularly relevent here in a discussion of industrial location and industrial landscspes, which have to be seen as the outcome of the process of the social and economic integration of space (rather than the other way round). There is a need for total historical geography, and it is here that geography and archaeology must come together. Historical geographers, archaeologists and anthropologists have already found common ground in the study of social organization and settlement (Green et al., 1978). A similar venture – based on the title of this chapter – would hopefully find many areas of common interest.

8 Spatial Models, Anthropology and Archaeology

R. Hodges

> Spatial models are the charts upon which social reality is projected, and through which it may become at least partially clear; they are truly models for all the different movements of time, and for all categories of social life.
>
> Paul Vidal de la Blache, *Revue de Synthese historique* (1903)

Introduction

For a decade or so spatial models were in vogue with archaeologists. The impact of Haggett's volume on locational analysis (1965) can be measured like waves emanating first from David Clarke's rather revolutionary *Analytical Archaeology* (1968) and then finding its way into less abstract works before, finally, being occasionally adopted by professional (technical) archaeologists as they grapple with the publication of an excavation and its wider meaning. Spatial models such as central-place theory were part and parcel of what Renfrew has termed 'the great awakening' (Renfrew, 1982a); they were being employed to reconstruct past landscapes and, most especially, to generate economic models. All of this has now become history. The struggle to find a new vogue has come and gone, and we might locate ourselves in a paradigm twice removed from the occasion when David Clarke pin-pointed spatial analysis as one of the central factors in archaeology's loss of innocence (Clarke, 1973: 17). Yet, while archaeological methodology has gained much from the ceaseless quest for new ideas, it has lost a good deal by failing to explore some of ideas with greater resolution. In this paper I shall not venture to claim that vogues are dangerous; instead I shall attempt to examine some central questions about spatial archaeology, beginning where Clarke so tragically left off at his premature death in 1976.

The Appropriate Model?

Clarke, in inimitable style, describes spatial archaeology as

... the retrieval of information from archaeological spatial relationships and the study of the spatial consequences of former hominid activity patterns within and between features and structures and their articulation within sites, site systems, and their environments: the study of the flow and integration of activities within and between structures, sites and resource spaces from micro to the semi-micro and macro scales of aggregation. Spatial archaeology deals, therefore, with human activities at every scale, the traces and artefacts left by them, the physical infrastructure which accommodated them, the environments that they impinged upon and the interaction between all these aspects. Spatial archaeology deals with a set of elements and relationships. (Clarke, 1977: 9).

Clarke's rather awkward definition was most readily expressed in his analysis of the pre-Roman Iron Age Glastonbury lake village (1972). In this seminal study, he endeavoured to re-examine the macro, semi-micro and micro levels of interaction (as he described them) explicitly using geographical models. Three models seemed appropriate to him at the time. First, von Thünen's model of relationships between spatial distributions of activities and land-use around a centre galvanized his attention, as it did many of his contemporaries then teaching and studying at Cambridge. The essence of von Thünen's model, published in 1826 in *Der isolierte Staat*, is the law of diminishing returns with distance. Archaeologists, much impressed by Chisholm's use of it in his *Land Use and Settlement* (1968), adapted it to what is familiarly called site-catchment analysis (Higgs and Vita-Finzi, 1970, 1972). A second model used by Clarke and his contemporaries was Alfred Weber's concept of minimum energy/least-cost locations (Clarke, 1977: 22–23). Hunter–gatherer (mobile) strategies have been described using this framework until the inception of ethno-archaeology applied a cautionary brake on the use of concepts like this (Binford, 1983: 202). Thirdly, the most influential and extensively used model has been Walter Christaller's central-place theory which endeavours to define an optimal, least-cost organizational structure within a network of related sites. In essence, Christaller contended that the sites in the network are likely to adopt a hexagonal territorial tesselation of space which may be altered by shifting the orientation of the hexagonal net, the size of each territory, and the number and variety of sites served by each central place.

Christaller's theory is constructed upon a number of assumptions. First, the population and (thus the) purchasing power are distributed over an undifferentiated and unbounded surface, and second, maximization of profits and minimization of costs (supply and demand)

regulated in some way through a structured market system existing in this space (Christaller, 1966; Haggett, 1965; Smith, 1976b). Central-place theory is as much concerned with the administration of spatial resources, as it is with the efficient distribution of commodities. Implicit in the model is the recognition of social mechanisms for controlling commerce and production. Clearly, it relates to complex, highly stratified behaviour.

Clarke rightly acknowledged, in a posthumously published paper, that all three models laid great emphasis upon maximizing benefits and urged the discovery of more appropriate forms of analysis (1977: 23–4). Almost a decade after the paper was written, few would argue with his point. Indeed, many archaeologists have appreciated the inherent assumptions in models borrowed from the burgeoning age of industrial expansion, and translated to prehistoric contexts at a time when, in the wake of President John F. Kennedy, the western world was at its richest and most expansive (Trigger, 1984a). In short, the assumptions which determined the theories of Christaller, von Thünen and Weber were rooted in behaviour that they could observe and test; obviously this is not the case in archaeology (e.g. Adams, 1975: 458, challenging Johnson's (1975) use of central-place theory in late prehistoric Iran). The more appropriate forms of analysis needed to place more emphasis upon social constraints determining economic behaviour. The maximization of benefits and the minimization of costs simply does not determine economic behaviour in many recent ethnographic contexts, and is unlikely to have done so in many prehistoric and early historic circumstances (cf. Dalton, 1981). But it is one thing to show the reasons why certain approaches to the past should be adopted; it is another (as Clarke was tacitly acknowledging) to construct spatial frameworks in which the interaction between society and its economy were satisfactorily taken into account. The attraction, after all, of Clarke's models, so ubiquitously adopted by archaeologists in the seventies, was that spatial data are the substance of material-culture studies. The maximizing frameworks offered an apparently straightforward opportunity to explain these 'former hominid activity patterns'. Innocence on this matter has been lost very slowly.

To advance this approach, as Clarke pointed out, models would have to be found from archaeology itself (with its advantage of a long time-depth to study spatial process) or from anthropology. Significantly, anthropology has devised the appropriate models, but these come from the neo-Marxists, whose work has reached a wider audience in recent years. There are two strands to this paradigm. The first, and by far the most familiar, school reject the economistic arguments of Marx's thesis on pre-capitalist formations, and propose instead a reformulated notion of social totality which gives greater weight to the political determination of material processes (Rowlands, 1982: 167–71). This approach owes much to the work of Jonathon Friedman and Maurice Godelier who, between them, have outlined the evolutionary process and a system of internal dynamics for pre-capitalist formations (Friedman, 1974; Godelier, 1977). They borrow some Marxist terminology, but essentially develop some of the early (unsophisticated?) aspects of substantavist economics (the work of Karl Polanyi, 1957; Paul Bohannan and George Dalton 1961; and Marshall Sahlins, 1974). This thesis, therefore, draws attention to social complexity in pre-capitalist conditions, and to the extent to which the economy is subsumed into what previously were regarded as discrete phenomena (such as political development, religion, etc.). As Mark Leone has pointed out, 'it is better to label such ideas as materialist and leave the political involvement with Marxism behind . . . The ideas can then be regarded most usefully as extensions of the successful materialist approach of the new archaeology, a move which will abandon the cumbersome and emotion-laden parts of Marxism' (Leone, 1982: 757). Leone rightly notes that this paradigm shift comes at a time when archaeology (including practising field/rescue archaeologists) is primarily concerned with more complex socities rather than with issues involving early man. The neo-Marxist or materialist approach provides the theoretical basis, rooted in anthropology, for extending archaeological theory beyond its over-whelming involvements in hunter–gatherer studies, successfully treated by the new archaeologists of Clarke's generation, and begins to link these complex, pre-capitalist formations to the ideology and issues which concern our times (Leone, 1982: 757).

The central problem, however, is how might archaeologists operationalize this neo-Marxist approach to the past? Ten years ago Clarke predicted that certain levels of socio-economic activity might generate replicable patterns which might be observed in the material-culture record. Indeed, the search for repeated behavioural manifestations in the archaeological record occurred alongside the implementation of those spatial models described above (Hodder, 1974; Renfrew, 1975, 1977b). However, the rise of 'social archaeology' (Bradley, 1984: 4–5), its great emphasis upon history (Leone, 1982; Rowlands, 1982), and the concomitant exploration of so-called middle-range theory (and ethno-archaeology, in particular (Hodder, 1982; Binford, 1983)) has drawn attention to this movement and away from the basic problem of relating archaeological data to anthropological models. Accordingly, the Great Synthesizer of Flannery's seminal volume, *The Early Mesoamerican Village* (1976), is either long in the tooth (i.e. grossly out of touch) or a very brave person indeed (cf. Bradley, 1984: 5). The trend towards particularism and away from synthesis, has instilled a cautionary attitude in the archaeological fraternity. There is a sense of pessimism that the goals for which Binford and Clarke were striving in the sixties cannot be achieved – archaeology needs to concern itself with less ambitious historical matters (Hodder, 1982b). Such pessimism needs to be challenged; the models appropriate to the (neo-Marxist) materialist approach do exist, although, as Clarke rightly predicted, these need to be qualified and developed using data from long-running processes well-documented by archaeology. My second strand, then, refers to Carol A. Smith's seminal work on the organization of stratification in agrarian societies and its promise for analysing pre-capitalist formations. It is first necessary to outline the essential elements of Smith's model, before examining those aspects which deserve some reconsideration.

Smith's model might be described as anthropological geography, which makes it highly relevant to archaeology. She takes a qualified neo-Marxist approach; that is, she maintains that economic stratification is a defining characteristic of agrarian societies. She also accepts Marx's explanation that the forces and relations of production structure differential control of the means of production; and, similarly, that economic classes are defined in terms of access to or control over the means of production. But she emphatically points out that agrarian societies exist where control of the means of production does not provide the basis for stratification. (In this respect she concurs with Friedman and Godelier.) Hence, she sought to construct a 'corollary to the theory of production anticipated by Marx' (Smith, 1976b: 309–10). She asserts that stratification in agrarian societies results 'from differential access to or control over the means of exchange; variation in stratification systems is related to types of exchange between producers and non-producers as they affect and are affected by the spatial distribution of the elite and the level of commercialisation in the region and beyond' (Smith 1976b: 310). In essence, it appears to be a corollary to the maximization models, appropriate to the anthropological data on pre-capitalist formations.

This model, according to Smith, is relevant to those agrarian societies where the great majority of the population is engaged in food production. In other words, it is relevant to pre-industrial societies, including west European societies before the eighteenth century. Social divisions in these societies are founded upon access to and control over resources. This might mean control over landed resources or, equally, control of military forces. Smith points out, however, that most exchanges across social divisions tend to be imbalanced; consequently, she refutes the substantavists (such as Polanyi and Dalton) who had maintained that some social commodity such as spiritual or physical protection, for example, might balance the exchange of gifts or commodities (Smith 1976b: 312). Indeed, imbalanced exchange, she contends, is a distinguishing feature of stratified agrarian societies, and the economic status of the elite is seen to depend upon their control of distribution and exchange rather than just production (Smith 1976b: 312).

Smith's model is a typology which is said to be of predictive value. The typology takes into account three frameworks, reminiscent in fact of George Dalton's pioneering work on peasant markets (Bohannan and Dalton, 1961); these are: (1) uncommercialized exchange (*non-market exchange*) where transactions are 'direct'; (2) partially commercialized, noncompetitive exchange (*controlled market exchange*) where transactions are administered (by the elite); (3) fully commercialized exchange (*competitive market exchange*). The exchange types are as follows (Smith 1976b: 314 ff.):

1 An unbounded network system where exchange is direct and no division of labour exists. This is an uncommercialized system found usually in aboriginal contexts.

2 A bounded hierarchical network system where exchange is direct, and in which the division of labour is very slight. The system is uncommercialized, with only the movement of a few scarce or prestige resources. Smith contents that this system typifies many 'feudal' societies in which power is based upon landed wealth.

3 A solar-central-place system in which an administered market exists at the centre of the region. In this system the division of labour is slight, and the network of relationships between central-place and satellite settlements is determined principally by administrative/decision-making forces. The system, as a result, is only partially commercialized.

4 A dendritic central-place system in which a monopolistic market (a gateway community (Hirth, 1978) or port-of-trade (Polanyi, 1957)) occurs on the confines of a region. This is a partially commercialized system in which exchange with another region is encouraged, but significantly is contained in an administered centre. These gifts and commodities are then used by the elite to sustain, or sometimes manipulate, the social system. One feature of this system is a limited increase in craft specialization at the market which has some influence upon a zone from which that community draws its subsistence. Smith contends that these systems occur on the periphery of what Immanuel Wallerstein has called 'world systems' (1974: 15). Following Wallerstein, she believes that the gateway communities indicate an exploitative, imbalanced exchange (Smith 1976b: 301–2).

5 Interlocking central-place systems of the type described by Christaller in which competitive markets are a prominent feature and maximization is the norm. In these systems, a high division of labour exists, and the implementation of tributary relations to mediate across the division means that the market fully extends to all parts of the region.

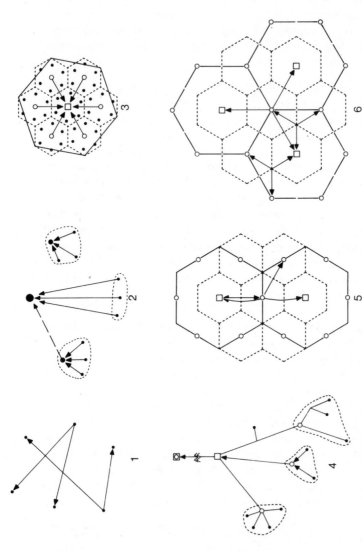

Figure 1 1 An unabounded network system where exchange in the region is direct and no division of labour exists; 2 a bounded hierarchical system where exchange in the region may be controlled by some central authority, but where the production and distribution of commodities is low; 3 a solar central-place system where an administered market exists in the region, maintaining a low level of commodity production and distribution, and an equally low level of social stratification; 4 a dendritic central-place system in which a monopolistic market (gateway community) occurs on the edge of the region to control prestige goods exchange and the production of limited commodities for external distribution; 5 Two variants of central-place systems in which interlocking competitive markets generate a high level of production and distribution in a well-regulated socio-economic system.

Smith's model is a highly appropriate framework for archaeology. Archaeologists, as Clarke stated, are concerned with the interaction between regional (macro) settlement systems measured at community (semi-micro) and micro (household) levels. Field survey on a regional basis, followed by selective excavations of communities and households provide data on the settlement structure (its hierarchy, function, etc.) and on production, distribution, consumption and cognitive interaction. In short, these regional patterns can be recognized in the material record (cf. Hodges, 1982); the typology as a result can be summarized in archaeological terms as follows:

Table 1   The archaeological correlates of Carol A. Smith's regional models

Network	Settlement hierarchy	Regional production	Regional distribution
1 Unbounded network	No hierarchy	Minimal	Minimal
2 Bounded hierarchical network	Small elite sites; minimal hierarchy	Minimal: at elite sites	Minimal: between elites
3 Solar central-place system	Large elite sites for administrative/ ideological purposes	Focused at central-place for its own ends; otherwise minimal	Minimal
4 Dendritic central-place system	Monopolistic trading sites and limited elite hierarchy	Large-scale at trading site; otherwise low-level production	Plentiful evidence of long-distance trade at monopolistic site, and limited evidence from regional elite sites
5 Interlocking central-place system	Hierarchy of competitive markets	High-level production at all levels of hierarchy	Distribution focused on market hierarchy

Nevertheless, Smith's models cannot be used as straightforwardly as Table 1 might imply; some aspects of her typology require reconsideration. The weakness of Smith's models is largely revealed by her data base – her research in modern Mesoamerica. The theory, in fact, relates principally to pre-capitalist contexts, while she appears to have in mind those peasant circumstances of the present Third World, in which the capitalist world is imposing itself (often discretely) upon Central American peasants. To use her approach as a corollary to the neo-Marxist or materialist anthropology it needs to be qualified.

First, she places undue emphasis upon exchanges which *appear* to be imbalanced. In this respect, she remains closer to traditional Marxist thinking, putting emphasis upon exploitation of one group by another. Neo-Marxists, as we have seen, like the substantavist economic anthropologists before them, placed greater emphasis on social exchange – on the spirit and the context of gift-giving, for example, and upon its wider social meaning. In non-market and controlled market exchange (as Smith defines them) a primary purpose of exchange is for social reproduction (to use the Marxist/neo-Marxist term). This point is of some significance, for example, in discriminating dendritic central-place systems. Certainly, there are occasions when a colonial power attempts to exploit a weaker, or primitive power (sustaining a less complex social regime) through a gateway community. There are plenty of historical examples as successive world systems obtained raw materials from under-developed contexts in exchange for manufactured goods of prestige value to the local (less primitive) regime (e.g. Wolf, 1982). There are also examples, however, of two comparable powers engaging in exchange at such places in which the balance of trade was deemed critical by both parties to it. In this latter circumstance, the traditional Marxist approach fails to take account of the significance of the exchange for both parties involved, and fails, accordingly, to recognize its role in social reproduction. This is an issue of some importance because it throws into relief the enormity of the social differences operating within partially commercialized and fully commercialized systems. Smith, by contrast, laconically indicates that the impact of a world system through a dendritic central-place (a gateway community or port-of-trade) leads to increased production and generates periodic markets which ultimately become fixtures as competitive markets. This economistic equation reduces the scale of social transformation to secondary occurrence, whereas, as I have maintained above, most anthropologists would place great importance on the dialetic between society and its economy in circumstances lacking fully commercialized markets.

These qualifications of Smith's models, and of her implementation of her thesis in central America lead me to make these proposals: First, Smith's framework – her theory – needs to be reconsidered in materialistic terms. Secondly, in the light of this, the dendritic central-place model needs to be redefined, placing greater emphasis upon the contol of the gateway community at which exchange of gifts and commodities (cf. Gregory, 1982) is transacted for the social benefit (not necessarily the *economic* benefit) of the native community in which the central-place is located. The relationship with aliens at the central-place will be governed to some extent by the idiosyncratic aspirations of the trade-partners engaged in the exchange (cf. Adams, 1974). Where non-market or partially commercialized societies are concerned, the balancing of gift with gift, commodity with commodity, will be of paramount concern.

Thirdly, Smith's theory and then her examples are an indication that her frameworks are too narrow. Regional networks 1–4 (see table 1), operating in pre-competitive market conditions, need to be complemented not only by an interlocking central-place system, (Christaller's classic model), but by variants of a fully commercialized system. Two major forms may be envisaged. One (6) in which the main consideration is the provision of efficient administration or the exercise of effective control over a territory (Smith, 1976b: 36–39), and the other (7) in which a hierarchy of commercial centres may be recognized, but progressive diminution in functional importance occurs with increasing distance from the monopolistic, highest-order centre. It is, in fact, a commercialized solar central-place system (6) and a commercialized dendritic central-place system (7) which Smith describes in Central America. However, the distinction between the partially commercialized and the fully commercialized is to be found in the degree with which manufacture of benefits and minimization of costs determine site location in the latter, while social formations may be pre-eminent in the settlement patterns of the former (Steponaitis, 1978). To make this dictinction still clearer, lower-order markets would be expected in the fully commercialized solar central-place and dendritic central-place systems, and so would a range of production–distribution features (such as mass-replication of standardized goods; exploitation of optimum agrarian resources; ranked distribution of goods according to market value, etc.); in the partially commercialized equivalents there can be no such expectations. Periodic markets might exist, but permanent ones would not; production and distribution would be related to the maintenance of social order, first, with the accumulation of private resources, for example, being an aspiration rather than the rationale of economic activity.

Bearing in mind these qualifications, however, we are coming close, as archaeologists, to possessing spatial models which are (anthropological) charts upon which social reality can be projected. Yet, it is one thing to discuss behavioural patterns which can be employed to model societies that exist today, or have recently existed and are well-documented in all these respects; it is another matter to measure the past using data that are mostly concealed from us and bear little physical resemblance today to the forms when these functioned. In other words, ruins, post-holes, shards of pottery and other refuse, buried beneath subsequent levels, pose many difficulties; how much easier it would be if complete buildings, storage facilities and inventoried data on production and consumption survived!

The Past Tense of Anthropology

Commonly, archaeologists contend that the real merits of archaeology are to be found in its capacity to investigate long-running processes of change. To some extent this is true; yet to some extent, too, the reality suggests nothing of the kind. Archaeology essentially consists of three inter-connected dimensions: settlement systems, production–distribution systems and cognitive systems. These three dimensions constitute the material-culture record. The optimum approach to this record is not to study a single site, or a single site and its wider/regional implications, but instead to examine the structure of regions in levels of analysis appropriate to implementing either Smith's models or, for example, central-place theory. This necessitates comprehending the relationship between regions, between the constellation of settlements that make up a region (i.e. communities), and between the constellation of households and other units that make up communities. Imagine the challenge posed by a living society if one was to study its material culture in this way; then imagine the challenge posed by (1) locating the sites; (2) uncovering/describing them; and (3) interpreting the material remains. The methodology appropriate to this challenge is only slowly being evolved, and the logistics and costs are, by and large, immense. Let us examine each stage of this enquiry – the methodology, the issues and the implications for using archaeology as the past tense of anthropology.

Regional analysis is obviously the appropriate framework in which to investigate past settlement systems. The intention is to identify the pattern of sites across the landscape and their environmental location. But, first of all, how is a region to be chosen? This is not just an archaeological problem; regions, after all, are units of analysis commonly used by anthropologists, geographers, historians and sociologists. Defining regions, of course, poses a significant challenge. Islands and ancient historical territories are often selected (e.g. Renfrew and Wagstaff, 1983; Hodges, 1985) because these spatial units betray cultural homogeneity in a predictable way. Very often, however, regional analysis starts from a definition formulated by modern or early modern observers, yet with little empirical basis on the ground in terms of cultural traits. Realizing this problem (cf. Clarke, 1968; Hodder, 1982b), archaeologists have increasingly selected spatial units that encompass several ecological zones. Questions about man–land relationships rather than cultural homogeneity tend now to take precedence. Hence, for instance, an essential feature of the archaeology of regions is the meaningful identification of long-running spatial processes in the material record. Type-fossils which make it possible to identify sites, as well as to date temporal horizons, are bound to be a vital element in any investigation and need to be taken into consideration when selecting a region.

Sampling regions is the next challenge. The past decade has witnessed the publication of an enormous amount of literature concerning this problem. If all regions were cultivated and accessible the problems might be less, but in the real world many sites will be buried by later deposits, beneath modern settlements, or they will be located in woodland or (modern) pasture where no surface remains can be detected. The methodology for sampling regions has had a somewhat amateurish dimension to it (cf. Mueller, 1975), and only recently have appropriate approaches (i.e. pragmatic approaches of a systematic kind) been considered. Given type-fossils, it should be accepted that all classes of site can be found; the challenge is to discover the relevant methodology (cf. Hodges et al., 1984). Field-walking, aerial photography, detailed mapping of surface monuments, extensive (as opposed to intensive) environmental mapping and the collation of miscellaneous historical information (such as place-name evidence) are all part of this task. Sampling regions successfully is, contrary to common belief, labour intensive and highly arduous, but it can be extremely productive (Cherry, 1983; Shennan, 1985).

The productivity, however, has to be measured in terms of the feedback between the other levels (community and household) of analysis. Community analysis is the next stage after regional settlement systems have been identified. To understand complex societies, as many archaeologists have pointed out, detailed documentation of the communities in a region is required. But the excavation of entire communities rarely occurs; as a rule, communities can only be sampled by excavation. Excavations, because of the expense involved, are the ultimate stage of the enquiry and rarely the means by which the scale and overall form of a settlement is established. Questions about the community must be ranked, and the means to answer each will depend upon the resources.

Commonly, a primary objective is to establish the extent of the settlement, any features which might indicate its form and possibly its formation through time, and the relationship of the place to its context. Surface indications may make it possible to postulate the size of the community; aerial photography or geophysical techniques may be deployed to achieve the same goal. In many cases, however, before the selection of excavation trenches/areas can be made, further data on its internal differentiation will be required. The systematic collection of surface materials (Redman and Watson, 1970; Hodges, Barker and Wade, 1980) may facilitate this. Geophysical work on such a scale is usually impractical. Where no signs of differentiation exist, systematic test-pitting, using units appropriate to the questions being asked, may be the only answer (Redman, Anzalone and Rubertone, 1979; Astill and Lobb, 1982). Undoubtedly, however, the traditional mainstay of British archaeology – a good survey of the area – remains an invaluable first stage prior to adopting some labour-intensive and potentially destructive technique.

But the archaeology of the living/occupation areas is only one dimension. The context of the community is equally significant. Archaeologists have resorted to two 'techniques' when investigating settlement context; these are site-catchment analysis and landscape archaeology. The two are rarely considered together. Site catchment analysis was introduced by Vita-Finzi (a geomorphologist) and Higgs (a prehistorian, principally concerned with subsistence production), but owed its basis to Chisholm's work on land use and, ultimately, von Thünen's law of diminishing returns with distance. Initially land-use was mapped in 1–3 km radii from a centre, but it soon became apparent that the appropriate soils were often as buried as the prehistoric sites at the centre of these territories. Consequently, mapping site catchments poses an enormous challenge, though one (if the buried soils like the buried occupation surfaces, etc. are dated by type-fossils) which can be of immense significance (cf. Hayes and Jones, 1985). However, as will be readily apparent from the previous section, von Thünen's theory may well be inappropriate to the analysis of many non-market societies. In other words, there is no reason to suppose that a community will utilize much more than a small fraction of its territory unless there exists the social necessity to do so (cf. Steponaitis, 1978). Only where the market principle exists will the territory be exploited and the law of diminishing returns be applicable to the creation of benefits and the minimization of costs. This point is often clearest when the fossilized remains of primitive agrarian systems survive and can be mapped. In these circumstances, it is salutary to discover the micro-element which determined the form of these systems; detailed soil analysis, where it has been carried out by 'landscape archaeologists', is most revealing and tends to emphasize the generalizations often made when using the catchment approach (Fleming and Ralph, 1982).

The third stage is to investigate communities in detail to discover the internal characteristics which invariably shed fresh light upon the interpretation of the community as a whole, as well as the regional system. Selection of excavation units remains the major problem faced by archaeologists today. As a problem it has largely been ignored by the new archaeologists (Cherry and Shennan, 1978: 155), and accounts for the tragic squandering of archaeological resources (Hodges, 1983). Strategies do exist for sampling communities, but these are still at a fairly primitive stage of development (Carver, 1983; Wade, 1978). The challenge of excavation is usually seen as obtaining data about the form and function of that part of a community (a dwelling, stable, workshop, cemetary), as well as data on production, distribution, consumption and the cognitive dimensions of the material record. But these are statics. Invariably these data pertain to broad time periods which, for example, accord with Smith's models. To undertake anthropological research – to operationalize the time-depth feature of archaeology – data pertaining to the changing configurations (the sequence) of the settlement is required. These data provide the dynamics. They indicate how forms evolve and change through time, and reveal how one form may be interpreted or erased by a subsequent generation. This form of settlement structural analysis offers the chance of investigating the archaeology of mind (Leone, 1982). Structuralist approaches in a temporal as well as a spatial context may have meaning, especially when examined in conjunction with other material data. However, stratigraphic excavation, nothing less, makes this approach possible. The quite astonishingly bad excavation techniques still to be found in the western world utterly undermines the opportunity to explore the dynamics of past spatial systems. Too few archaeologists have appreciated the challenge not only of reconstructing the evidence of static behaviour, but the opportunity to shed light on temporal dynamics. This brings one back to Flannery's parables in his *Early Mesoamerican Village*: there are thinkers (theorists) and there are fieldmen, and the two remain quite separate. To resolve the issues posed by Clarke and to test Smith's models, this predicament must be ended. Here lies the challenge today if one is to frame the appropriate spatial models for past societies.

Conclusion

> The settlement pattern – the arrangement of population upon a landscape – may be taken as the material isomorph of the entire mode of production in its broadest sense, and one of the core features of social and political organisation.
>
> (Price, 1978: 165)

The use of space through time is the key asset in the archaeologist's armoury. It is a measure of behaviour at regional, community and household scales of activity. Central-place theory has successfully offered a set of assumptions appropriate to market-based societies in the modern world. However, if archaeologists are to formulate assumptions of similar economic and social significance which enable them to interpret fossilized patterns of spatial use, some fundamental problems must be resolved. The first is that archaeologists lack ethnoghraphic data commesurate, for example, with the ethno-archaeological data on hunter–gatherer behaviour (cf. Binford, 1983), which might serve as an analogy for the regional patterns of sedentary, ranked societies detected in the archaeological record. Instead, archaeologists have had to work with models founded upon anthropology, geography and ethno-history. (Carol Smith's work, needless to say, falls into this category; she might be surprised by its application to the archaeological past.) These models have served as the analogies which archaeology chooses to adopt or adapt to its data. This approach, however, is not satisfactory. It has already led to many inferences being made about past societies which the data do not substantiate on closer scrutiny. In many respects, it appears that a decade after Clarke's untimely death that archaeology itself must construct its own models (as he predicted). These must, then, be subjected to further archaeological scrutiny. The reason for this will almost certainly be plain to the anthropologist, geographer and historian. Only the archaeologist will be working simultaneously on extensive (regional) and intensive (sub-household) scales of spatial use; both scales, as I have pointed out above, need to be used systematically (using rigorous sampling procedures) to offer a possibility of reconstructing and, indeed, explaining past behaviour. In addition, only archaeology will have the data on *world-wide* patterns of behaviour in pre-modern and early modern times: other works, the best record of the use of space in pre-state times lies in the archaeological record. Robust models founded upon this record must be constructed.

As great a challenge as this is translating the static imprint of the settlement pattern into a dynamic record that not only records behaviour at one point in time, but also the process of that behaviour. We have to employ the spatial record to study not only change (the primary concern of the new archaeology), but to appreciate periods of stability. We need to know more than when a structure was built and when it was destroyed. We must conquer long-running processes, rather than time-slices within these processes (cf. Plog, 1979). This is clearly a challenge, which is only really apparent when actually excavating and phasing archaeological remains. At this point the chronological 'ifs' and 'buts', the leaps of faith, and Okkam's razor become prominent features in the decision-making/analytical process. The dichotomy between change and process has become most telling in historical archaeology where certain horizons are emphasized and where it is tempting to diminish the processes which generated these horizons. Hence, archaeologists inevitably place great store by the 'invention' of towns, changes from dispersed to nucleated settlement patterns, the switch from accommodation in one domestic unit to units composed of multiple structures. The switch from one to another, in one temporal horizon must not be underestimated – it is the measure of behaviour at all levels of society – *but* it needs to be documented as part of a process, and each horizon of that process has to be explored not only in terms of its settlement system, but also its production–distribution capacity and its expressions particular to that cultural horizon. Historical archaeology may offer the appropriate analogies for individual components of such systems; for example, the archaeology of towns, the archaeology of monetary systems, the archaeology of mixed agrarian systems may shed light on prehistoric circumstances. But it is too early as yet to use analogies of this kind uncritically (*contra* Binford, 1983: 25–6); the documentary sources need to be critically evaluated, the archaeologist needs to use his methodology on the appropriate scale and the two sources must be evaluated rigorously prior to the formulation of models that have general applicability. In this respect, it is becoming all too apparent that invasions and migrations in historical times have to be treated with as much caution as those in prehitory; the historical process is a suspect model for prehistoric events.

David Clarke, it may be argued, lead us in some wrong directions; he was a dynamic contributor in an academic revolution that encompassed many disciplines other than archaeology in the late sixties. Yet his final essay on spatial archaeology betrays his growing awareness that the methodology for using this central asset – man's imprint on the landscape – has to be generated by archaeologists themselves with reference to other disciplines. A good many geographers may not be surprised by this conclusion. On the one hand, archaeology is restricted by the nature of its data, primarily lacking the direct testimony of those whose behaviour we are intending to analyze. On the other, to paraphrase Eric R. Wolf (1982), archaeology accounts for the people for whom history has been denied, as well as those who make history. With appropriate methodology, pre-capitalist spatial formations can be identified and interpreted. This may seem pragmatic alternative to the heady belief in studies by Walter Christaller and Michael Chisholm, for example. The new geography certainly stimulated archaeologists to give fresh consideration to spatial behaviour and its implications, and to develop stategies for documenting spatial relations through time. To some extent, Smith's work represents the direction archaeologists were taking, even though her studies were aimed at anthropologists and geographers. Now, however, we are becoming aware of a more complex fossilized past which requires us to refine archaeological strategies still further. Clearly, archaeological methodology must be developed on a scale appropriate to formulating spatial patterns of settlement, production, distribution, and cultural systems through time at regional, community and household levels of interaction. Research on this scale promises important results on man's attitude to space through time. This, inevitably, may enable archaeologists to re-calibrate the models currently used by geographers. In the meantime, though, the challenge faced by archaeology calls for resources constant with the spatial scale that is the strength of the discipline.

9 Converging Traditions: The Search for Symbolic Meanings in Archaeology and Geography

I. Hodder

In both archaeology and geography the search for mind was long-relegated to the lower divisions of the intellectual game. Until recently it was possible to identify those writings which dealt specifically with symbolism, identity and culture as opposed to other areas of analysis and theory building. Now, however, the development of theory in both disciplines is characterized by attempts to tackle directly meaning, subjectivity and experience, and place them in the forward line. This essay, then, will necessarily move into a consideration and comparison of general theoretical discussions within the two disciplines. First, however, a brief résumé of the history of work on symbolism in the two disciplines is needed.

In the nineteenth century, the boundaries between the humanities were often blurred and there was certainly much mutual influence between geography and archaeology in the identification of cultural areas. The important Austro-German 'anthropo-geographers' (Clarke, 1977) between 1880 and 1900 developed the mapping of cultural items in order to locate regional complexes and to search for social and environmental correlates. In both disciplines an empiricist emphasis meant that inadequate attention was paid to social meanings.

In archaeology this concern with defining cultural entities remained as the main method of placing assemblages into time–space 'box of drawers' until the main impact of radiocarbon dating was felt in the 1960s. Childe (1951) had clready made it clear that cultural trait distributions could not be equated with tribes and ethnic groups, but the debate continues to the present day (Clarke, 1968; Renfrew, 1977a; Hodder, 1982c).

As the theoretical debate about symbolism gained momentum, archaeologists and geographers tended to obtain insights from rather different sources. There was a common backcloth of anthropology, philosophy and social theory, but the ideas were used and emphasized differently. For example, both disciplines became aware of structuralism, but Lévi-Strauss has been applied more widely in archaeology than in geography. Individuals in both disciplines could have read Weber, but there is, as far as I am aware, no single reference to Weber in the archaeological literature. Geographers have widely discussed phenomenology and hermeneutics. But, again, I know of no referenes to either in archaeology.

There were also differences in timing. Tuan (1975: 205) suggests that 'in the last fifteen years geographers have shown increasing interest in mental phenomena'. In 1960 in archaeology, however, the behaviourist, functionalist and positivist 'new' archaeology had not yet started and attempts to get at mind and meaning were soon decried as 'palaeopsychology' (Binford, 1965), unattainable through material archaeological remains. In contrast to Tuan's statement, visible and coherent discussions of reconstructing mental phenomena in archaeology are rare before 1980 (Leone, 1982; Renfrew, 1983c). Certainly, archaeologists prior to the 1960s often talked of artefacts as embodiments of ideas (as will be discussed below), but their approach remained decidedly empiricist. Hawkes (1954) described a 'ladder of inference' in which it was deemed feasible to reconstruct past technologies and economies, whereas the reconstruction of past social organization and certainly past beliefs was deemed to verge between the difficult and the impossible.

Despite these variations in the character and timing of renewed attempts to reach symbolic meanings in archaeology and geography, there is now a common reaction against the positivism of the 'new' movements of the 1960s and early 70s. In both disciplines, questions of the subjective individual, mind, meaning and symbolism have played a central role in this reaction. At the same time, convergence is seen in the common incorporation of Marxism and history within theoretical debate. This convergence has occurred with little direct influence between the two disciplines, but results from a common reading of and interest in certain social theorists. Heightened theoretical awareness in the two disciplines has led to the common discovery of central debates in philosophy and social theory which affect all who work in the social and human sciences.

Divergencies

First, I wish to concentrate on work in the 1960s and 70s which shows the different ways in which archaeologists and geographers have approached symbolic meanings. In a sense, however, one is not comparing like with like. Geography is a spatial science, whereas space only constitutes a small part of the domain of archaeology. Most work on symbolism in archaeology has not been about space at all, but rather about typology, art, style, burial, ritual and so on. While I shall try to restrict the archaeological account to those symbolic studies which have concentrated on past spatial relationships, much of the support for my argument lies in other realms.

The archaeological directions

In geography, territoriality has been studied as a form of behaviour displayed by individuals or groups seeking to establish, maintain or defend specific bounded portions of space. Human symbolizing behaviour is here examined by analogy with animal territory. This emphasis on territoriality as regulative of resources is also found in archaeology. Indeed, the behavioural and systems-theory approaches to symbols and ideology (the ideational sub-system) dominate the discipline.

Wobst (1977), in particular, emphasized the way in which material culture or style boundaries might be more marked when competition between groups over the control of resources increased. This theory has been tried and tested in ethno-archaeological and archaeological studies (Hodder, 1979b, 1982; Wiessner, 1983). More generally, Wobst (1977) was concerned with the adaptive advantages that artefacts provide in information exchange. 'Learned behaviour and symbolising ability greatly increase the capacity of human operators to interact with their environment through the medium of artifacts. This capacity . . . improves their ability to harness and process energy and matter' (1977: 320). 'Style' is defined as the participation of artefacts in information exchange, and on this basis Wobst is able to suggest a number of cross-cultural generalizations. For example, artefact style gains in value if the potential receivership is neither too close socially (since emitter and receiver will be acquinted) nor too distant (since decoding of the message is unreliable). Thus, as the sizes of social units increase so that there is more interaction with socially intermediate receivers, artefact stylistic behaviour will increase. Such theories have been widely applied in archaeology; to the increases and decreases in the spatial and typological variability of pottery styles, for example (Plog, 1980).

The 'information-exchange' approach is a welcome replacement for earlier ideas – that cultural similarities provided a direct reflection of degrees of social interaction. The more contact one individual or group had with another, the more similar it would be in terms of artefact styles (e.g. Longacre, 1970). Nevertheless, the functionalist basis of both 'interaction' and 'information-exchange' models leaves artefacts and symbolism as passive and responsive rather than active and creative.

Flannery and Marcus (1976), in following an approach to symbolism and ritual derived from human ecology, also emphasize that human ecosystems involve the exchange of matter, energy and information. In their reconstruction of the past Zapoteck cosmology in the Valley of Oaxaca, Mexico, ritual activities are seen as regulating natural events and the distribution of resources. The functional, adaptive approach to symbolism in archaeology is dominant because of the all-pervasive influence of the 'new' archaeology. Indeed, as will be shown below, several structuralist studies of past spatial relationships have been couched within adaptive arguments.

There is increasing debate about the ability of such adaptive approaches to account for particular historical circumstances. In geography, Gold (1982) has noted that territoriality varies enormously and that it is not always combative and regulatory of resources. An important function is to create a stable and unobtrusive framework for the orderly conduct of daily life. Similarly, in archaeology, Flannery and Marcus (1976) suggest that

. . . the Zapoteck world was an orderly place in which human activities were based on empirical observations, interpreted in the light of a coherent body of logic. Once that logic is understood, all Zapoteck behaviour – whether economic, political or religious – makes sense as a series of related and internally consistent responses based on the same set of underlying principles. In other words, one very non-Western metaphysic regulated exchange of matter, energy and information. (1976: 383)

The notion that some component of symbolic behaviour is simply to provide an ordered framework within which to live and think and which is passed on within historical traditions has been discussed most fully in archaeology by Sackett (1982) in reaction against purely ecological and adaptive models.

But how is the ordering in such traditions to be studied? Within both geography and archaeology there has been some embracing of formal and structuralist methods. In the realm of formal studies of spatial structure there has been some direct influence from geography on archaeology. The generative grammar outlined by Hillier et al. (1976) was reprinted in an archaeological publication (Green et al., 1978), and David Clarke's (1977) *Spatial Archaeology* contained an article by Dickens on Medieval house forms. However, neither of these pieces of work have been followed up within archaeology. Most archaeological and ethno-archaeological formal studies have been in the realm of pottery-design analysis, and the major work by Fletcher (1977, 1981) on settlement form is highly individual in nature. Fletcher shows that, using ethnographic and archaeological examples, settlement space can be shown to be constructed according to mathematical progressions, such as the Fibonacci series. In addition, in a massive cross-cultural study, Fletcher suggests that there is a mechanical limit in the human brain which prevents densities rising above a ceiling, a ceiling which remains the same whether one is talking of urban centres or agricultural camps.

Such studies are little concerned with assigning symbolic meanings to structures and to the components located within structured sets. This is the domain of structuralism, and there is certainly much structuralist anthropology which gives the lead in studying the structure of settlement space in terms of, for example, inside/outside, culture/nature, left/right, front/back oppositions. Surprisingly, as Gregory (1978b) implies, structuralism has not been a major influence in geography. This is perhaps because it often seems difficult to apply such oppositions in western contexts.

Whatever the reason, structuralism has been more widely applied in archaeology, although again this is as much to decorative and iconographic data as it is to spatial arrangements. Since deep structures are supposed to lie behind several realms of activity, however, spatial patterns on pots are often seen as transformations of settlement and land-use patterns. Thus, Arnold (1983) argues that in Quinua, Peru, the horizontal bedding of ecological zones around a potting community leads to a horizontal organization of decorative designs on ceramic pots. Tilley (1984) suggests that the drawing of boundary lines around the decoration of Neolithic pottery from southern Scandinavia can be related to a concern with the boundaries of social groups.

Other archaeological structuralist studies, however, focus on settlement alone, attempting to substantiate the hypothesized structures by showing that they occur at different spatial scales (see, for example, Huffman, 1981). Fritz (1978) identifies symmetrical relationships in the archaeological evidence for settlement in Chaco Canyon in the southwestern United States. On an east–west axis the number and arrangement of settlements and settlement structures is symmetrical, while on a north–south axis there is asymmetry. As already noted, such studies in archaeology often adopt an adaptive framework. Thus, Fritz argues that the structural arrangements have adaptive advatages in regulating symmetrical social relationships, on the one hand, and hierarchical social structure, on the other. Similarly, David Clarke's (1972b) identification of major/minor, male/female halves of houses and settlements in the Iron Age of Somerset, England, forms part of what is widely considered a classic example of the application of the 'new' archaeological systematic, ecological emphasis.

Rather than having adaptive, defensive functions alone, the boundary around an archaeological settlement can be seen to separate culture from nature or to have other symbolic connotations (Hall, 1976). Indeed, the overall organization of artefacts and settlement traces across the landscape can be shown to be amenable to structuralist analysis. McGhee (1977) considers prehistoric archaeological remains from the

Thule culture of arctic Canada. He notes that ivory was used for items associated with sea-mammal hunting (snow goggles, harpoon heads, kayak mountings), whereas antler is used for arrows to hunt land animals. Other items made from ivory are those connected with women and with winter activities. Thus,

land:sea :: summer:winter :: man:woman :: antler:ivory.

The division of the landscape into land and sea is thus given symbolic significance. Since there is continuity between the prehistoric archaeological remains and the historic Inuit, McGhee is able to support the structural model in ethnographic and historic evidence.

Indeed, it is in historical periods, within which it seems particularly difficult to differentiate historical archaeology from historical geography, that structuralism has been most convincingly applied in archaeology. In particular, Glassie (1975) has described the codes lying behind eighteenth-century housing in America. He shows that types of building, façade, room space, can be said to be 'public' or 'private', and that through time the varying emphasis on asymmetry and symmetry in the layout and appearance of Georgian-style houses can be related to 'nature' and 'the organic' on the one hand, and to 'culture' on the other.

The application of structuralism in archaeology lays bare the difficulty the method has in dealing with change through time. While Glassie (1975) and Deetz (1977) show how symbolic structures change in line with social, economic and religious changes in eighteenth-century America, their structuralist analyses do little to account for or explain those changes. Similarly, in discussing the change from Neolithic to Bronze Age in Orkney, it is possible to show how a structure which generated domestic, ritual and burial space became transformed through time (Hodder, 1982b). The mechanism of change had thus been more fully discussed, but the reasons for change remained unclear.

Thus, recent structuralist applications in archaeology have begun to link up with Marxism in an attempt to provide fuller accounts of agency and change. In this there begins to be a convergence with recent developments in geography. For the moment, however, the divergent directions taken in geography need to be explored.

The geographical directions

While archaeology has entertained structuralism, geography has listened to a debate about the application of phenomenology. The difference here may partly relate to the mute nature of archaeological data in contrast to the additional oral and written testimony available to geographers. Structuralism provides a method for the examination of structure in any form of communication, verbal or non-verbal. Archaeologists, however, can less obviously probe into subjective thoughts and intentions.

However, an opposing explanation can be given for this difference between archaeology and geography. Prior to the 'new' archaeology, it was widely held that prehistoric artefacts do represent ideas. Daniel's (1962) *Idea of Prehistory* was based on Collingwood's (1946) *Idea of History*. Although Collingwood is mainly known in archaeology for his strictly archaeological writings about Roman Britain, his historical idealism did have some impact on a generation of British archaeologists. In America, Taylor (1948) emphasized the artefact as idea. The 'new' archaeology grew up specifically to argue against idealist and 'normative' approaches. The conflict was its *raison d'être*. This may be part of the reason for archaeology's recent lack of involvement in approaches which emphasize intentionality and subjectivity.

In geography, on the other hand, Collingwood, Vico and idealism have recently been brought into the reaction against positivism. It seems likely that a rediscovery of such authors, along with a discovery of phenomenology, will occur in archaeology as its attempt to integrate mental and material phenomena matures and catches up with developments in geography. At the moment, the haunting spectre of 'normative' archaeology stands too close in many archaeologists' memories.

Guelke (1974) has tried to break down the positivist suspicion of historical idealism by emphasizing that Collingwood's explanation, through reconstructing the thoughts behind human actions, can be tested rigorously. Similarly Mills (1982), in introducing the eighteenth-century philosopher, Giambattista Vico, to human geographers, stresses that Vico offers the possibility of reconciling the positivist concern with systematic explanation with the phenomenological demand for reflexivity. Vico was searching for a metaphysical theory which would allow the human past to be known without denying its historical and conditioned character. Whether Vico's solution to this problem is acceptable today must await further debate. But clearly there is today in geography a need for some such solution, since phenomenology itself often appears more as a framework for criticisms than as a starting point for productive interpretations.

Phenomenology is often referred to as providing a philosophical background to humanistic approaches in geography (Entrekin, 1976; Relph, 1970; Ley and Samuels, 1978), as a kind of romantic revival. Derived primarily from Edward Husserl, it is concerned with the investigation of people's 'lived world' of experience (Relph, 1970). Contemporary humanism in geography emphasizes the study of meanings, values, goals and purposes. 'Space' is converted into 'place', defined as a centre of meaning or a focus of human emotional attachment (Entrekin, 1976: 616; Tuan, 1974; Buttimer and Seaman, 1980). Place gives a person a sense of identity. Subjective perceptions of the built environment are important in satisfing human goals and safeguarding the quality of life.

Lowenthal and Bowden's edited volume *Geographies of Mind* (1976) may have a title similar to Renfrew's *Towards an Archaeology of Mind* (1983c), but the content is clearly different. While the latter work searches for universal instruments and methods to measure mind, the former geographical text unashamedly searches for the subjective and historically conditioned. For example, Bowden's (1976) paper in the former volume shows how perceptions of a Great American Desert in the American Plains have shifted through time according to a variety of factors.

As well as the impact of phenomenology, increasing public awareness in the 1960s and 70s about the quality of the environment encouraged geographers to undertake surveys on public attitudes, opinions, preferences and values relating to the environment. For example, Lowenthal (1972) conducted a questionnaire survey of the difference between people's ideal environments (how they would like to live) and their perceptions of the real environment in Boston, Massachusetts.

Clearly, archaeologists cannot have access to this type of data and this difference between geography and archaeology has already been identified above as one possible reason for the lack of discussion of phenomenology in archaeology. On the other hand, the inadequacies of the phenomenological approach recall the limitations long identified in traditional 'normative' archaeology. To what extent can descriptions of subjective thoughts lead to a better understanding of social action?

It is in contemporary critique of phenomenological, positivist and structuralist approaches in the two disciplines that a convergence is detectable. Despite the fact that interest in symbolic and subjective meanings took very different paths in both geography and archaeology in the 1970s, the current critique that has been engendered by them has much in common. In both disciplines there is a concern to ground subjectivity in contexts, to re-centre the individual, and to re-emphasize the importance of history. Equally, there is a common basis for these critiques in contemporary Marxism.

Convergencies

Marxist perspectives are now widely debated in both disciplines (e.g. Kohl, 1981; Taylor, 1982), but it is Marxist contributions to the debate about ideology which are relevant to the present discussion. At different scales, spatial relationships can be said to mask, naturalize or mystify contradictions either between social groups with different interests or between the forces and relations of production (e.g. Kus, 1982).

An example from historical archaeology (or is it historical geography?) is provided by Leone's (1984) analysis of the spatial ordering in an eighteenth-century garden in Annapolis, Maryland. In the eighteenth century, social control by plantation owners was being weakened in a number of ways and wealthy members of the planter-gentry, such as William Paca, the owner of the Annapolis garden, held contradictory beliefs. On the one hand, individuals such as Paca based their substantial inherited wealth in part on slavery, but, on the other hand, they passionately defended liberty. To mask this contradiction and to naturalize the social order, Paca's position of power was placed in nature, in the garden. The ideal of Georgian order in the house and carefully laid-out garden conformed to rules of bilateral symmetry and perspective. In this way the arbitrariness of the social order is naturalized, the gentry are isolated and distanced from attack on the established order. The balance and organization of the garden appear convincingly both natural and culturally ordered, thus making the elite the natural centre of social control.

Here the materialist conception of ideology is clear: the ideology functions in relation to growing contradictions within eighteenth-century society. While the extent of dominance accorded the infra-structure varies in different Marxist perspectives on ideology (Spriggs, 1984), the approach as a whole suffers from four criticisms which can be only briefly described here (Hodder, 1984b). First, it is difficult to oppose ideology and a social reality since the identification of the reality must itself be subjective and ultimately ideological. Equally, ideas are themselves part of the real resources used in power relations. Ideology is not separate from social reality but it is involved in the definition of that reality.

Second, not all members of society share the dominant ideology or accept it with equal conviction. Subordinate groups may have different perspectives on material symbols and spatial relationships, and Paca's garden may have been at the same time naturalizing and socially divisive. We cannot assume that individuals are duped by the ideas of the dominant class, although they may have to express such ideas overtly.

Third, can ideology be subjected to universal theories and categories of analysis? If ideology is a part of symbol systems, dependent on context, how can we assume that terms such as masking, naturalization and ideology can be applied cross-culturally? If the analyst pays sufficient regard to social and symbolic context, *a priori* terms developed for the study of Western industrialized socieites may be seen to be inappropriate and inexact when applied elsewhere.

Fourth, where does the ideology come from? Ideologies, once they exist, may be said to mask appropriation by dominant groups. But can we derive the ideology from this social function? Clearly, the description of social function does not provide a complete explanation of the generation of ideology. There are many ways in which William Paca could have naturalized his arbitrary position of power.

The Marxist approach to ideology clearly allows structuralist and phenomenological emphases to be linked into social process. Yet the critique of the Marxist perspective itself leads to further changes in outlook which have now come to play a central role in theoretical debate within archaeology and geography. Gregory (1981a), for example, has criticized humanistic geography for paying insufficient attention to the 'boundedness' of human life (see also Ley, 1982). His critique is very close to that seen in archaeology (Miller and Tilley, 1984; Hodder, 1984 a and b). These similarities derive largely from a common grounding in contemporary social theory, particularly the work of Anthony Giddens (1979, 1981), and in French social anthropology, particularly Pierre Bourdieu (1977).

The critique has two central themes: the relationship between the individual and society; and between idea and practice. The first is the dominant theme. As Duncan (1980) points out, geography has generally accepted a holistic view of culture, even when it has long been criticized in anthropology. Social totalities are studied, with their own causes and structures in which the individual is a passive, controlled part. The totality, not the individual, is the active determining force. The same point can be made in reference to processual, structuralist and Marxist archaeology. The individual is either controlled by regulative systems, universals of the mind, or structures of society. By re-centering the individual in geographical and archaeological theory, we can begin to see individuals making choices, interacting, negotiating different and opposing interests, using strategies to manipulate the spatial and temporal world around them, with its varied contexts and meanings.

Deriving from and parallel to this reassertion of the role of individuals in society, is an emphasis on the duality between idea and practice and hence the new central role for mind, meaning and symbolism in archaeological and geographical theory. For Duncan (1980), culture is a context for, not a determinant of action. Equally, Tilley (1982) stresses that culture and ideas are 'enabling' not 'constraining', and that the verb 'to act' involves both intention and practice.

These ideas have now been widely applied in the spatial realm, particularly in view of Bourdieu's (1971) analysis of spatial relationships in the Kabyle house. For example, Donley (1982) has shown how the organization of space in Swahili houses on the east African coast plays a part in the negotiation of power relationships between men and women. Moore (1982) and Okely (1979) have emphasized that the category 'rubbish', and its spatial ordering within settlements, are both culturally relative and socially active. In all these instances, spatial structures is both the medium and outcome of social practices. It is neither ideology nor social reality but it integrates both in the moments of daily life.

Conclusion

I have tried to show that although archaeology and geography have, until recently, developed rather different approaches to symbolic meanings, the contemporary critique of these older positions has drawn the two disciplines together – not as the result of direct contact, but as a result of a common reading of anthropology and social theory. The main lines of this critique, which applies equally well to processual, structuralist and classical Marxist archaeology as it does to 'new' and humanistic geography, centre on conceptions of the relationship between the individual and social totalities and between idea and practice. Within this new position symbolic meanings are to be adequately grounded in 'contexts', by which are meant the practical, situational contexts of action, the expediently created lived world, as well as the broader cultural codes through which such activities occur.

To re-centre the individual, then, is to re-centre meaning and symbolism within archaeological and geographical theory. As the old divides between process and norm, agency and structure are broken down, so 'the symbolic' and 'the subjective' move up the league table and play an active role at the centre.

There are a number of implications of this new position: First, there is the possibility of greater dialogue between the two teams, since at least now they are playing the same game. As already indicated, the present commonality of approach derives little from direct contact between the two disciplines. Yet the potential does now exist for fruitful contact and discussion as the contextuality (Hodder, 1982c) or boundedness (Gregory, 1981a) of spatial meanings is explored.

Against this, however, is the second implication that there is an undercurrent which threatens to draw away from this potential dialogue. As the theoretical debate continues, it has tended to focus increasingly on context, so that the difficulties of generalization, using universal categories, are becoming more widely recognized. As the concrete is emphasizesd so general theory is undermined. The argument against theory has been made by Guelke (1974) and is rife in archaeology amongst Flannery's (1973) 'young fogeys'. If this emphasis on the particular continues, geographical studies of the modern world may be seen to have little relevance to the very different contexts excavated by archaeologists.

A third and still further twist reawakens the likelihood of still closer ties. The contextual binding of social action leads to the embrace of history. In anthropology the need to situate present realities within historical frameworks of meaning has been unambiguously identified (e.g. Sahlins, 1981). Students of contemporary society, including geographers, may well ask 'where do the meanings, the ideologies come from?' and may well look to history, historical geography or archaeology for the answer. Thus, Leone (1982) has argued that the origins of contemporary American 'taken-for-granteds' can be found, in the archaeological and historical data, in the growth of capitalism in eighteenth-century America. Whether the spirit of western industrialism can be seen to originate in Bronze-Age Europe, as Childe (1925) claimed, has yet to be debated. Yet the interdependence between archaeology and geography, given a contextual perspective, becomes clear; the boundaries between the two disciplines become blurred.

As long as symbolism, meaning and action are thought to be separable and subject to cross-cultural universals of various forms, and as long as the individual is seen to be subordinate to such laws or generalizations, the two disciplines have little direct contact. They can borrow each other's laws, throw them back and forth at abstract level with little direct contact with no consideration of each other's data. But, as the individual is re-centred, it is the context which becomes important, not the discipline with its accompanying body of theory and its own line of approach. Through context and history there is the potential for a close interdependence rather than occasional and asymmetric borrowing between the disciplines.

10 Power in Space: Archaeological and Geographical Studies of the State

J. F. Cherry

Introduction

A theme of importance to all social scientists is the effective modelling of the spatial operation of power and dominance. As Wagstaff (1983: 324) recently noted: 'Whatever our primary concern as archaeologists and geographers, we cannot proceed very far before we are up against questions of power in society. There is, therefore, a shared interest in what constitutes economic and political power, how it is spatially organised and, more important, how its configuration and articulation can be recognised.' Until recently, however, the extent of such mutual interest has been limited, confined for the most part to the use by archaeologists (e.g. Hodder and Orton, 1976) of work in economic and locational geography, which in general pays little attention to overtly political factors. This may be attributable, as Renfrew (1981: 268–72; 1983a: 322) has claimed, to the odd absence of rigorous, quantitative analyses in most traditional political geography. If we follow the definition of that field offered by Kasperson and Minghi (1969), as *the spatial analysis of political phenomena*, then it is indeed possible that current *archaeological* work may be able to throw some light on the sorts of general problems that interest political geographers. This chapter, therefore, selectively reviews some instances, and assesses the potential, of what one might call 'political geography in the past tense'.

To the geographer, it probably seems that archaeological study of past socio-political systems – what Trigger (1974) calls 'the archaeology of government' – requires a disproportionate research effort merely to ascertain basic factual matters, such as their territorial extent or hierarchical patterns of power. These aspects, if not self-evident, are at least much more accessible to observation in the modern world using external, operational evidence: why, then, struggle with bad archaeological data? To the archaeologist, on the other hand, it appears counter-intuitive that geographers have shown so little interest in the origins and development of early states and imperial systems, and that they seem generally to lack any coherent or distinctive theories of the state and its origins (Dear and Clark, 1978; Johnston, 1982). It should be frankly acknowledged that there are many topics of interest to political geographers where archaeological data can make little or no contribution. If the pages of, say, the *Political Geography Quarterly* hold little for the archaeologist, this is largely because of the recent surge of work by geographers on local-level processes (e.g. electoral behaviour or fiscal policy) among spatially or hierarchically segregated interest groups *within* states – what Johnston (1982: 187–260) terms 'the local state'. Trigger (1974: 96) rightly commented that 'there is probably little hope of using archaeological data to study any significant problems related to interpersonal competition for power'.

I would maintain, nonetheless, that there remains a hard core of common problems about the ways in which human socities tend to organize their activities in space–time and that this could foster parallelisms in approach going far beyond the mere borrowing of data or analytical techniques. For the study of the state is fundamentally one of power and political potential. The variables suggested by Sprout (1968: 118) as basic to such studies – 'location, distance, space, the configuration of lands and seas, and the distributions of population, raw materials, technology, institutions, ideologies and other phenomena' – are amenable to archaeological examination in the past, as well as geographically in the present.

The Study of the State

Some brief preliminary remarks are necessary on the concept of the state itself, as seen archaeologically and geographically, for the different perspectives adopted here have fostered distinct and only partially overlapping traditions of enquiry. Geographers, naturally enough, concentrate on contemporary states, and their interest in origins for the most part extends only to European capitalist nation-states (Johnston, 1982); the sea-born colonial empires subsequently developed by several of these states, and their subsequent dismantling, have stimulated some interest in the geopolitics of empire (e.g. Fawcett, 1957) and the geographical aspects of the formation of independent nations as a result of decolonialism (e.g. Fisher, 1968). Archaeologists, in contrast, have access to low-grade evidence on a far wider range of types of state reaching back over the past four or five millenia. In practice, however, their chief interest has been the few earliest 'pristine' states – despite the obvious importance of secondary states in attempting to explain cross-culturally why states emerge only in some times and places, and not others (Cherry, 1978; Claessen and Skalník, 1978). A contrast thus exists between the archaeologist's interest in the origins and spread of states and the geographer's emphasis on the role of the state in geographic processes and the impact of its intervention in different sorts of modern policy settings.

Neither side would find much to disagree with in Harvey's description of the state as 'a relation, or process, for the exercise of power through certain institutional arrangements' (1976: 87). Sovereignty, buttressed by the legal use of force, is the key element of anthropological writing on the subject: Service (1962: 171), for instance, sees the state's main characteristic as 'the presence of that special form of control, the consistent threat of force by a body of persons legitimately constituted to use it'. This conception of the state as an institution for suppressing class conflict arising from economic inequality could be taken as Marxist, though Service (1975: 282–6), Friedman and Rowlands (1977), Haas (1982) and many others prefer to see such ineqaulity as arising rather from the economic implications of competition for political power in systems with weak, but permanently constituted, offices. On the other hand, certain actions by state powers can be construed, in functionalist terms, as maintaining cohesion, ensuring security and stimulating economic opportunity for society at large. Thus, most archaeological theories of the origin and role of the state can be classified as stressing either co-operation or conflict, or – more usually – some mix of the two (Cohen and Service, 1978: 21–34). This distinction seems to apply equally to geographic writing. Dear and Clark (1978) isolate five major classes of analytical interpretation of the role of the state: as supplier of public goods and services; as facilitator and regulator of the economy; as social engineer; as arbiter; and as agent of some ruling elite.

One could cite numerous archaeological studies of now-extinct states, dealing with each of these five aspects. What perhaps helps distinguish them from geographical writing is their strongly materialist basis. The exercise of power is, after all, an abstract concept that requires translation into terms which might be archaeologically visible and intelligible. Consequently, recent research has tended to emphasize states as societies with relatively complex, centralized bureaucratic organizations, involving hierarchically ordered and spatially segragated personnel who perform specialized administrative tasks and make decisions (Johnson, 1973: 1–4; Wright, 1978). This is very much more than the Childean view of the emergence of bureaucrats and priests in urban civilizations, and it goes well beyond the earlier insights of, for instance, Naroll (1956: 690) and Murdock (1957) on the relationships between community size, the number of authoritative officials and the growth of socio-political complexity. Since the impact of systems models on archaeology in the late 1960s and, in particular, of

Flannery's (1972) seminal paper on the systems behaviour of complex polities, there has been much interest in states as power structures which dictate the existence of characteristic patterns of circulation of matter, energy and information. These patterns have an on-the-ground component, for example in terms of the mobilization and allocation of resources, or functional types of settlement systems. In a number of important respects, studies undertaken within this framework converge with the spatial and functional analyses of location in economic geography, and many of the same types of data or analytic technique have proved to be relevant.

Considerations of space clearly proclude any review here of the burgeoning archaeological literature on state origins: useful overviews, in any case, may be found elsewhere (e.g. Webb, 1973; Service, 1975; Wright, 1977, 1978; Cohen, 1978; Sanders and Webster, 1978; Haas, 1982). The trend over the past two decades, in a nutshell, has been a distinct shift *away* from a search for allegedly universal 'prime movers' – population pressure, the managerial requirements of irrigation projects, warfare, environmental/social circumscription, redistribution, the organization of long-distance trade for the importation of prestige goods, and so on – and *towards* more complex models of multilineal evolution, in which it is not the variables themselves but the interaction between a number of locally relevant variables and their interaction with various elements of regulatory systems which are important. This shift, it may be noted, was prompted not by changing theoretical fashions, but by careful empirical research in both the Old and New Worlds, aimed at testing the validity of certain prime-mover explanations (e.g. Wright and Johnson, 1975; Wright, 1977, 1978). There has also been a concomitant reaction against 'stage' typologies of socio-political complexity (such as Service, 1962), since the accumulation of archaeological data has forced the realization that most empirical societies, past and present, exhibit features which draw them away from any prescriptive 'ideal' type, such as the state: some archaeologists thus lay emphasis on the measurement and explanation of changes in complexity itself (e.g. van der Leeuw, 1981a; McGuire, 1983). On the other hand, it is perhaps insufficiently appreciated that an element of cross-cultural taxonomy is still essential (Cherry, 1978), for if one cannot specify when the state begins, one cannot attempt the rejection of explanatory hypothesis for it.

Lastly, it may be useful to geographical readers to point to several growth areas in current archaeological research on states, since aspects of them recur in the sections that follow.

1   Earlier this century, much theorizing about the organization and exercise of power in early civilizations was based on the results of large-scale urban excavations in areas such as Egypt, Mesopotamia or

Mesoamerica. While the results of excavation are no less important today, it would be true to say that most current work has been stimulated by, and relies heavily upon, data acquired by purely surface *survey* conducted over hundreds of square kilometres. Sites offer a uniquely detailed perspective from points in the landscape, but only survey can provide data on the regional distribution of populations and of functionally differentiated settlements, seen in their changing environmental contexts. The most successful work, indeed, has been in circumstances where it has been possible to pool the results of a number of such surveys in neighbouring areas to provide detailed diachronic information at macro-regional scales (e.g. Adams, 1981 in Mesopotamia; Blanton et al., 1981 in Mesoamerica). The vastness of more imperial systems generally precludes work at this level of spatial resolution.

2   Despite critics who label such work as unduly taxonomic or functionalist, there is a continuing tradition of cross-cultural or cross-temporal *comparative* studies of past power systems. In one sense, this is both enforced and facilitated by the important role of regional data, just noted: surveys often reveal the spatially overlapping traces of several state or imperial systems which replaced each other within a single area, allowing controlled comparison with many aspects of environment held constant. But systematic comparative studies of regional (e.g. Larsen, 1979) or global (e.g. Claessen and Skalník, 1978; Renfrew and Cherry, 1968) scope have also come to the fore. In this regard, an important individual paper is that by Renfrew (1975) in which he notes the recurrent tendency for nation-states to be preceded by the emergence of clusters of autonomous 'early state modules', often closely comparable in size and geographical separation, united by many institutional and cultural features, and in close and regular interaction with each other (see figure 1). Combined with the interest (mentioned above) in states as information-processors and the realization that even mundane trade goods can convey information about power and hierarchy from one political system to another, this insight has led to the more thorough consideration of the range of interactions within and between emergent 'peer-polities' and the ways in which such interaction influences the manner in which power comes to be exercised in them (Renfrew and Cherry, 1986).

3   There has recently been a marked waning of interest in accounts of state formation cast solely, or dominantly, in terms of ecological variables and of the state's managerial capacity for dealing with the problems posed in a widely divergent set of specific socio-environmental contexts. Once again, it was the paper by Flannery (1972) that first set out clearly the arguments for widening this perspective. The outcome has been the resurgence of an explicitly political (and loosely Marxist) approach, examining structural transformation over time, in which the

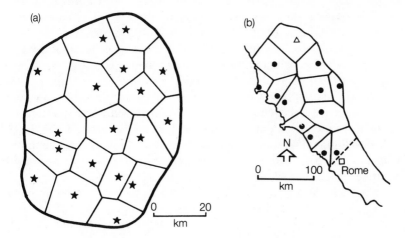

Figure 1 The early state module: (a) an idealized map of the territories and centres of a cluster of early stage modules, within an overall area of cultural homogeneity; (b) the twelve cities of ancient Etruria, with hypothetical territories defined by Thiessen polygons.
(After Renfrew, 1975: figures 2 and 5.)

trajectory of change is determined by the structural properties of the initial system, notably the social and economic conflicts rooted in the internal political dynamics of pre-state polities (e.g. Friedman and Rowlands, 1977; Spriggs, 1984). Putting such an approach into operation archaeologically poses many problems and, naturally, the most convincing studies so far have been those in contexts with good historical controls – for instance, Brumfiel's (1983) study of Aztec state formation. However, work in this vein should encourage some *rapprochement* between anthropological archaeologists and political geographers. A renewed interest in state ideologies and the 'iconography of power' has accompanied this trend, as discussed below (pp. 168–72).

4   Finally, we may note a marked increase in what might be called 'high-level' modelling and theorizing about the emergence of structure – or 'morphogenetic change' – in complex political systems (cf. papers in Renfrew and Cooke, 1979; Renfrew et al., 1982: 281–464). For instance, interest in information flows and decision-making in states has led to the development of general theory, akin to Hierarchy Theory in general systems thinking, about the role of scalar stress in the rise of decision-making organizations (Johnson, 1978, 1982). A similar origin can be seen for the growing influence of the 'Brussels School' (Nicolis and Prigogine, 1977), and its whole approach to the spontaneous emergence of structure via the self-organizing properties of non-

equilibrium systems (e.g. van der Leeuw, 1981b; Allen, 1982). Large-scale computer simulations, using systems models, of culture change (Cooke and Renfrew, 1979) and of the rise/collapse of states (Hosler et al., 1977), have been strongly influenced by parallel geographical work, and especially by dynamic models of urban growth (e.g. Allen and Sanglier, 1979); but there has been justifiable criticism of the mechanistic assumptions and inflexible algorithms involved in such studies. This may account for the attraction felt in some quarters for topological models such as Catastrophe Theory (Renfrew, 1978, 1979) – a development which again has recent parallels in geography (Wagstaff, 1978) – and also explains recent attempts to introduce the cognitive processing of invividual political actors into simulations of dynamic socio-cultural systems (Doran, 1982). In fact, current archaeo-logical theory about the development and operation of complex political structures in past societies is a rich *farrago*, drawing not only on different strands of archaeological thought, but also on biology, physics and chemistry, mathematics, the computer sciences, and – of course – geography.

In the remainder of this paper, I have arbitrarily chosen to focus on just four aspects of this vast field: the recognition of states and empires as territorial units in the landscape; the spatial expansion of polities; the constraints imposed by space upon the effective exercise of power within them; and the ways in which the ideological and cognitive aspects of power find material manifestation. My hope is that this emphasis on the spatial aspects of power and polity will strike a chord in geographical readers and indicate some of the ways in which archaeologists have made use of geographical concepts.

Mapping the Territorial Extent of State Power

Political geographers have engaged in extensive discussion of appro-priate units and scales of analysis (P. J. Taylor, 1984). Likewise, a fundamental requirement for a political study in archaeology is the ability to define and demarcate clearly the entity under consideration – that is, to partition the landscape and its population in political terms. For the geographer, this poses no major problems: the whole world is divided clearly among many states whose boundaries, if often disputed, are nonetheless readily ascertained with some precision from maps or on-the-ground features such as customs posts and militarily defended lines. Were it necessary, he or she could interrogate the resident population in an area in order to establish under whose ultimate jurisdiction they live; their answers would provide a unique solution, since an individual or a tract of land cannot be subject at once to more than one supreme power. The study of territoriality and boundaries among geographers (e.g. Jones, 1959; Pounds, 1963: 56–97) has thus concentrated on the classification of different types of boundary, the precision with which they are drawn and defended, their historical development and degree of permanence, and their viability (in terms of defensibility, coincidence with natural boundaries, incorporation of whole functional economic units (such as oil fields) and degree of separation of already-distinct cultures).

The archaeologist, however, even when working with societies with extensive written records, usually has to start from scratch. It is true that actual maps are known archaeologically from northern Mesopotamia as early as 2400 BC, and there are sets of plans of later date showing an organizational centre in relation to its hinterland. But these are schematic in the extreme and generally indicate territory in terms of the positions of peoples or places which are, or are not, considered to be under the jurisdiction or military control of the state in question, rather than by the drawing of actual boundary lines: this is more a personal than a territorially based sovereignty. Expansionist empires, moreover, often claimed authority over regions they could not in practice fully control, so that boastful campaign accounts or manifestly political artistic scenes depicting 'tribute-bearers' from distant provinces must be treated with great caution. Even the most physical and precise indications of ancient boundaries – the Great Wall of China, the *limes* systems of the Roman empire, Offa's Dyke – in many ways served more as psychological or cultural divides ('us' versus 'them', 'civilized' versus 'barbarian') than as absolute, defensible territorial markers, and they did not greatly impede flows of goods, people and information across them. Despite these complicating factors, it is nonetheless an advantage to the archaeologist that states are *organized* territorially as pieces of land on which people live under public authority. It is accordingly recognized by the rulers, by the ruled and by neighbouring states alike that there exists some sort of political unity extending to the boundaries of a specified territory, irrespective of the kinship or ethnic affiliations of those defined as citizens in this way (Claessen and Skalník 1978: 18, 537–8).

How, then, have archaeologists set about reconstructing areas of landscape that fell under a single polity's territorial jurisdiction at specific periods in the past? The simplest solution, in the absense of any explicit indications of political hierarchy, would be to contemplate a regional distribution of contemporaneous highest-order sites and partition the landscape in which they lie by drawing (weighted) Thiessen polygons around each of them. Examples include the mapping of clusters of early state modules (Renfrew, 1975), of the territories controlled by Iron-Age hillforts in southern England (Cunliffe, 1971), and by Mayan ceremonial centres (Hammond, 1972). But Thiessen polygons simply enclose areas closer to the site in question than to any other and, while this may be a useful concept for consideration of purely economic interactions, it takes no account of political *dominance* expressed territorially. An alternative approach has been to consider archaeological site distributions not in locational terms, but as rank–size distributions of centres (see figure 2), and to look for 'naturally' emerging separations between large (dominant) and smaller (subordinate) sites, from which spheres of political influence might be deduced. Work in this vein has been reviewed by Trigger (1974), Crumley (1976) and Hodder (1979a), while Johnson (1975) and Alden (1979) provide detailed and statistically sophisticated practical applications, However, the correlation between the size of a centre and its power or administrative importance is far from perfect.

It is logical to suppose that the consolidation of a state in a region should result in a zone of relatively homogenous style or material culture, and some archaeologists have certainly attempted to trace the territorial growth of prehistoric states on such grounds alone. States, however, generally expand by incorporation, rather than replacement,

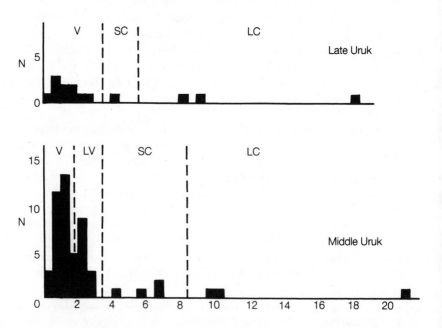

Figure 2   Site histograms for sites of the Middle and Late Uruk periods (c. 3500–3150 BC) on the Susiana Plain of Lower Mesopotamia. Breaks in the size distribution indicate a settlement hierarchy which may correlate partially with relative political influence; V = village, LV = large village, SC = small centre, LC = large centre
(After Johnson, 1975: figure 17.)

of populations, regardless of their cultural background: imperial states are almost invariably multi-ethnic in character, including societal segments that are diverse in language, economy and culture. Conversely, there are many instances where distinctive patterns of material culture extend well beyond the territorial limits of a single government. The city-states of Classical Greece, for instance, were small-scale autonomous territorial units, self-governing, subject to unique constitutions, issuing their own coinage, and so on; yet they were bound together by spoken language and written script, by the structure of religious belief, by comparable political institutions, by competition in international religious games and military co-operation against common threats – indeed, by a cultural conception of Hellenism which amounts, in material terms, to what archaeologists normally call 'a civilization'. It has only recently come to be realized that such civilizations, and the emergence of larger-scale units under a single unified jurisdiction, are very often the outcome of an extraordinarily wide range of interactions among staunchly autonomous 'peer polities' (Renfrew, 1982c; Renfrew and Cherry, 1986) and that these *can* be monitored archaeologically.

In many cases, the most useful indications of the spatial extent of state powers will come from some combination of different types of evidence for the asymmetry in access to goods and services characteristic of such systems, and for a distinctively high-status material culture serving as a badge of political identity. Thus, the distribution of palaces, temples, elaborate burials, fine art, prestige manufactured goods, etc., together with the bureaucrats, priests, artisans and other full-time specialists responsible for them, constitutes a spatial mapping of the personal glory of high-status individuals and of the power of the state itself. Likenesses of the ruler(s), represented in statuary or on coinage and found well away from the centre, generally testify to deliberate promulgation of that same power; coins, however, may diffuse well beyond the limits of empire, while the display of imperial portraiture may be impolitic in certain sensitive regions which are no less under imperial control than others. The discovery of lawcodes erected in public places would constitute a more straightforward indicator of who ruled whom. Likewise, large-scale, labour-intensive construction projects – canal irrigation schemes, road systems, frontier defences and, of course, monumental, self-aggrandizing architecture – tend to be co-extensive with state powers and, by their very man-power requirements, testify to the state's ability to wrest significant surpluses from the polity at large.

Severe operational difficulties, however, arise in the study of the territorial extremes of imperial states, for (as discussed below) there is inevitably some diminution with distance in the centre's capacity for the exercise of effective control: the fuzzy boundaries that result are not easy to study archaeologically. It has widely been found useful to distinguish between zones of direct and indirect rule (e.g. Larsen, 1979: 96–7). The former is characterized by features which should be partially recoverable archaeologically, such as direct territorial conquest and annexation, tightly controlled provincial administration, taxation, land exploitation, trade monopolies, etc. (Garnsey and Whittaker, 1978: 63). In the latter, which should certainly be seen as part of the imperial structure, the internal power structure and means of production are left to function relatively intact, but under the supervision of the centre, and these would exhibit little archaeologically detectable change as a result of incorporation. Egyptian imperial policy in Syria and elsewhere in south-west Asia in the New Kingdom provides a typical illustration: a series of clientage treaties existed between Egypt and hereditary Asian kings of long-established city-states, whereby the king maintained local control while swearing allegiance to the Pharoah and 'offering' regular tribute, extracted locally by his own techniques (Kemp, 1978). Similar client kingdoms and buffer states along the borders of the Roman empire have long been a focus of interest for historians (e.g. Millar, 1967) and archaeologists (e.g. Dyson, 1985) alike. At still further spatial removes, an equilibrium of power was sometimes maintained by treaties, for instance with pastoral nomads, to stop border raids and to promote trade. The archaeological record in such cases would probably amount to little more than written treaty documents (preserved at the centre of power) and relatively feeble flows of trade goods across the boundaries.

This discussion may indicate why the material culture evidence for complex processes taking place at frontiers and boundaries has become an important field of study in its own right within archaeology (e.g. Hodder, 1978; De Atley and Findlow, 1984; Green and Perlman, 1985). Much work has stemmed from the suggestion (cf. Soja, 1971) that political boundaries may act as barriers to interaction and that the edges of polities may thus be reflected in observable diffusion patterns (see figures 3a and 3b). But the hope that there might exist easily recognizable sharp distributional fall-offs at the boundary between the areas of dominance of two autonomous centres is rarely fulfilled (figure 3c); this may be because the archaeological data is too coarse and incomplete, or because boundaries shifting over time produce blurred aggregate patterns. Indeed, recent work by archaeologists in ethnographically or historically controlled contexts has shown that the circumstances under which political (or ethnic and linguistic) boundaries find clear expression in material culture are highly variable and very complex (e.g. Hodder, 1978: 199–269, 1982c). This should not engender extreme pessimism, however. Historical case studies provide the critical link in the development of better methods for the detection of territoriality and boundaries in fully prehistoric situations.

A good exemplification of this point is Alden's (1979) study of

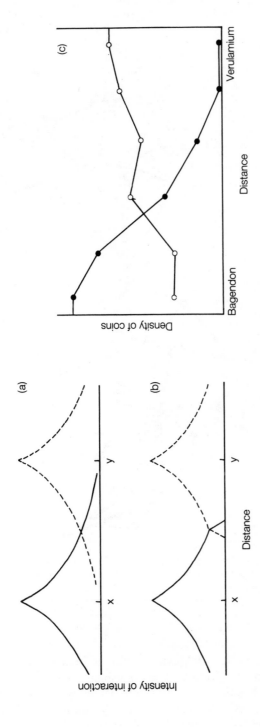

Figure 3 A model for the fall-off in intensity of interaction with increasing distance from two centres x and y, under conditions (a) of non-territorial and (b) territorial behaviour; (c) shows the fall-off in the density of coins from two centres of pre-Roman Iron Age southern England, suggesting the blurred distributions that may in practice occur towards the edges of two political areas
(After Soja, 1971; and Hodder and Orton, 1976: figure 5.82.)

158   J. F. Cherry

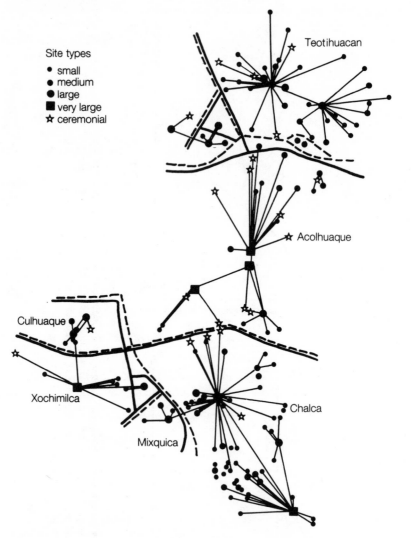

Site types

- • small
- • medium
- ● large
- ■ very large
- ☆ ceremonial

Teotihuacan

☆ Acolhuaque

Culhuaque

Xochimilca

Chalca

Mixquica

Figure 4 A political map of the Valley of Mexico in the Early Aztec period, based on archaeological site distributions clustered in terms of nearest interacting neighbours. Note the very close correspondence between the territorial boundaries reconstructed from ethno-historical data (solid lines) and from a computer model of political interaction (broken lines)
(Simplified from Alden, 1979: figure 7.2)

political units in the Valley of Mexico in the early Aztec and Toltec periods. Alden adopted a standard gravitational model of political interaction between locations, whereby interaction is seen as directly proportional to the populations at each location and inversely proportional to their separation (i.e. $I_{ij}=C(P_i.P_j)/f(d_{ij})$). Important assumptions were that a site's size and its population are closely related, and that the population affects the amount of information to be processed by administrators interacting with other places in the political hierarchy. Using archaeological survey data, Alden was able to derive strengths of interaction between pairs of sites and thus to generate clusters of sites, based on nearest neighbours defined in terms of strongest interaction. For the early Aztec period (c. AD 1300–1418), however, it is also possible to reconstruct political divisions using ethno-historic records of settlements, conflicts and alliances, and some of these settlements are identifiable with known archaeological sites, included in Alden's study. This overlap allowed the manipulation of exponents in the gravitational model to produce an excellent fit between the ethno-historically derived political map and that predicted by the strictly archaeological dataset (figure 4). The clear success of this exercise encourages the application of the method for the retrodiction of political boundaries in the preceding Toltec periods, for which similar historical data do *not* exist. It may be noted that a rather similar approach, using as a proxy for interaction the contiguous occurrences of place-names on inscribed clay tablets, underlies attempts at the computational mapping of political geography in prehistoric Greece (Cherry, 1977) and in Anatolia (Tobler and Weinburg, 1971).

The Spatial Growth of States and Empires

Almost all accounts of the historical development of modern political geography begin with Friedrich Ratzel (e.g. Pearcy et al., 1957: 14–26; Dickinson, 1969: 69–71). The territorial ranges over which the industrialized states of the late nineteenth century could now exercise effective political control encouraged Ratzel (1896) to conceptualize the state in ecological terms as an organism, whose spatial growth could be seen to follow Darwinian-style 'laws'. Later perversions of his notion of states engaged in the struggle for *Lebensraum* have had the unfortunate effect of discovering serious consideration of the fundamental questions raised by Ratzel: Why do states seek to expand their territories? What governs their growth rates? Are there limits to growth and 'natural' boundaries? Although Ratzel's own work now seems naïve and excessively determinist, such questions are not themselves distasteful.

Eighty years later, archaeologists have returned to these matters, armed not only with a far better temporal database, but also with sophisticated ecological theory (e.g. Odum, 1971) and a more flexible multivariate approach to causality in complex systems (e.g. Flannery, 1972). An influential paper in this 'neo-Ratzelian' vein is that by Gall and Saxe (1977). These authors follow Flannery in considering the state as one class of living system with distinctive types of information, matter and energy transfers, and they seek to understand why agriculturally-based states have a selective advantage that always allows them to expand at the expense of less complex systems. But they also introduce an organic metaphor – the greater maturity of the state in terms of ecological succession. States, of course, have a far greater energy budget than non-states; equally important, however, is the imbalanced spatial distribution of that energy, with much of it stored in the central managerial sub-systems in the form of monumental architecture, bureaucracies, sumptuary goods, etc. This is 'paid for' by specialized agricultural primary producers at some remove from the centre, and it is a part of state strategy to drain energy into the centre from the periphery (for instance, by taxation of corvée labour), keeping it in a continual condition of ecological instability and political dependence. (Arguably, the dendritic settlement and marketing patterns seen in many early states (Smith, 1976a: 34–5) represent a spatial consequence of this strategy.) The control span of such systems is limited by transport technology and the increasing costs with distance of exploitation; but as energy is regularly transmitted from the 'immature' outer zones to the buffered, 'mature' core, it becomes increasingly possible for the managerial elite of a state to meet the costs of exploitation beyond their previous range. This leads inexorably to territorial conquests and economic/political subordination of formerly independent societies. In short, the state grows, along with its energy budget and its structural complexity.

These ideas are much more than Ratzel's 'laws' dressed in new clothes. They offer much insight into the factors which condition the economic and territorial stability or instability of states, and help explain why there is a temporal trend towards domination of the world political map by fewer, larger states (Carneiro, 1978). They also open up new vistas and help integrate current research on matters such as the energetic aspects of states (Cherry, 1978: 426–31); their locational and network characteristics (Crumley, 1976; Taylor, 1975); strategies of imperial conquest by warfare (Webster, 1975; Browman, 1976); demographic levels and the spatial distribution – even the relocation – of population (Parsons, 1968; Sanders, 1972; Morris, 1972); contrasts in the territorial properties of market-oriented versus exploitative administrative institutions (Christaller, 1966; Smith, 1976b; Blanton et al., 1981: 234–42); and many other specific aspects of the study of states. Although such topics could be construed as geographical in character, most of these examples draw heavily on purely archae-ological data from both the Old and New Worlds. Clearly, Ratzel's original questions are now producing some fresh answers.

A corollary of Gall and Saxe's explanatory approach to state expansion is that the universal principles they adduce should lead to some cross-cultural comparability in temporal patterns of spatial growth. Taagepera (1968), following earlier work by Hart (1945), has examined the growth curves of the areas under the political control of various imperial systems. Despite many uncertainties in the historical and archaeological data available, it was found that all the cases examined followed the same pattern of slow initial rise, a period of more rapid growth, and a slower approach to a plateau which is more or less maintained for a long time (see figure 5). The data can be fitted best to a time-lagged logistic growth curve of the sort that would apply equally well, for instance, to a bacterial colony grown in isolation on a limited food supply. The constraints on growth in the case of empires, of course, are likely to be those imposed by the frictional effects of distance on internal matter/energy/information shunts (see below pp. 163–68). As usual with diachronic, cross-cultural studies, pattern recognition in itself explains nothing and deviations from the norm can be at least as informative: weak or strong leaders can affect the area under tributary status, and it is quite possible for territory to be lost in one part of the empire while gains are being simultaneously made elsewhere. Moreover, the growth curves described by Taagepera seem to apply best to compact and relatively isolated land-based empires, and they are seriously perturbed by conditions of competition with other strong states or of maritime fragmentation. Such specifically historical considerations, however, do not impugn the principle, already well known to systems theorists, that the large number of individuals comprising something so complex as an empire can actually make it *simpler* to describe and explain the system's holistic behaviour.

This modest study is a nice illustration of Renfrew's assertion (1981: 268) that 'the very activity of examining the spatial correlates of early social structure has the useful effect of posing important problems in general and simple terms'. Renfrew himself has recently provided another relevant instance in his so-called X-TENT model (Renfrew and Level, 1979; Renfrew, 1981: 268–72), which is an attempt to tackle the reconstruction of political organization from purely archaeological data, using an explicitly political framework (cf. Soja, 1971) rather than economic and locational modelling (Johnson, 1972; 1980; Crumley, 1976; Hodder and Orton, 1976). The key concept is the potential for poitical dominance (i.e. unique territorial jurisdiction) of major settlements; the problem is to predict which sites dominate which. It can be assumed that there is some positive correlation between the size (in area or population) of a centre and the territorial extent of the polity it controls; but the partitioning of the political landscape among a number of such centres cannot be achieved using gravitational or Pareto models, since these always require an equilibrium point where competitive influence is equal – a condition manifestly inappropriate when power, rather than economic influence, is being mapped (see figure 6).

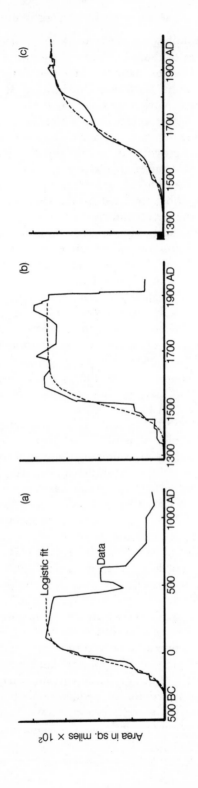

Figure 5 Patterns of growth in (a) the Roman Empire; (b) the Ottoman Empire; and (c) the Muscovite-Russian Empire, with the best-fitting logistic growth curves superimposed (Data from Taagepera, 1968: figures 1–3.)

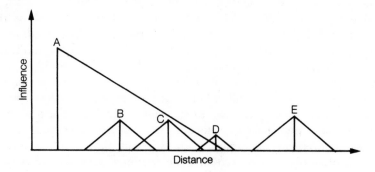

Figure 6   The X-TENT model, showing how the radius of dominance of five centres A–E depends on their size or influence and the slope (k) of fall-off in influence. Note that centres B and C are dominated by A, while D remains independent, even though it is smaller than, and closer to, B and C
(Modified from Renfrew and Level, 1979: figure 6.4.)

This insight encouraged simulation based solely on the size of centres and the slope (k) of the distance fall-off of their influence. Details of the model cannot be described here, nor its test applications to archaeological data-sets and to a controlled modern situation – the 117 largest cities of Europe in 1960 (using as input data their population and location, but *not* their national affiliation). Though obviously simplistic and static as it stands, it has implications of real interest to archaeologists seeking to 'retrodict' the political landscape, as well as to political geographers concerned with how state power is expressed in spatial dominance. Equally important, however, the ideas behind the X-TENT model contain the potential for the dynamic mapping of the *growth* of polities: consideration of a macro-regional settlement system at successive points in archaeological time could lead, by these means, to the prediction of changing political configurations and boundaries, and even of the conflicts they might entail. There is scope for much work here, both archaeological and geographical.

Centre–Periphery Relationships

The inherent tendency of states to expand their territories brings in its train an unremitting and worsening struggle against the obstacle of distance. The evolution of new mechanisms of dominance underlying the elaboration in scale and integration of territorial political units inevitably generates a new dynamic of spatial relations between 'core' and 'peripheral' areas, irrespective of whether we are dealing with compact, small city-states or with vast empires. The archaeologically and historically documented change in the ancient Near East, for instance, from localized systems of 'early state modules' in the third millenium BC, to territorial states and federations in the second, to very large empires (such as the Assyrian) in the first, implies major advances in the technology of interaction over distances measured in many hundreds of kilometres – administrative techniques, communication and transport systems, military operations, effective taxation, and so on. The fact that there *do* exist some spatial regularities in the disposition of power relationships in such societies must relate, in part, to the convergent development, at different times and in different places, of devices for overcoming the frictional effects of distance on interaction. This is one reason why (as noted above) many archaeologists find it helpful to conceptualize states as institutions with specialized, complex and hierarchically organized mechanisms for information processing and decision-making.

The political and economic implications of social location within complex systems are, of course, a fundamental concern of political geography. It is thus of considerable interest that there has emerged a parallelism between geographical works such as Gottman's *Centre and Periphery: Spatial Variations in Politics* (1980) and recent archaeological perspectives of the kind reflected in, for instance, *Centre–Periphery Relations in the Ancient World* (Kristiansen et al., 1986). Some form of distinction between core and peripheral areas is, of course, characteristic not only of imperial studies, but also of archaeological studies at other scales: for instance, 'civilized' versus 'barbarian'; urban versus non-urban; sedentary versus nomadic; agriculturalist versus pastoralist. A pervasive influence over such studies, in both geography and archaeology, has been exercised for the past decade or more by the 'world-systems' perspective of Wallerstein (1974), and by the French *Annales* school of social and economic history, especially the work of Braudel (1972).

The sheer bulk of archaeological studies falling under this general rubric precludes any useful review of them here. Moreover, it has to be admitted that in many cases archaeologists have paid attention only to the material flows which underlie 'world' politico-economic systems, or worse, have automatically *assumed* the existence of such systems merely on the basis of a few finds of traded items in areas remote from the manufacturing centre. On the other hand, as both Gledhill and Rowlands (1982) and Gall and Saxe (1977) have emphasized, the institutionalized acquisition of significant resources from peripheral areas, via inter-regional networks of trade and productive specialization, is a condition for the consolidation and growth of political power in expansionary systems. In archaeological and historical cases as diverse as ancient Mesopotamia, Mesoamerica, north China or Carolingian Europe, it can be argued that the collapse of extended political territories and their replacement by more nucleated city-states was a function of loss of control by earlier centres over resources flowing through large-scale core–periphery exchange networks (Adams, 1981; Ekholm and Friedman, 1979; Hodges, 1982).

Thus, a very significant factor in the study of core–periphery relations at almost any scale is the way in which 'distance, the first enemy' (Braudel, 1972: 355), imposes significant constraints on direct intervention or exploitation by the centre. In a world shrunken by instantaneous satellite communications and high-speed air travel, it is now difficult to imagine the political impact of time-lags of the order of weeks or months in the transmission of news, directives and commodities between the heartland and remote border zones, and back again. Braudel (1972: 365) speaks of a Mediterranean world 70 or 80 days across, even in the late sixteenth century, and his map (figure 7) of despatch times to Venice provides a graphic indication of the ways in which the landscape of political interaction was distorted by 'time-geography'. It is a specific instance of a circumstance that must obtain,

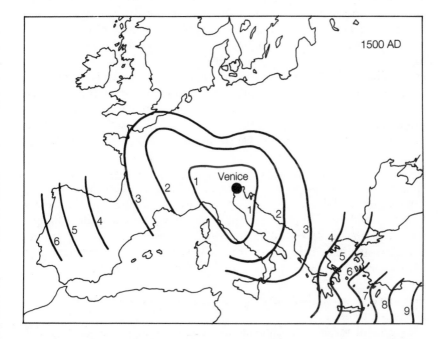

Figure 7 The frictional effects of distance on communication. The isochronic lines indicate intervals of one week in the time required for the dispatch of letters travelling to Venice in the period AD 1496–1534. Time-lags of this order must have been normal in all large-scale polities before the Industrial Revolution
(Simplified from Braudel, 1972: figure 28.)

to a greater or lesser degree, in all states and empires: that is, the inverse relationship between distance and the strength of political and economic intervention by the centre, analogous in a sense to the von Thünen rings of economic geography.

There are certainly on-the-ground, material consequences of the differential spatial strategies that a state must adopt in dealing with the problem of distance, but they have not been much studied in any generalized, cross-cultural sense. One obvious instance is the attempt to reduce travel times by the construction of well-engineered and carefully maintained road systems, equipped with staging posts and supply stations along the way, along which imperial couriers could travel at great speed. The roads of the Roman empire are perhaps the best known example, though other equally impressive systems exist (e.g. in Inca Peru: Hyslop, 1984). Other devices seem designed to safeguard loyalty to the centre among local elites or governmental officials located in provinces sufficiently remote to have a propensity for insurrection. These include the sending of spies to serve as 'the king's eyes' (e.g. in the Assyrian and Persian empires); the taking of noble children from the provinces to be 're-educated' in the capital, essentially as guest–hostages ensuring good behaviour back home (e.g. in the Roman empire); and royal or dynastic intermarriages linking political centres of primary and secondary importance (e.g. among the Classic lowland Maya). Archaeological evidence for such devices usually comes in iconographic or epigraphic form. Even more draconian measures were sometimes adopted: boastful Assyrian campaign accounts, for example, speak of close to half a million Chaldean and Aramean tribesmen taken as prisoners or forcibly uprooted in southern Babylonia during four decades of the eighth century BC (Brinkman, 1979: 227). Such acts of population relocation (which must surely have archaeologically visible consequences) had as their purpose not only the military subjugation of regions showing entrenched resistance to empire, but the economic exploitation of labour. The latter was also the objective of the Chimu kingdom and Inca empire in Peru, where purpose-built state administrative centres were set up in outlying regions to co-ordinate tribute labour, sometimes brought in from elsewhere, in the construction of massive irrigation canal systems and in agricultural production on the state's behalf. Such systems leave very obvious archaeological traces that have been studied in detail in recent years (e.g. Morris, 1972; Keatinge, 1974).

In general terms, it is difficult to disagree with Eisenstadt's (1963) view of empires as parasitic: maintaining and reinforcing core–periphery relations politically, by the extraction of tax and tribute from conquered areas and peripheries. Some doubt that the balance-sheet of empire is so simple or that 'exploitation' necessarily entails massive transfers of wealth and produce from periphery to centre: there are costs involved in the financing of local administration and in existing state ideologies and these may consume much of the revenue actually raised locally, as Kemp (1978) has argued for the Egyptian expansion into Nubia during the New Kingdom. Lattimore (1951) has even claimed that Central Asian pastoral nomads (or at least their elite) were the material beneficiaries of the tributary relationship imposed on them by the 'core' Chinese civilization. Whatever the case, state exploitation of the peripheries is seldom accompanied by a replacement of those local economic mechanisms of production and circulation which have been undermined in the process of domination; the result is frequently an economic decentralization allowing a prosperity, outside state control, that may ultimately lead to shifts in the focus of power from the old centre to the former periphery. The Roman empire is undoubtedly the instance best documented archaeologically and historically, though the spatial shifts in the location of regional power centres in various parts of Mesopotamia over the course of the two millennia before European contact are perhaps also understandable in these terms.

Much of the foregoing may seem trivially obvious, to archaeologists and geographers alike. It amounts to the assertions   (1) that there exist characteristic spatial arrangements for exploitative, centripetal political/ economic systems, in which a central elite is, to varying degrees, parasitic on peripheral populations, so that the majority of resource and information flows within the system are inward, coerced and im- balanced;   (2) that there is a 'cost' incurred in transferring resources and information, which is a function of the distance involved; and (3) that there are cross-cultural regularities in the devices developed by political hierarchies to minimize these costs, and these devices leave material, archaeologically recoverable traces. These may indeed be lamentably simplistic ideas; but to the extent that they require the development of methodologies for the recognition of spatial patterns in the exercise of power, using mute archaeological data, they have the potential to make a contribution to the study of political systems more generally. They can perhaps also serve as a corrective. For instance, in a polity exploiting a socio-political, as well as environmental and economic, landscape – one where other people's labour and energy are important commodities at stake, where adherence to a central political ideology is spatially variable as a result of cultural, ethnic, linguistic, historical and many other factors – a crucial element is the cost incurred to those at the top/centre of the political hierarchy in enforcing exploitative decisions at a distance from the centre. Such a situation is in some important respects almost the inverse of that presupposed in central-place theory, which is predicated on the assumption that the location of centres providing retail services is a satisfying solution to demand and the costs incurred by those at a distance from centres who must travel to them. It could be argued that economic geographers have tended to operate with landscapes that are politically too uniform, while political geographers have paid inadequate attention to the spatial irregularities in economic costs which operate at different scales. This leads me to agree strongly with Renfrew's conclusion that

... a unified field theory of political geography will establish separate fields for political and economic interactions. Any effective models will, however, have to cope with the evident yet subtle relationships between the two. The long time perspective of archaeology should facilitate the development and testing of such models, some of which may be of use to the geographer, even in the modern industrial world. (Renfrew, 1981: 272).

State Legitimation: The Iconography of Power

Much of the archaeology of archaic states and empires concentrates on the spectacular monuments – temples, palaces, tombs, statuary, paintings, and the like – of its urban places, rather than on the wider settlement patterns needed for the types of macro-regional spatial analysis considered above. Nonetheless, this traditional emphasis does provide material evidence for the expression and communication of ideologies via conventionalized symbolic systems, and this can tell us much about the organization of power in the past. Not all governments are equally self-conscious in this respect: the Indus Valley and Minoan civilizations, for instance, are notably poor in explicitly political symbolic art, or what Marcus (1974) calls 'the iconography of power', whereas the Roman and many Near Eastern states and empires, or the lowland Classic Maya polities of Mesoamerica, are exceptionally rich.

Even when accompanied by written texts, the interpretation of highly formalized state iconography is not a straightforward matter. Fortunately, detailed contextual analysis reveals a limited number of themes, with juxtapositions, similarities or contracts in the attributes of the figures depicted, which frequently appear to symbolize their non-egalitarian relationships and differential access to power. Thus, the relative size and positions of figures, the elaboration of their dress, their association with iconic paraphernalia (crowns, head-dresses, earplugs, sceptres, crosses, swords, etc.), the presence of defeated enemies depicted naked, supine or undertaking acts of obeisance or forced labour – these are all symbolic representations of a socio-political hierarchical order. They therefore constitute a powerful source of evidence for archaeologists seeking to reconstruct the configuration of political power in extinct polities.

Political institutions in the archaic power-based systems tend not to be sharply distinguishable from religion, ideology and its iconographic representation. One reason for this is that states are based upon the exercise of legitimized power in areas such as military affairs, the exaction of tribute, and even decisions about life or death. Rulers need to establish their credentials to use such sweeping powers, and they do so especially in terms of descent from divine and/or real or mythical ancestors; as Rappaport (1971a; 1971b) has shown, sanctified legends come to be regarded as history which the ruling class manipulates to gain or maintain power. 'The critical contribution of state religions and state art styles is to legitimise [the hierarchical arrangement of members and classes of society], to confirm the divine affiliation of those at the top by including religious experience' (Flannery, 1972: 407). This is not a bland reassertion of Hegelian-Marxist views on the state as an agent within society seeking to misinterpret itself, by mystification, in order to maintain class divisions and inequality. Nor does it imply – as a growing body of idealist geographers and archaeologists insist – that understanding can come only by disentangling the full 'meaning' of complex symbol-sets to those who conceived and manipulated them. In my view, the most useful recent archaeological work on the functioning of symbols in coercive polities is not that which aims to decode systems of signification, but that which focuses on how symbol systems *work* (e.g. Larsen, 1979, for the Old World; Jones and Kautz, 1981: 157–227; Marcus, 1976; Flannery and Marcus, 1976, for the New World; Renfrew and Cherry, 1986, more generally).

There is a convergence here with writing in political geography (e.g. Hartshorne, 1950; James, 1968) which has concentrated on the importance of the 'state-idea' for the viability or administrative effectiveness of states. James defines this as

a set of purposes to which the citizens of the state can subscribe, which has the necessary appeal to command widespread support, and which is sufficiently distinct from the purposes formulated by other states ... It is made up of written history, folklore, stories of national heroes, religious beliefs, and the language and art forms in which these things are communicated ... [as well as] the characteristic economic, social and political institutions. (James, 1968: 33)

This is analogous to the position taken in Renfrew and Cherry (1986) that the very act of acceptance of power (which is always held by a few, yet accepted by many) implies acquiescence in a belief structure or political philosophy.

In that volume, however, the discussion is not confined to nation-states, but concentrates on the ways in which belief systems in groups of neighbouring polities may converge, or at least influence each other, as a result of processes of symbolic communication and interaction, for which there exists an unsuspected wide range of hard archaeological data. Since the acceptance of power involves a willing suspension of disbelief, a related question (of considerable interest to archaeologists studying state origins), is whether the preoccupation of early state rulers with iconographic display and monumental architecture reflects a concern to use propaganda to impress their subjects and contemporaries and especially to suggest powers which, in practice, were not yet fully effective or institutionalized (Marcus, 1974: 83; Cherry, 1978: 429–31). It is certainly relevant that most archaic states were theocratically organized (Webster, 1976). Moreover, the relationship between the degree of their investment in ideology and the strength of political authority is open to empirical investigation using archaeological data: the chronological construction sequences of Egyptian pyramids, Mayan ceremonial plazas and Minoan peak-top sanctuaries offer just three instances. Growing numbers of archaeologists are arguing that religion and ideology are not epiphenomenal, nor merely an *ex post facto* development to justify a previously established political hierarchy, but rather a crucial factor in the self-representation of power relationships (e.g. Freidel, 1981; Conrad and Demarest, 1985).

Iconography and ideology have important implications for spatial organization, too, though there is space here to mention only two. The first stems from the obvious heterogeneity of states and imperial systems: they expand by subordinating and incorporating within their structure increasingly distant and differentiated ethnic, linguistic and cultural units. But if state religion and ideology constitute the codified and idealized reality of government, they will also be the symbols of identity *of the central core* – a dominant (but not universal) ideology which often proves difficult to uphold in the peripheries (as we know well from the activities of religious nationalists and secessionist movements in the contemporary world). The spatial distribution of archaeologically recoverable, material symbols allows some insight into the variable strategies adopted, and the degree of success achieved, by ancient empires in dealing with this problem. For instance, a group of papers on propaganda and art in the Assyrian, Achaemenid, Egyptian and Roman empires (in Larsen, 1979: 295–390) reveals a spectrum ranging from the univeral imposition or acceptance of a highly cohesive set of conceptions (as in the Egyptian case), to extreme regional differentiation in cosmology, the image of kingship and receptivity to foreign ideologies.

The second point is essentially another expression of the fact that archaeology *can* recover hard evidence relating to the expression of legitimacy and authority in traditional states. For, in many cases, secular power relationships are conceptualized as a specific exemplification of a more universal, celestial order and it is the role of ritual specialists (whose temples and other paraphernalia form such a conspicuous feature in the archaeological record of early states) to establish an ontological link between these sacred and profane realms.

Indeed, the imitation of cosmological archetypes in thoroughly material symbols can result in power transformations of the landscape itself, by means of planned cities, monumental architecture and the distribution of settlements according to ordained schemata.

Wheatley (1971) has provided one of the best examples in his study of Shang and Chou Chinese cities as 'cosmo-magical symbols', and he notes (1971: 417) the very general tendency throughout Asia, India and the Near East for 'kingdoms, capitals, temples, shrines, and so forth, to be constructed as replicas of the cosmos': an *imago mundi*. It is important to note that such cognitive factors underlying the layout of these Chinese urban centres do not stand in conflict with principles of a more general kind suggested by urban geographers.

Another important study along similar lines is Marcus's (1973) demonstration of relationships between lowland Classic Maya cosmology and territorial organization. Hieroglyphic inscriptions (see figure 8) indicate that the Maya viewed heaven as a quadripartite region

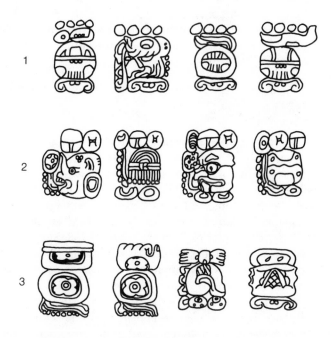

Figure 8   Polity and cosmology, reflected in Mayan hieroglyphic inscriptions on part of Stela A, Copán, Honduras (AD 731). The emblem glyphs of the four supreme capitals at that date (Copán, Tikal, Calakmut(?), and Palenque) are shown in line 2, together with the world-directions (E, W, S, N) with which they are associated, in line 3; line 1 shows the glyphs of the four sky-bearers of the Maya world, as an indication of the political supremacy of the four capitals named in the following line
(After Marcus, 1973: figure 3.)

supported by four divine brothers or *bacabs*, each associated with a particular colour, set of rites, and particular gods; earth was regarded as similarly partitioned. Marcus was able to show that the Maya conceived their political geography as dominated by four capital ceremonial cities, each located in one quadrant of the Maya lowlands; that these were seen as occupying the four quadrants of the Maya universe, for which the royal dynasties employed the appropriate cosmological emblems; and that there were never more than four such centres, even though power shifted from one centre to another over the centuries. Moreover, no secondary centre even mentions any capital except that to which it was a subsidiary. The political mapping made possible in this way reveals a nested five-level hierarchy of hexagonal lattices of the kind predicted by the strictly economic considerations of central-place theory. Again, Marcus (1973: 915) wrote that 'there was no real conflict between the lattice-like network predicted by locational analysis and the cosmological four-part structure predicted by epigraphy and ethnology'. Other comparable studies include Fritz's (1978) work on the ideational significance of symmetries in the architectural design and spatial distribution of Puebloan towns in Chaco Canyon, New Mexico, and Kus (1981) on the spatial ordering of the Merina kingdom of central Madagascar during the eighteenth and nineteenth centuries.

Conclusion

This has been a very partial and partisan review of a small corner of a vast subject. The study of the ways in which power is exercised in human socieites is too important for a single discipline – or even a pair of disciplines in collaboration – to claim a monopoly on insight. For the wider issue of the problems and prospects for further co-operation between archaeologists and geographers in the field of power and polity, I would refer the reader to Renfrew (1981; 1983a) and Wagstaff (1983), or to those geographers, such as Johnston (1982), whose writings on the state pay some attention to current archaeological thinking. My own enthusiasm is, I hope, obvious. However, Adams (in Larsen 1979: 403) ended a recent symposium on ancient empires by quoting Sir Robert Boyle in *The Sceptical Chymist*: 'Our present business is not to exchange compliments, but arguments.' The remark is equally apposite here. The existence of overlapping areas of interest, supported by a long tradition of mutual appropriation of data, methods and paradigms, ought to engender both criticism and self-reflection.

11　The Contemporary Past

P. J. Fowler

He had no control over the past – could only shine it up here and there and shut up as to the rest. From now on he would keep his mind on tomorrow . . .

Bernard Melamud, The Assistant (1957)

Introduction

'The Disappearance of England' fairly dramatically heads chapter 2 of *Vanishing England*, a sincere if unscientific book published three-quarters of a century ago (Ditchfield and Roe, 1910: 15). Both titles echo the anxiety about the destruction of Britain's heritage which runs through antiquarian and, increasingly, politically motivated writings from the seventeenth century (e.g. Turner, 1979) to the present day (e.g. Christian, 1977; Cormack, 1976). John Aubrey expressed his regret (in 1670): 'I am heartily sorry I did not set down the Antiquities of these parts sooner, for since (1659) many things are irrecoverably lost' (P. J. Fowler, 1972: 96). Compare a present-day geographer's plea that 'for cultural, as much as economic, reasons, the need to record and conserve historic landscapes is urgent . . . over half of the known legacy of man's activities in shaping our countryside up to 1945 has been lost in the past 30 years' (Brandon and Millman, 1980: 16). Hunter (1975) puts the former observation in its biographical and intellectual context; the latter preludes (along with much else which I shall attempt to review) the blunt, overtly political and aggressive statement in the Countryside Commission's *News Supplement* for July, 1984 under the front page headline 'Last chance for Agricultural Landscapes': 'The problems which beset the countryside . . . can be tackled and solved. The key is co-operation. (But now) is the last chance for the voluntary approach.'

A discussion of preservation and conservation of man-made heritage can appropriately begin with land, literally the common ground of geography and archaeology. The cultural landscape, crudely definable as the result of man's occupancy of land, is essentially a function of time and, therefore, an historical concept; but it exists today and, therefore, also has a spatial dimension in geographers' terms. Furthermore, it is an inheritance which is present on and in land, all of which (in Britain at least) is property, in the sense of having a legal existence allocating its ownership to persons or institutions. Inevitably, therefore, consideration of the present and future of this inheritance is a political matter, and potentially a highly charged one, both in terms of political philosophy and of the expediences of day-to-day government (e.g. Williams-Ellis, 1937; Haines, 1973; Wigens, 1980; Shoard, 1980). Does the landowner own the heritage items on his land? Who pays for conservation for the communal good on private land? What dilution of private property rights is reasonable on the occasion of receipt of public money for conservation in the national interest? Who says what the national interest in these matters is, anyway? Historic preservation, cultural conservation – call it what you will – far from being a peripheral matter, is an issue central to a nation's view of itself and of its most precious non-human resource – land (MacEwen, 1976).

Components of the Cultural Heritage

The 'cultural heritage' consists of far more than the items normally attributed to archaeology. The phrase is therefore preferred here, despite a certain pomposity in its sound, for we cannot be limited to archaeology's conventional material of sites and monuments. The 'cultural heritage', too, is the exact verbal counterpart of 'natural heritage', a phrase which has come to be accepted fairly generally. 'Cultural' here means man-made and is used in opposition to natural. In this sense, cultural activities, be they the building of a house or the manufacture of an artefact, can produce cultural debris – archaeological evidence in time – though without necessarily doing so; many of man's activities, after all, do not leave a physical residue. On the other hand, cultural heritage, however incomplete a reflection of past activity it may be, is, by definition, man-produced. Of course, where man has affected a natural heritage nature has influenced cultural activity at the time and, in many cases, has conditioned the way in which the physical remains of that activity have survived to the present. In a curious paradox archaeological evidence (by definition 'cultural'), by and large, can only survive to be recognized as such through natural agencies. Even at the fringe of what can be argued to be archaeological evidence, say in the case of an eighteenth-century portrait and a nineteenth-century silk curtain hanging in a country house, while familial care and an avoidance of death duties may have ensured their survival *in situ*, their physical preservation will be as much due to atmospheric and light conditions, as anything else.

This is, of course, more obviously true of the survivals on which conventional archaeology as an academic discipline is based. 'Sites and monuments' have already been mentioned; the phrase is generally understood to embrace the stone ruins of castles, abbeys and other large, mainly medieval structures and the more obvious earthwork remains, principally banks and ditches, of Roman camps and pre-historic fortifications and burial mounds. It includes, too, that ever-interesting group of stone but prehistoric structures, the stone circles, standing stones and other megalithic features from the, to some, dim and distant past (Bord and Bord, 1974); and also, at the other end of the time-scale, some of the major installations of the Industrial Revolution, including canals and bridges as well as defunct factories. This assortment may well seem broad enough and certainly to range adequately through time; but, of course, it is only the tip of the archaeological heritage iceberg, even when narrowly defined. The point is made if comparison be made between the Department of the Environment's *Map of Historic Monuments* (1982) and, singly or together, the *Period Maps* produced by the Ordnance Survey. On the former we see a few hundred sites and monuments, mainly medieval and of stone, preserved and, in general, open to the public (Sturdy and Sturdy, 1977); on the latter we see the great rash of sites, monumental or not, which the OS knew about at the time of compilation. It is no criticism of a great cartographic agency to observe that compilation is always bound to lag behind discovery and the availability of new information so that, inevitably, far more sites are known to exist than appear on even the *Period Maps*. Here, we are writing not of the main upstanding remains, but the tens of thousands of settlements with their related landscape features from prehistoric, Roman and medieval times – tracks, field systems, boundaries, cemetries and so on, all the occupational litter spread across what were, then as now, much-used agrarian landscapes (Taylor, 1983). Nor is all such evidence only agrarian, for much small-scale industry was carried out in the pre-eighteenth century countryside. Quarrying and mining (Beresford and St. Joseph, 1979), brick and tile-making (Cox, 1979) and pottery manufacture (Swan, 1984) leave detectable signs; those of a whole range of other activities, such as leather-working or salt-manufacture, are often less evident, on the ground or from the air, though evidence of them nevertheless exists.

Two major forces have brought about this relatively recent realization of what archaeological 'sites and monuments' actually exist in the landscape. One is the increasingly intensive use of the landscape by modern society, a trend which while involved in the very act of heritage-damage also acts as agent of discovery; the other, a reactive force, is the consequential application of larger resources to anticipatory reconnaissance, recognition and record, and to data-recovery during destruction.

On the first, intensified land-use means, in archaeological terms, two things. To begin with, it means an *extension* of different, even new, uses of land into areas where heritage was 'safe' or at least survived relatively unthreatened by existing practices. Moorland containing characteristic botanical and archaeological resources, now threatened by an extension of forestry, is a case in point (Allaby, 1983). Further, it also means greater demands made of the particular *locale*: deeper plough-ing in a field where buried deposits were previously below share-depth, for example, or more drastic alteration to a standing historic building to adapt it to new uses, including, perhaps, removing the ground beneath it to make a car park or provide modern services. Such intensification of land-use, justified by a society trying to earn its keep, nevertheless often has implications for the community and its cultural heritage beyond the intentions, indeed even the awareness, of those seeking to intensify the land-use.

The reaction to this usually unavoidable situation has included the creation of a heightened awareness of the range and extent of archaeology's responsibilities and, to an extent, the means to underpin them. In the field, literally following the plough and the JCB in many cases, the fairly systematic application of air photography country-wide has opened professional eyes at least to the near-ubiquity of man-made phenomena in much of the landscape (Maxwell, 1983). Simultaneously, and sometimes in concert, field-walking, field survey and salvage excavation have picked up the artefactual remnants which support the general thesis of extensive former occupancy of the British landscape. This landscape is dotted liberally with visible nodes of intensive settlement such as hillforts (Palmer, 1984) and crop-mark complexes like those round Dorchester-on-Thames (Benson and Miles, 1974: 91–4). Much of this development of response and consequential data-acquisition has been carried out in Britain under the umbrella-term 'rescue archaeology', a term initially regarded as too emotive and treated with contempt in some quarters but subsequently enshrined in the language of officialdon (ultimately fossilized and difficult to erase despite having outlived its usefulness as a concept. (Rahtz, 1974; Jones, 1984; English Heritage, 1984).

While these development have been taking place at and below ground level (as it were) that part of the cultural landscape which many regard as *the* historic heritage – medieval and later buildings – has also expanded. Castles, churches and country houses are obvious enough; the range now includes buildings into the 1930s and, in terms of social scope, vernacular architecture, industrial buildings, workers' housing, urban houses and farm buildings as well as dwellings (e.g. Hampshire

County Planning Department, 1982). This expansion has, in simple quantitative terms, enormously increased the heritage estate as perceived by conservation interests, the public and officialdom. It is, for example, difficult for the last to cope with the increase in the number of items under their control. A rapid country-wide sweep is, at the moment, attempting to identify for official purpose all the buildings deserving statutory protection, and a haul of over half a million is expected. Particular interests such as barns (Pearce, 1982) and historic gardens have emerged from this general expansion, some with their own pressure groups concerned with preservation, e.g. the Thirties Society.

Beyond these by and large 'respectable' developments, the waves of heritage interest with some form of institutional expression ripple even wider. Marine archaeology began with a scientific concentration on old wrecks, then expanded to include shore installations and almost anything connected with sea-farings. The 'Mary Rose' saga and the creation of a Trust to preserve the Chatham naval dockyard both reflect and channel such interest, one which, linked with political will, public money, social problems and another popular growth subject, industrial archaeology, has resulted in a massive investment – of hope as much as resources – in, for example, Liverpool's South Docks (Ritchie-Noakes 1984). On land the range now stretches from the Society for Landscape Study to the Brick Study Group, and embraces practically everything in between; while representing preservation above, as it were, is the like of the RAF Museum at Hendon and the branch of the Science Museum at Duxford with its not always very antiquated flying machines (Concorde 001 rests in a museum at Yeovilton, Somerset). Less respectably, perhaps, fervent amateur groups trace and dig up the mangled remains of Second-World-War combat planes and, more properly, the 1984 Shire Aware for the best piece of archaeological work by a schoolchild went to a study entitled 'Archaeological Evidence for the American Air Force 94th Combat Wing in North Northamptonshire between 1943 and 1945'. A copy of the paper now rests in the National Monuments Record, the public archive of the Royal Commission in Historical Monuments, beside records of Palaeolithic flint implements, the earliest artefacts in England. Of the past, there is no end . . .

The Agencies of Preservation and Conservation

In Britain the institutions involved with heritage, together with their powers and functions, form a complicated pattern. The situation shows features with that elsewhere but in some aspects is idiosyncratically insular. The structure is described and comparisons made in two very recent and wide-ranging publications (Cleere, 1984, for the world, selectively; Lehni, 1984, for Europe, comprehensively), so there is no need to elaborate here.

There is, in fact, no single heritage agency for Britain, let alone the United Kingdom. Organizationally, separate bodies cover England, Scotland, Wales and Northern Ireland geographically; different bodies also divide the heritage by subject (e.g. 'nature' is split from 'historic buidings'); there is also a divide between statutory and non-statutory bodies, between central and local government bodies, between parts of central government proper and (quasi-) independent but publicly-funded bodies, and between official and voluntary bodies. Furthermore, while England and Wales operate in the same legal framework (though exercised through different central government Departments), Northern Ireland is different and Scotland proudly preserves its own legal tradition. The whole structure lacks an organizational credibility; yet, in a curious sort of way, it works, and who is to say that a more uniform, rational but larger structure would be more effective?

Mention of some of the names in the present structure must begin with the three main central government Departments: the Department of the Environment (DOE) for England, the Scottish Development Department and the Welsh Office. Taking England alone, 1984 saw the setting up of a Heritage Sponsorship Division within DOE through which funds go to the main agencies, namely the National Heritage Memorial Fund, the Nature Conservancy Council, English Heritage (the Historic Buildings and Monuments Commission) and the Royal Commission on Historical Monuments. The existence and status of these (and other) bodies represents the policy of the present government to remove to 'arm's length' matters which it believes are not appropriate to in-house central government consideration. Reference here can only be made for further explanation to the *Annual Reports* which all these bodies produce. In the historic buildings and ancient monuments field, however, all accounts in print (including Cleere, 1984; Jones, 1984; Lehni, 1984) have been superseded by the formal existence from, 1 April 1984, of a new 'quango', officially the Historic Buildings and Monuments Commission for England (HBMC). Its promotion of a more popular label for itself, 'English Heritage', reflects the hopes and, indeed, statutory functions invested in it. Chief among these is an educational/interpretive/presentational role which was not specifically a charge upon its predecessor, the Directorate of Ancient Monuments and Historic Buildings within DOE. The new Heritage Commission has to concern itself with exercising most of the statutory responsibilities of (and on behalf of) the Secretary of State for the Environment in the heritage areas covered by the Town and Country Planning Act, 1972, and the Ancient Monuments and Archaeological Areas Act, 1979. The necessary definitions and powers are laid out in the relevant sections of the National Heritage Act, 1983, which also, incidentally here but central to the purposes of the Act, changed the status of and provision for several national museums, including the Science Museum, with major concerns in other aspects of the man-made heritage. Only a selection of the most important of HBMC's duties can be mentioned here. Through its statutory Historic Buildings Advisory Committee, it dispenses a fairly large sum (currently about £15 million p.a.) in a variety of grants designed to preserve and restore the fabric of some of the hundreds of thousands of buildings which, by a number of national criteria, can be regarded as 'historic'. Not only do major ecclesiastical and secular buildings receive aid in this way, but grants can also go to Town Schemes, for streets or other groups of urban buildings, and to individual churches, chapels and houses, and even ancillary buildings, such as stables, or structures such as park gateways, especially when they have a 'group value' or 'merit by association'. No such grants, it must be emphasized, are for 100 per cent of the costs involved; the general level is in the 25–50 per cent range, much of the point of the provision being to encourage other, often local or private, money to be applied to preservation when it might otherwise not have been forthcoming at all.

One of the devices for sifting out acceptably historic buildings is the compilation of a Statutory List. Acquisition of listed status in no way guarantees favourable receipt of a grant application, much to the disappointment of many householders; rather, listing is a planning provision whereby the owner has a considerable constraint put on his personal freedom of action in the public interest. Essentially, he has to seek permission from the local Planning Authority and ultimately the Secretary of State to do what he will with his own property if he wishes to change it.

Similarly, on the Ancient Monuments side, HBMC inherits a heavy load of administration. It has to look after the 400 or so Guardianship sites – that is, the major ruins such as Dover Castle and Stonehenge, which came into State care before 1984. A fairly important exception is the royal palaces, including the Tower of London, the most-visited monument in Britain (2,182,000 visitors in 1983). The 1979 Act also made significant changes, two of which are still working their way through the system. In the first place, as its title implies, the concept of 'Areas of Archaeological Importance' was introduced, though not, as many had hoped, in imitation of Conservation Areas. Nevertheless, the Act necessitates the precise definition on large-scale maps of areas within which developers are obliged to allow archaeological recording, including excavation, if necessary, by recognized agents acting on behalf of the Secretary of State. So far, parts of only a few historic towns such as Canterbury, York, Chester, Exeter and Hereford have been thus designated. Secondly, the 1979 Act shifted the 'onus of proof' in respect of proposed changes to Scheduled Monuments onto the landowner by introducing the requirement of obtaining consent for such works from the Secretary of State; previously the owner merely had to give notice of his intent and it was up to the DOE to react as it chose. The Scheduled Monument Consent procedure does indeed appear to be giving greater protection to sites but, particularly as it now involves applications going through two bodies, HBMC and DOE, only at the cost of a considerable bureaucratic load. Nevertheless, by putting Scheduled Monuments, in effect, on the same footing as Listed Buildings under a different Act, the 'consent' requirement represents a very significant development in Ancient Monuments legislation. It makes it worthwhile, for example, to consider extending the Schedule from its present number of roughly *c.* 13,000 sites to a much larger and more representative proportion of the approximately half a million archaeological sites already known to exist.

This national resource, and the official national bodies dealing with it, overlap with many other institutions. Of the examples listed here, the National Trust has to be mentioned first because it is now the largest archaeological landowner in England and Wales, albeit with inadequate in-house resources to cope. Merely by acquiring such large land-holdings, it has acquired many archaeological sites as well as its better-known country houses and parklands. Indeed, the parks themselves, being fossilized bits of landscape, contain much of heritage interest and value besides the landscaping of Repton/Brown type which immediately attracts the eye: the medieval landscape of deserted settlements and fields at Wimpole is a case in point (RCHM, 1968: 226–7). The moorlands and coastal properties, although perhaps acquired primarily for scenic and recreational purposes, are similarly well-endowed archaeologically. Much the same is true of the National Parks (e.g. Hart, 1981) and great estates, like that of the Duke of Cornwall. In all these there are now advisory/managerial mechanisms to protect, even enhance, the cultural as well as the natural heritage – of course, they do not always work. Nevertheless, an awareness, even a recognition, of the existence of landscape heritage, including individual archaeological sites, exists where it did not ten years ago. This is, perhaps particularly so at the local level, where County and District Councils and voluntary bodies, such as Naturalists and Historic Buildings Trusts, are now working at least within the same parameters by and large. The 'conservation ethic' is in general acknowledged, even if some do not like it and more find it difficult to practice (Baker, 1983).

Unfortunately, so far, the professional geographical input to the archaeological aspects of preservation has not been particularly influential, though the shade of O. G. S. Crawford has infused much endeavour. The writings of, for example, Chisholm (1968), Newcomb (1979) and Roberts (1977) have elucidated the problem, but there seems to have been little direct involvement with the few geographers concerned with matters of conservation (e.g. Lowenthal, 1979; Prince,

1982). On the other hand, much that archaeologists and environ-
mentalists have been thinking and doing could be argued to be
essentially geographical and especially of an historico-geographical
nature (e.g. Heighway, 1972; Ellison, 1983; Fowler, 1972, 1977).

Of course, as Goudie demonstrates (chapter 2, above), there is a long
history of interplay between geography and archaeology, and there is
no denying the tremendous influence that the 'new' geography (and
other social sciences') had on archaeology in the 1960s and 70s.
Furthermore, these changes have affected the day-to-day work of
practical archaeologists as well as the lectures and papers of their
university-based colleagues. Nevertheless, archaeologically-motivated
developments in Britain, in preservation and conservation, have been
stimulated much less by geographical influence than by the natural
sciences (Nicholson, 1970; Stamp, 1974; Ashby, 1978), by Town and
Country Planning in terms of prefessionalism (Rowley and Breakell,
1975, 1977), and by both European practice (Lehni, 1984) and
transatlantic concept in terms of external inspiration (McGimsey, 1972;
McGimsey and Davis, 1977; Schiffer and Gumerman, 1977).

Principles of Conservation

For present purposes, 'conservation' is used as a wide-ranging and
positive concept which embraces the older, narrower meaning of
'preservation' – that is, preventing further deterioration taking place.
Conservation, being a dynamic concept, demands rather than allows
change but, and this is crucial, primarily in the interests of that which is
being conserved. This principle applies, too, in the narrow meaning of
the word when it is being used in scientific terms about the (laboratory)
conservation of metalwork, fabric and the like.

Archaeologically speaking, the philosophy and methods of preserving
ancient monuments are clearly expressed in Thompson (1981). This is a
view stemming from a century of state care of monuments based on
principles of consolidation and documentarily allowable restoration but
an avoidance of on-site reconstruction. This explains the present well-
maintained but ruinous appearance of so many of our Guardianship
Monuments, now in the hands of the HBMC. Given the new
Commission's brief to make such monuments more attractive to the
public and to use them for educational purposes, it will be interesting to
see how traditional preservation policies fare in the light of presen-
tational needs (Fry, 1984). Faced with the same problem, the National
Trust, for example, has no doubt whatsoever that its primary
responsibiity is in the care of its houses and their contents, so public
access can be considerably constrained where necessary in the interests
of that which is being preserved.

In fact, while constructional preservation of major monuments like castles and abbeys as ruins has continued, major shifts in thinking and practice have followed from the developments already outlined. 'Preservation', in the traditional sense, of even a statistically acceptable sample of the archaeological heritage is not possible, for too much survives of what once existed, despite the destructive practices of recent decades. Indeed, in realistic terms, it currently seems unlikely that the national portfolio of Guardianship sites will be significantly increased at all. Local authorities and a few other bodies may bring a small number of sites into similar care but while these may be individually important, they are hardly likely to affect the unrepresentative nature of the whole. One of the problems here is that most building in prehistoric Britain was in timber and earth, while monuments capable of consolidation and public display tend to be medieval or later and of brick and stone.

Furthermore, with both the simultaneous recognition and destruction of so much archaeology in the landscape has come the development and acceptance of other modes of 'preservation'; these include total site destruction. As a short-term expedient under the 'rescue archaeology' programme, the destruction of a site – by gravel quarrying or urban development, for example – has in practice become acceptable, provided that the evidence is first recorded adequately: a non-existent site can survive, as it were, in its archive. As a result, archive-preparation and the maintenance of record systems has become an essential component of archaeological professionalism and a major employer of both archaeological and untrained labour, (see below, p. 185).

At the other end of the range, facilitated now by the 1979 Act, is the archaeological management agreement, similar in all respects to the technique developed in efforts to protect natural environmental interest. Archaeologically speaking it was stimulated by the 1972 Field Monuments Act (now defunct) whereby the DOE undertook to pay the owner of a Scheduled Monument for not damaging it; for example a farmer could be paid £20 a year for not ploughing a scheduled Bronze-Age burial mound. Now linked to the Scheduled Monument Consent procedure the idea is that a landowner wishing, say, to plough up an area of moorland which contains Scheduled Monuments, could be invited to be party to a management agreement whereby he would not only carry out his immediate proposals but would agree to pursue a land management practice sympathetic to the archaeology which was on his property. In return, as compensation of a kind, he would receive an annual grant from the DOE. In practice, this could mean, for example, that he would maintain a flock of sheep on relatively poor quality herbiage rather than plough up the moorland to carry a more remunerative herd of cattle feeding on a new and faster-growing ley.

Though some may well have doubts about the principle of paying a landowner *not* to do something (particularly now that the 1979 Act puts the onus on him to show why he should do it in the first place), the principle of building archaeology into land management is clearly very good for the archaeological sites themselves. This is particularly so where the same areas of land contain a botanical or other scientific interest, as well as a cultural value. In fact, just as a hilltop preserved for its fine views may also be enclosed by a hill-fort, so a number of archaeological sites are on land which is already designated in some way or other for its scientific value. Since nature conservation and archaeological preservation tend to result from the same state of relatively undisturbed ground, this is perhaps not surprising; but there is clearly considerable scope in this area for joint preservation within a land management programme.

Archaeology has indeed watched with both admiration and some envy as the natural history lobby, on the one hand, and scenic and recreational interests, on the other, have advanced in a way which the cultural heritage has not, except under state aegis. This is the matter of actually owning land (Sheail, 1976). The National Trust with its large holdings, the National Parks, the Nature Conservancy Council and the many Naturalists' Trusts have all moved into the landowning or land-leasing field (although the creation of a National Park as such does not, of course, mean a change of ownership). With a few exceptions, for example where the National Trust has consciously acquired a specifically archaeological property, archaeology has been brought into the landowning conservation lobby by accident or as a secondary consideration, the decision to acquire the land having been made. This is perhaps the effect of archaeological effort some 10–15 years ago which, in Britain, came to be primarily directed towards raising more money in order to excavate more sites, rather than to preserve them according to the, at that time unknown, precepts of the 'conservation ethic'.

Nevertheless, a lot of good came out of the 'rescue archaeology' movement in the early 1970s. It was, in part, inspired by another strand held in common with geographers: it played to one of the great strengths in the antiquarian tradition, topography, and looked to the many exemplars of people going out into the field to see and record sites both as direct monuments and as parts of an evolving landscape (Moir, 1964; Fowler, 1972: 38–74; Piggott, 1976). Many of those involved had been fired by the vision of the landscape enshrined in Hoskins' book, *The Making of the English Landscape* (1955). It was the basic concept of that book – that the whole of the landscape is man-made – that underlay many of their actions as a new approach to conserving the heritage, rather than merely preserving sites, began to develop. It was realized that it was only by looking at sites in their environmental, as well as their topographical context, that they could be appreciated; in conservation terms, it therefore became necessary to think of 'archaeological landscapes' rather than merely of single archaeological sites.

The discoveries made by the activity of 'rescue archaeology' and from air photography reinforces this line of thinking (Darvill et al., 1978). As a result, within rescue excavation itself, the practice of project-based work developed (preceded by proposals for academic and financial approval), embracing an examination of the surrounds of a site as well as the site itself. It has become common to survey, to commission air photography and to draw up maps based on its results, to carry out topographical research and to involve a host of scientific disciplines, rather than merely to carry out an excavation as if the site existed in isolation (Keeley, 1984). Various names have been bandied around to label this approach: 'landscape archaeology', even 'total archaeology'. This approach was, and still is, constantly fed by the thinking from the 'environmental bandwagon', that is, an awareness within the archaeological profession that cultural conservation was very much bound up with a series of questions about how society used and now wished to use not just its variegated heritage but its other resources too.

Archaeological sites themselves, following American precedent, came to be regarded as resources, each site a resource the exploitation of which had to be carefully considered from several points of view, not just that of the digging archaeologist. In this regard, especially, archaeology grew up: just as an early argument had been that the developer must take account of the archaeological interest in carrying out his proposals, so archaeologists came to see that what they had regarded as their own special interest site was, in fact, a communal resource on which others had just as much a claim as themselves. In this atmosphere the American concept of 'cultural resource management' came to be discussed and even applied, though always to a limited extent. Although rescue excavation has continued, it has increasingly been within the concept of a research design and a project (often regional) lasting over several years, as often as not in a pre-emptive action rather than merely reacting to a discovery accidentally made on a motorway or along a pipeline (Silvester, 1984).

Excavation, itself an expensive business, has come to be regarded as 'a last resort', that which it is necessary to do *in extremis*, when all other means of conserving the site have failed. This is a very far cry indeed from the days when every bump on the landscape was assumed to be fair game for the archaeologist's spade and for no one else's; and when an unstated assumption was that all sites would be excavated (and the truth therefore known). In contrast, the management of a cultural resource has as its objective the prolongation for as long as possible of the life of that resource by whatever means are most appropriate. Those means have come to range widely over a variety of mechanisms in a conceptual, as much as a practical, development which has rapidly taken those involved a long way from sticking together the stones of a Guardianship monument with DOE mortar.

This great spurt of activity has unfortunately found archaeological organization, and to a certain extent those who man it, lacking. In particular the speed, number and size of projects increased at such a rate that one of the major end-products of this activity (that is, publication) has come to lag far behind the activity in the field. Yet publication at various levels and in various forms is a crucial part of the conservation process, if only because the aims of conservation can only be achieved if the results are communicated to both peer groups and the wider public. Millions of pounds of 'rescue archaeology' money have been spent on as yet unpublished excavations, though the HBMC and the profession is now making a concerted effort to reduce this unfortunate and embarrassing backlog. Indeed, so great is the effort at the moment and so large a proportion of the available money is it absorbing, that it has had a marked impact upon the amount of fieldwork and excavation being carried out in the mid-1980s. This situation has brought to the fore the need not just to publish in a conventional sense, but also to prepare an archive which others can use and to deposit that archive in a publicly accessible repository. It is in this context that the National Monuments Record is coming to have an even greater significance. Not only does it contain records from fieldwork of the externally visible features of a site, as are also contained in local sites and Monuments Records, but increasingly it is coming to hold the multifarious documentation of major excavations which so far have either been published only in part or not published at all. Indeed, the archive itself is being used as a major support for whatever form of printed publication a report takes. The analogy here is, nationally, with the Public Record Office, and, locally, County Record Office the relevant contents of which an historian will refer to as support for his published research. He will not feel it necessary to quote in extenso every piece of evidence that he knows when readers will be able to consult it if they so require. Exactly the same process is beginning to develop in archaeology and is a far more significant development than the issues behind the current endless arguments about the use or non-use of microfiche. In any case, the developing technology of information storage and retrieval in various media will increasingly come to play a major part in resolving the problems of data-dissemination.

Meanwhile, research continues along several allied lines, all bearing in one way or another upon conservation. The conservation of the materials from excavations themselves, for example, is now a much more sophisticated procedure than used to be the case; many objects now have an added lease of life and an extra potential for study as a result of modern techniques, whether or not they are going to be shown in a museum showcase. Similarly, research continues (internationally rather than just in Britain) on building materials and the effects of erosion upon them (National Materials Advisory Board, 1982). This is particularly important in countries other than Britain which tend to place more emphasis upon restoration than the much more conservative conservation tradition in this country. Nevertheless, since major parts of the British heritage are invested in, for example, external sculpture and stained glass, scientific laboratory-based research into the effects of such items to exposure (particularly in these days of acid rain) are absolutely crucial if such are to survive into the next century and beyond. Though superficially involved in different fields, experiments carried out primarily for farming reasons in, for example, types of grass and, by those with interests on recreational pursuits, on the effects of wear on different types of grass, are directly relevant to the preservation in the field of archaeological sites surviving as earthworks. Though this may seem a recondite matter, the major damage to stretches of Hadrian's Wall and to such a huge hill-fort as Badbury Rings, Dorset, caused by over-visiting, or the similar damage caused by motor-bikes to another hill-fort at Barbury, Wilton, point to the relevance of these experiments. In both cases only careful land-management, including control of visitors can restore such sites to an acceptable condition.

Underlying much of the English response to the conservation of ancient monuments and historic buildings is another principle. This is the belief that retaining the owner-occupier is the best way of ensuring the long term conservation of a monument. Certainly, this is part of the convenant of beliefs enshrined in the National Trust, an understandable point of view since it is much more concerned with buildings in use than with the ruins which characterize the state's holdings. It is, nevertheless, a curious principle, one indeed which some find socio-politically unacceptable. The idea that an owner-occupier, likely already to be better-off than most, should receive public funds enabling him to continue living on his own property is a curious one; but, of course, the situation is usually not quite as simple as that, since the owner would normally have to give up part of his proprietorship as the condition for receiving such aid. The merit of the idea is that it is far better to have a building being lived in (and lived in by someone taking a personal interest in it) rather that for it to survive merely as an empty shell, which would accentuate the maintenance problems; or for it to be owned by an institution like the state. Certainly, too, tourists seem to like the idea of visiting a family house which is still occupied. Unfortunately, it is easy to justify adherence to the principle as far as field monuments are concerned, although the very first Act in 1882 was based upon precisely that. It was genuinely believed until fairly recently that an owner would be proud to be told that he had a monument of national importance on his land and would take steps to look after it. The development of the landscape under the pressures of post-War agriculture has shown that this is, by and large, an unjustified belief (Hinchliffe and Schadla-Hall, 1980).

A medley of principles is, therefore, being followed in a variety of ways to conserve the historic heritage. In general, there seems to be a growing recognition that this heritage is a communal resource, even though the land on which it sits may be a private or corporate possession. Increasingly, public bodies buy land, make land-management agreements, or manage their land with a conservation awareness (Countryside Commission, 1980; Pritchard, 1981; Swain, 1982; Sinclair, 1983; Hampshire County Planning Department, 1984). Yet damage and destruction continue, while public 'heritage awareness' continues to increase and expectations of that heritage grow.

Uses of the Heritage

There is now a desire to do so much in such a variety of ways with our tangible past, that the 'expectation factor' is one which itself has to be taken into account in trying to manage this patrimony. Conversely, appeals for heritage action inevitably produce counter-attitudes. The architectural profession, for example, has never been much interested in conservation, tending to see an empty space as an opportunity for one of its own creations, just as archaeologists used to see each site as the potential *locus* of an excavation. Now, with conservation of buildings very much in the minds of public and officialdom, the point is being put that such attitudes are actually inhibiting the creation of modern architecture of the sort which will become regarded as the monuments of tomorrow. In a way, this is a version of the old materialistic argument in the days of belief in economic progress – that 'the past' was obstructing, literally sometimes, the rightful and inevitable way ahead to a better future. We may be wiser now, but the pendulum of attitudes to the past continues to swing this way and then that. The past is an intellectual concept, not to be confused with its physical monuments, and our reactions to it are chameleon-like.

That past is always with us; but as with art, we can take it or leave it as we wish – at least, in terms of visiting it. There were roughly 167 million visits made in the U.K. in 1983 (English Tourist Board, *English Heritage Monitor 1984*), protecting it (there are 1.3 million members of thr National Trust) or actively supporting its investigation (there are roughly 100,000 members of archaeological societies in England). The first of these figures is certainly an underestimation. It cannot include visits to unmanned sites, town and historic trails, where access is free and the whole point is to be self-guided, or ordinary historic sightseeing out and about in town and country ('heritage browsing'); it specifically excludes visits to sites which have no official public access (thereby excluding most archaeologists' visits!). Nevertheless, although there is a considerable degree of guesswork about such figures, in England alone we are faced by a situation in which, probably, several hundred million visits each year are made to our stock of visible history, sufficient to justify the *Monitor's* sub-title – 'a vital tourism asset'. As it remarks (1984: 37), 'the income and employment generated directly at historic buildings is, of course, only part of its total economic benefits ... hotels, cafes, shops, pubs, and garages all benefit directly from spending by visitors who would not otherwise have visited their area.' One has only to cite places like Winchester, Windsor and St Albans to demonstrate the obvious: take away their visible historic interest and there remains undistinguished smallish towns which hardly divert the column of money-bearing tourists moving between Oxbridge, Chester and York. That some erstwhile towns of historic distinction have done their best, short of dismantling their cathedrals, to join the ranks of the undistinguished – Gloucester, Worcester, Newcastle-on-Tyne come to mind (cf. Amery and Cruikshank, 1975) – and yet remain viable shows, on the other hand, that there is more to an urban economy than tourism and the tangible and even promoted history that attracts it.

As an assistant in a Tourist Information Office at the last-named said to me, *apropos* a poster of Tyneside's recently invented industrial heritage: 'This isn't a tourist area, y'kna – ah cann't see people wantin' t'cum an' see that. It divvent seem right t'cal them things a tourist attraction.' Yet sympathy for that viewpoint should not blind one to the apparently insatiable curiosity of the tourist: '*Even* [author's italics] northern industrial cities', records the English Tourist Board (1984: 36) from its address in Grosvenor Square, London 'are now being affected by tourism as, for example, Bradford City Council attracted 30,000 package holiday buyers spending £1.5 million in 1983 to view Bradford's industrial heritage.' Let us hope they had not all made the same mistake in thinking they were being packaged to the Brontë country, to which Bradford also lays patrimonial claim.

The statistics of heritage are now, thanks to the monitoring of the ETB and its punctuality in publishing, almost overwhelming. There are now 22 heritage centres in England. Unsurprisingly, the 'vast majority are housed in historic buildings and located north of a line from the Bristol Channel to the Wash'. Could this possibly be an unconscious reflection of a 'let them eat cake' attitude in the areas of highest employment? Why should not the 'undivided nation' south from Watford have heritage centres too? Has northern England cottoned on to something NLIL ('not learnt in London')? Probably not for, setting aside the fact that 8 (36 per cent) of the 22 centres are actually south of the Bristol Channel–Wash line, a heritage centre has as its purpose 'architectural interpretation through the use of a variety of display techniques'. The cynic would doubtless say, therefore, that the average southern sightseer, having made the effort to get out of his chair and then out of his car, would prefer to see the real thing, be it Canterbury or St Paul's Cathedral, rather than an 'audio-visual presentation in a special theatre'. He can, after all, watch his videos at home and a visit to Canterbury is meant to be a day *out*, that is, different from all the other days *in*. Are we, too, seeing here the beginnings of a heritage differentiation in popular perception? At a certain level of perception, Canterbury Cathedral needs no heritage centre or interpretive intercession between itself and a visitor: it is big, beautiful, obviously old and important; dull would be of soul indeed, who could not perceive and be affected by these obvious attributes. It would be understandable, too, if that experience was of itself enough for many who do not therefore want to need to know that the lancet clerestorey of the choir is the work of William of Sens (1177–8) or that in the south-west transept (*c.* 1405) the vaulting dates from 1414. On the other hand, with presumably less obvious 'heritage' to play with, centres to identify and explain in ways unnecessary for some needs at Canterbury may well be welcomed at places like Rawtenstall, Lancashire, by native and visitor alike.

Let us look at some different but equally provoking figures. In 1980, the General Household Survey found that seventeen per cent of adults in Britain had visited historic towns and/or buildings in the month before the interviews; five per cent had visited museums and art galleries and three per cent had been to a zoo (*English Heritage Monitor*, 1984: 36). The average frequency of historic buildings visits per person (excluding children and foreign tourists) over the whole year was 3.8 (which gives roughly 200 million visits per year for the population, in line with the figures above (p. 187). This frequency was greater than 'for any other sightseeing activity or any out-of-home visual entertainment (ibid.) 'In Britain as a whole it is likely that historic buildings and gardens attracted about £85 million in revenue from visitors in 1983, and the vast majority of this would have been earned in England' (ibid.). It is virtually impossible to put a figure to the national expenditure on heritage-related work in 1983 but one can infer that it must have been of the order of at least £100 million.

Clearly, the conservation, management and exploitation of 'heritage' is big business and, to a certain degree, as such it is quantifiable. Yet that is certainly not a simple matter. That this is so should be technically and professionally self-evident. Furthermore just below the surface of 'heritage consideration', whether they be to destroy, conserve, exploit or ignore, are deeper issues of communal psychology, academic judgement, public policy, individual freedoms, and ethics. Archaeology, in a narrow sense, can be regarded as but one small part of this heritage world, or it can be used as an umbrella-concept covering all that has been man-made and that survives as evidence to become heritage; either way, it is inevitably concerned with such deeper issues.

Statistics of the type quoted from the English Tourist Board – and there are many more (e.g. Hanna, 1984) – are useful but, of course, they can only relate to that which is quantifiable. Tourism is not the only use of heritage, and not even all tourist use can be counted. Numbers, for example, cannot express pleasure (*cf.* Bainbridge, 1979); the difference in a person before and after seeing Canterbury Cathedral cannot adequately be entered in a column. Monuments are a resource indeed; but they also contain resources, notably a great deal of information and a power to trigger human response. With today's emphasis on the latter, particularly as it is the secondary effects of human reactions which produce the financial and bureaucratic figures, it is necessary to reassert the importance of the research potential of that which we inherit. So much about the past is unknown and the unwritten, silent fragments from it are the only evidence we and posterity shall ever have about it (e.g. Taylor and Muir, 1983; The Prehistoric Society, 1984). Artefacts are human signals in the time dimension, like radio-activity in interstellar space – unintended messages recordable and sometimes decodable but always with a changing significance as research and interpretation themselves change.

To strike such an astronomical note hardly provides a terminal point in terrestrial geography; yet it is precisely in astro-archaeology that many would seek origins and explanations for early monuments and prehistory (Devereux and Thomson, 1979). By the prevailing professional standards of scientific rationalism they are misguided, but science has not yet explained everything and there is a case for an element of irrationality in deciding what to preserve (Michell, 1982: 125). Just because a single standing stone, for example, does not at the moment apparently relate to anything else is not in itself sufficient to dismiss it; an aerial photograph of tomorrow might show the traces of its timber counterpart. Just because an earthwork or crop-mark does not accord with current classification, that is, we do not know what it is, it should not automatically fall through the net of official protection merely because bureaucracy deals only with the known. The early, and often underground history of sites later manifest in the assessable architecture of churches and, especially in towns, of historic buildings is an area which has particularly suffered in this regard. Misunderstanding is one thing, however; to argue that anyone in the name of their hobby, be it with a metal-detector or not, has the right as an individual freedom to pillage, for personal curiosity, survivals from the past seems contrary, in general, to the communal interest. Yet, here again, we see a conflict over the use of heritage, albeit on a minor scale compared to the damage it suffers daily from normal land-use, tourist wear and tear, and natural erosion.

In a pioneer post-industrial society, with often unwanted time on its hands, a tangible and accessible past may be increasingly significant, to us and for that posterity in whose name we tend to justify our principles and practice to mitigate the preservation of the landscapes, artefacts and monuments of the past – the visible evidence of its culture.

Bibliography

Abel, O. 1935: The Pleistocene mammals of Europe and their relations to the religion of the palaeolithic man of Europe. *Proceedings of the Linnean Society London*, 147, 58–70.

Aberg, F. A. (ed.) 1978: *Medieval Moated Sites*. London: Council for British Archaeology Research, Report 17.

Adams, R. E. W. and Jones R. C. 1981: Spatial patterns and regional growth among classic Maya cities. *American Antiquity*, 46, 301–22.

Adams, R. M. 1974: Anthropological reflections on ancient trade. *Current Anthropology*, 15, 239–58.

Adams, R. M. 1975: The emerging place of trade in civilisational studies. In J. Sabloff and C. C. Lamberg-Karlovsky, (eds), *Ancient Civilization and Trade*, Albuquerque: University of New Mexico Press, 451–65.

Adams, R. M. 1981: *Heartland of Cities*. Chicago: Chicago University Press.

'After Altusser' 1981: *New Society*, 55, 224.

Agrawal, D. P. 1970: Archaeology and the Luddites, *Antiquity*, 44, 115–29.

Ainsworth, W. 1833: *Researches in Assyria, Babylonia, and Chaldea, forming part of the labours of the Euphrates Expedition*. London: Parker.

Alden, J. R. 1979: A reconstruction of Toltec period political units in the Valley of Mexico. In C. Renfrew and K. L. Cooke (eds), *Transformations: Mathematical Approaches to Culture Change*, New York: Academic Press, 169–200.

Allaby, M. (ed.) 1983: *The Changing Uplands*. Cheltenham: Countryside Commission.

Allchin, B., Goudie, A. S. and Hegde, K. T. M. 1978: *The Prehistory and Palaeogeography of the Great Indian Hedge Desert*. London: Academic Press.

Allen, P. M. 1982: The genesis of structure in social systems: the paradigm of self-organisation. In C. Renfrew, M. J. Rowlands, and B. A. Segraves, *Theory and Explanation in Archaeology*, New York and London: Academic Press, 347–74.

Allen, P. M. and Sanglier, M. 1979: A dynamic model of growth in a central place system. *Geographical Analysis*, 11, 256–72.

Allison, K. J. 1976: *The East Riding of Yorkshire*. London: Hodder and Stoughton.

Amery, C. and Cruikshank, D. 1975: *The Rape of Britain*. London: Elek.

Ammerman, A. J. and Cavalli-Sforza, L. L. 1971: Measuring the rate of spread of early farming in Europe. *Man (N. S.)*, 6, 674–88.

Andrews, J. H. 1980: Degrees of generality. *Journal of Historical Geography*, 6, 203–7.

Arnold, D. 1983: Design structure and community organisation in Quinua, Peru. In D. Washburn (ed.), *Structure and Cognition in Art*, Cambridge: Cambridge University Press.

Arnold, T. 1847: *The History of the Peloponnesian War by Thucydides.* 3rd edn, 3 vols, Oxford: Parker.

Ashby, E. 1978: *Reconciling Man with the Environment.* Oxford: Oxford University Press.

Astill, G. and Lobb, S. 1982: Sampling a Saxon settlement site: Wraysbury, Berks, 1980. *Medieval Archaeology*, 26, 138–42.

Aston, M. and Rowley, T. 1974: *Landscape Archaeology.* Newton Abbot: David and Charles.

Atkin, R. 1981: *Multidimensional Man.* Harmondsworth: Penguin Books.

Austin, D. 1985: Doubts About Morphogenesis. *Journal of Historical Geography*, 11, 201–9.

Bailey, G. N. and Davidson, I. 1983: Site exploitation territories and topography: two case studies from Palaeolithic Spain. *Journal of Archaeological Science*, 10, 87–115.

Bailey, G. N., Deith, M. R. and Shackleton, N. J. 1983a: Asprochaliko and Kastritsa: further investigations of palaeolithic settlement and economy in Epirus (North-West Greece). *Proceedings of the Prehistoric Society*, 49, 15–42.

—— 1983: Oxygen isotope analysis and seasonality determinations: limits and potential of a new technique, *American Antiquity*, 48(2), 390–403.

Bainbridge, S. 1979: *Restrictions at Stonehenge: the reactions of visitors to limitations in access.* London: HMSO (for Social Survey Division, Office of Population Censuses and Surveys, for the Dept. of Environment).

Baker, A. R. H. 1972: *Progress in Historical Geography.* Newton Abbot: David and Charles.

—— 1977: Historical geography. *Progress in Human Geography*, 1, 465–74.

—— 1978: Historical geography: understanding and experiencing the past. *Progress in Human Geography*, 2, 495–504.

—— 1979: Historical geography: a new beginning. *Progress in Human Geography*, 3, 560–70.

—— 1982: On ideology and historical geography. In A. R. H. Baker and M. Billinge (eds), *Period and Place*, Cambridge: Cambridge University Press.

—— and Butlin, R. A. (eds) 1973: *Studies of Field Systems in the British Isles.* Cambridge: Cambridge University Press.

——, Butlin, R. A., Phillips, A. D. M. and Prince, H. C. 1969: The future of the past. *Area*, 4, 46–51.

——, Hamshere, J. D. and Langton, J. 1970: Introduction. In A. R. H. Baker, J. D. Hamshere, and J. Langton, (eds), *Geographical Interpretations of Historical Sources*, Newton Abbot: David and Charles.

—— and Harley, J. B. (eds) 1973: *Man Made the Land.* Newton Abbot: David and Charles.

Baker, D. 1983: *Living in the Past. The Historic Environment.* Bletsoe, Beds.: D. Baker.

Barker, G. W. W. 1975: Early neolithic land use in Yugoslavia, *Proceedings of the Prehistoric Society*, 41, 85–104.

Barker, P. 1977: *Techniques of Archaeological Excavation*, London: Batsford.

Barley, M. W. 1961: *The English Farmhouse and Cottage*, London: Routledge and Kegan Paul.

Baskin, L. M. 1974: Management of ungulate herds in relation to domestication. In J. Geist and F. Walther (eds), *The Behaviour of Ungulates and Its Relation to Management*, Morges.

Beaufort, F. 1818: *Karamania, or a Brief Description of the South Coast of Asia-Minor and the Remains of Antiquity*, London Hunter.

Behrensmeyer, A. K. and Hill, A. 1979: *Fossils in the Making*. Chicago: University of Chicago Press.

Bell, M. 1983: The effects of land-use and climate on valley sedimentation. In A. F. Harding (ed.), *Climatic Change in Later Prehistory*, Edinburgh: Edinburgh University Press.

Bender, B. 1975: *Farming in Prehistory*, London: Black.

Bennet, J., Jones, J. H. T. and Vyner, B. E. 1980: A medieval and later water mill at Norton on Tees, Cleveland. *Industrial Archaeology Review*, 5, 171–6.

Benson, D. and Miles, D. 1974: *The Upper Thames Valley: An Archaeological Survey of the River Gravels*. Oxfordshire Archaeological Unit, Survey no. 2.

Beresford, M. W. 1954: *The Lost Villages of England*. London: Lutterworth.

—— and Hurst, J. G. 1971: *Deserted Medieval Villages*. London: Lutterworth.

—— and St Joseph, J. K. S. 1979: *Medieval England: An Aerial Survey*, 2nd edn, Cambridge: Cambridge University Press (originally published 1958).

Berry, B. J. L. 1964: Cities as systems within systems of cities. *Papers of the Regional Science Association*, 13, 147–63.

Binford, L. R. 1965: Archaeological systematics and the study of cultural process, *American Antiquity*, 31, 203–10.

—— 1973: Olorgesailie deserves more than the usual book review, *Journal of Anthropological Research* 33, 493–502.

—— 1977: General introduction. In L. R. Binford, (ed), *For Theory Building in Archaeology*, New York and London: Academic Press.

—— 1979: Organisation and formation processes: looking at curated technologies, *Journal of Anthropological Research*, 35, 255–73.

—— 1981: *Bones: Ancient Men and Modern Myths*, New York: Academic Press.

—— 1983: *In Pursuit of the Past: Decoding the Archaeological Record*, London: Thames and Hudson.

Bintliff, J. L. 1975: Mediterranean alluviation: new evidence from archaeology. *Proceedings of the Prehistoric Society*, 41, 78–84.

—— 1981: Archaeology and the Holocene evolution of coastal plains in the Aegean and circum-Mediterranean. In D. Brothwell and G. Dimbleby (eds), *Environmental Aspects of Coasts and Islands*, British Archaeological Reports, International Series 94: Oxford, 11–31.

Bird, J. H. 1983: Transactions of ideas: a subjective survey of the *Transactions* during the last fifty years. *Transactions of the Institute of British Geographers*, 8, 55–69.

Bishop, W. W. and Clark, J. D. 1967: *Background to Evolution in Africa. Systematic Investigation of the African Later Tertiary and Quaternary*. Chicago: Chicago University Press.

Blanton, R. E., Kowalewski, S. E., Feinman, G. and Appel, J. 1981: *Ancient*

Mesoamerica: A Comparison of Change in Three Regions. Cambridge: Cambridge University Press.

Bohannan, P. and Dalton, G. 1961: *Markets in Africa*, Evanston: Northwestern University.

Bond, C. J. 1975: The Estates of Evesham Abbey: A preliminary survey of their medieval topography. *Vale of Evesham Historical Society*, Research Paper 4, 1–62.

—— 1979: The reconstruction of the medieval landscape: The estates of Abingdon Abbey. *Landscape History*, 1, 59–75.

Bord, J. and Bord, C. 1974: *Mysterious Britain*. St Albans: Paladin.

Bourdieu, P. 1971: The Berber house or the world reversed. In J. Pouillon and P. Maranda (eds), *Exchanges et Communications*; The Hague: Mouton.

—— 1977: *Outline of a Theory of Practice*, Cambridge: Cambridge University Press.

Bove, F. J. 1981: Trend surface analysis and the lowland classic Maya collapse, *American Antiquity*, 46, 93–112.

Bowden, M. J. 1970: Review of C. T. Smith's *An Historical Geography of Europe before 1800*. *Economic Geography*, 46, 202–3.

—— 1976: The Great American Desert in the American mind: the historiography of a geographical notion. In D. Lowenthal and J. J. Bowden (eds), *Geographies of Mind*, New York: Oxford University Press.

Bowler, J. M. Jones, R. Allen, H. and Thorne, A. G. 1970: Pleistocene human remains from Australia; a living site and cremation from Lake Mungo, western N.S.W. *World Archaeology*, 2, 39–60.

Bradford, J. 1957: *Ancient Landscapes*, London: Bell.

Bradley, R. 1979: *The Prehistoric Settlement of Britain*, London, Henley and Boston: Routledge and Kegan Paul.

—— 1984: *The Social Foundations of Prehistoric Britain: Themes and Variations in the Archaeology of Power*, London: Longman.

Braidwood, R. J. 1973: The early village in southwestern Asia. *Journal of Near Eastern Studies* 32, 34–9.

—— and Howe, B. 1960: *Prehistoric Investigations in Iraqi Kurdistan*, Chicago: University of Chicago Press (Studies in Ancient Civilisation, 31).

Brain, C. K. 1969: The contribution of Namib Desert Hottentots to an understanding of Australopithecine bone accumulations, *Scientific Papers of the Namibian Research Station*, 39, 13–22.

—— 1981a: The evolution of man in Africa: was it a consequence of Cainzoic cooling? *Annex to Transactions of the Geological Society of South Africa*, 84, 1–19.

—— 1981b: *The Hunters or the Hunted? An Introduction to African Cave Taphonomy*, Chicago: University of Chicago Press.

Brakenridge, G. R. 1978: Evidence for a cold, dry full-glacial climate in the American southwest, *Quaternary Research*, 9, 22–40.

Brandon, P. and Millman, R. (eds) 1980: *Recording Historic Landscapes*. Polytechnic of North London: Dept. of Geography, Occasional Publications, 2.

Braudel, F. 1972: *The Mediterranean and the Mediterranean World in the Age of Philip II*. 2nd edn, London: Collins.

Braudel, F. 1980: *On History*. London and Chicago: University of Chicago Press.

Breasted, J. H. 1916: *Ancient Times*, Boston: Ginn and Co.

Brice, W. C. (ed.) 1978: *The Environmental History of the Near and Middle*

East since the Last Ice Age. London: Academic Press.

Bridges, E. M. 1978: Interaction of soil and mankind in Britain. *Journal of Soil Science*, 29, 125–39.

Brinkman, J. A. 1979: Babylonia under the Assyrian Empire, 745–627 BC. In M. T. Larsen (ed.), *Power and Propaganda*, Copenhagen: Akademisk Forlag.

Britnell, R. H. 1982: Review of Rowley 1981, *Economic History Review*, 35, 111.

Brookes, I. A., Levine, L. D. and Dennell, R. W. 1982: Alluvial sequence in Central West Iran and implications for archaeological survey, *Journal of Field Archaeology*, 9, 285–99.

Brookfield, H. C. 1975: *Interdependent Development*. London: Methuen.

Brothwell, D. and Higgs, E. eds 1969: *Science in Archaeology*. 2nd ed, London: Thames and Hudson.

Browman, D. L. 1976: Demographic correlations of the Wari conquest of Junin. *American Antiquity*, 41, 465–77.

Brumfiel, E. M. 1983: Aztec state making: ecology, structure, and the origin of the state. *American Anthopologist*, 85, 261–84.

Brunskill, R. W. 1971: *Illustrated Handbook of Vernacular Architecture*, London: Faber and Faber.

Bryan, K. 1941: Pre-Columban agriculture in the southwest as conditioned by periods of alluviation, *Annals Association of American Geographers*, 31, 219–42.

Bryson, R. A. and Barreis, D. A. 1967: Possibility of major climatic modifications and their implications; Northwest India, a case for study. *Bulletin American Meteorological Society*, 48, 136–42.

Buchanan, A. 1982: *Industrial Archaeology in Britain*. 2nd edn, Harmondsworth: Penguin.

Buckle, H. T. 1857: *History of Civilization in England*, 3 vols, London: Richards.

Bull, W. F. 1979: Threshold of critical power in streams. *Geological Society of America Bulletin*, 90, 453–64.

Bunn, H. T. 1981: Archaeological evidence for meat-eating by Plio-Pleistocene hominids from Koobi Fora and Olduvai Gorge. *Nature*, 291, 574–7.

Burgess, C. 1980: *The Age of Stonehenge*. London: Dent.

Butt, J. and Donnachie, I. L. 1979: *Industrial Archaeology in the British Isles*. London: Elek.

Buttimer, A. 1971: *Society and Milieu in the French Geographical Tradition*. Association of American Geographers, Monograph Series 6, New York.

Buttimer, A. and Seaman, D. (eds) 1980: *The Human Experience of Space and Place*. London: Croom Helm.

Butzer, K. 1965: Acheulian occupation sites at Torralba and Ambrona, Spain: their geology, *Science*, 150, 1718–22.

—— (1965; 1972) *Environment and Archaeology: An Introduction to Pleistocene Geography*, London: Methuen.

—— 1978: Towards an integrated contextual approach in archaeology: a personal view. *Journal of Archaeological Science*, 5, 191–3.

—— 1982: *Archaeology and Human Ecology: Method and Theory for a Contextual Approach*. Cambridge, Cambridge University Press.

Cameron, K. 1965: *Scandinavian Settlement in the Territory of the Five Boroughs: The Place-Name Evidence*, Inaugural lecture, University of Nottingham.

Cantor, L. (ed.) 1982: *The English Medieval Landscape*, London and Canberra: Croom Helm.
Carlstein, T. 1983: *Time Resources, Society and Ecology. On the Capacity for human interaction in space and time* vol. 1, *Pre-industrial Societies*. London: Allen and Unwin.
Carneiro, R. L. 1978: Political expansion as an expression of the principle of competitive exclusion. In R. Cohen and E. R. Service (eds), *Origins of the State: The Anthropology of Political Evolution*, Philadelphia: ISHI.
Carpenter, R. 1966: *Discontinuity in Greek Civilisation*. Cambridge: Cambridge University Press.
Carr, M. 1983: A contribution to the review and critique of behavioural industrial location theory, *Progress in Human Geography*, 7, 386–401
Carver, M. O. H. 1983: Valutazione, strategia ed analisi nei siti pluristratificati *Archaeologia Medievale*, 10, 49–72.
Carson, M. A. and Kirkby, M. J. 1972: *Hillslope Form and Process*, Cambridge: Cambridge University Press.
Caton-Thompson, G. and Gardner, E. W. 1932: The prehistoric geography of the Kharga oasis. *Geographical Journal*, 80, 369–409.
Champion, T. (ed.) 1984: *Prehistoric Europe*. London and Orlando: Academic Press.
Chappell, J. E. 1970a: Climatic change reconsidered: another look at 'The Pulse of Asia'. *Geographical Review*, 60, 347–73.
—— 1970b: Review of 'Northern Mists' by C. O. Sauer. In *The Historian*, 32, 662.
Cherry, J. F. 1977: Investigating the political geography of an early state by multidimensional scaling of Linear B tablet data. In J. L. Bintliff (ed.), *Mycenaean Geography*, Cambridge: British Association for Mycenaean Studies, 76–83.
—— 1978: Generalisation and the archaeology of the state. In D. Green, C. Haselgrove and M. Spriggs (eds), *Social Organisation and Settlement*, Oxford: British Archaeological Reports, International Series, 47, 411–37.
—— 1981: Pattern and process in the earliest colonisation of the Greek islands. *Proceedings of the Prehistoric Society* 47, 41–68.
—— 1983: Frogs around the pond: perspectives on current archaeological survey projects in the Mediterranean region. In D. R. Keller and D. W. Rupp (eds), *Archaeological Survey in the Mediterranean Area*, Oxford: British Archaeological Reports, International Series, 155, 375–416.
——, Gamble, C. and Shennan, S. J. (eds) 1978: *Sampling in Contemporary British Archaeology*, Oxford: British Archaeological Reports, British Series 50.
—— and Shennan, S. 1978: Introduction: strategies for sampling intrasite variability. In J. F. Cherry, Gamble, C. and S. Shennan (eds), *Sampling in Contemporary British Archaeology*, Oxford: British Archaeological Reports, British Series 50.
Chibnall, A. C. 1965: *Sherrington: Fiefs and Fields of a Buckinghamshire Village*. Cambridge: Cambridge University Press.
Childe, V. G. 1925: *The Dawn of European Civilisation*, London: Routledge and Kegan Paul.
—— 1928: *The Most Ancient East. The Oriental Prelude to European Prehistory*, London: Routledge and Kegan Paul.
—— 1930: *The Bronze Age*. Cambridge: Cambridge University Press.

198 Bibliography

—— 1936: *Man Makes Himself.* London: Watts.

—— 1945: Rational order in history. *The Rationalist Annual,* 21–6.

—— 1949: *Social Worlds of Knowledge,* Oxford: Oxford University Press.

—— 1951: *Social Evolution,* London: Nelson; New York; Schuman.

—— 1952: *New Light on the Most Ancient East,* 4th edn, London: Routledge and Kegan Paul.

Chisholm, M. 1962: *Rural Settlement and Land Use,* 1st edn, London: Hutchinson.

—— 1968: *Rural Settlement and Land Use,* 2nd edn, London: Hutchinson.

Chorley, R. J. 1978: Bases for theory in geomorphology, In C. Embleton, D. Brunsden and D. K. C. Jones (eds), *Geomorphology: Present Problems and Future Prospects,* Oxford: Oxford University Press.

——, Beckinsale, R. B. and Dunn, A. J. 1964–73: *The History of the Study of Landforms,* London: Methuen.

—— and Haggett, P. 1965: *Frontiers in Geographical Teaching,* London: Methuen.

(eds) 1967: *Models in Geography.* London: Methuen.

Christaller, W. 1966: *Central Places in Southern Germany.* (Originally published 1933; translated by C. W. Baskin.) Englewood Cliffs: Prentice-Hall.

Christian, R. 1977: *Vanishing Britain.* Newton Abbot: David and Charles.

Claessen, H. J. M. and Skalník, P. (eds) 1978: *The Early State.* The Hague: Mouton.

Clark, J. G. D. 1933: Review of 'The Personality of Britain'. *Antiquity,* 7, 232–4.

1969: *Kalambo Falls Prehistoric Site.* Cambridge: Cambridge University Press.

—— 1970: Mesolithic times. *Cambridge Ancient History,* 3rd edn, Cambridge: Cambridge University Press, pp. 90–121.

Clarke, D. L. 1968: *Analytical Archaeology,* London: Methuen.

1972a Models and paradigms in contemporary archaeology. In D. L. Clarke, (ed.), *Models in Archaeology,* London: Methuen.

—— 1972b: A provisional model of an Iron Age society and its settlement system. In D. L. Clarke, (ed.), *Models in Archaeology,* London: Methuen.

—— 1973: Archaeology: the loss of innocence, *Antiquity,* 47, 6–18.

—— (ed.) 1977a: *Spatial Archaeology,* London: Academic Press.

—— 1977b: Spatial information in archaeology, in Clarke, D. L. (ed.) *Spatial Archaeology,* London: Academic Press, 1–32.

Clarke, R. 1935: The flint-knapping industry at Brandon. *Antiquity,* 9, 38–56.

Cleere, H. (ed.) 1984: *Approaches to the Archaeological Heritage. A Comparative Study of World Cultural Resource Management Systems.* Cambridge: Cambridge University Press.

Cliff, A. D. and Ord, J. K. 1973: *Spatial Autocorrelation,* London: Pion.

Cohen, R. 1978: State origns: a reappraisal. In H. J. M. Claessen and P. Skalník (ed), *The Early State,* The Hague: Mouton.

—— and Service, E. R. (eds) 1978: *Origins of the State.* Philadelphia: Institute for the Study of Human Issues.

Collingwood, R. G. 1946: *The Idea of History,* Oxford: Oxford University Press.

Conrad, G. W. and Demarest, A. A. 1985: *Religion and Empire: The Dynamics of Aztec and Inca Expansion.* Cambridge: Cambridge University Press.

Cooke, K. L. and Renfrew, C. 1979: An experiment on the simulation of culture changes. In C. Renfrew and K. L. Cooke (eds), *Transformations: Mathematical Approaches to Culture Change*, London and New York: Academic Press, 327–48.

Cooke, R. U. and Reeves, R. W. *Arroyos and Environmental Change*, Oxford: Oxford University Press.

Cooke, R. U. and Robson, B. T. 1976: Geography in the United Kingdom, 1972–76. *Geographical Journal*, 142, 81–100.

Cormack, P. 1976: *Heritage in Danger*. London: New English Library.

Cosgrove, D. E. 1984: *Social Formation and Symbolic Landscape*. London: Croom Helm.

Countryside Commission 1980: *Protecting Ancient Monuments and Historical Features*. Cheltenham: Countryside Commission (Leaflet 8 in Countryside Conservation Handbook).

Cox, A. 1979: *Brickmaking: a History and Gazetteer*. Bedford: Bedfordshire CC/RCHM.

Cramer, J. A. 1828: *A Geographical and Historical Description of Ancient Greece*, 3 vols, Oxford: Clarendon Press.

Cramer, J. A. 1832: *A Geographical and Historical Description of Asia Minor*. 2 vols, Oxford: Oxford University Press.

Crawford, O. G. S. 1912: The distribution of early Bronze Age settlements in Britain. *Geographical Journal*, 40, 184–203.

—— 1921: *Man and His Past*, Oxford: Oxford University Press.

—— 1922: Prehistoric geography. *Geographical Review*, 12, 257–63.

—— 1953: *Archaeology in the Field*. London: Phonenix House.

Crossley, D. 1975: *The Bewl Valley Ironworks, Kent, c. 1300–1730* AD. London: Royal Archaeological Institute.

—— Ed. 1981: *Medieval Industry*. London: Council for British Archaeology, Research Report 40.

Crumley, C. L. 1976: Towards a locational definition of state systems of settlement. *American Anthropologist*, 78, 59–73.

Cunliffe, B. W. 1971: *Some aspects of hill-forts and their cultural environments. In M. Jesson and D. Hill (eds), The Iron Age and its Hill-Forts*, Southampton University: Department of Archaeology, 53–69.

Cunliffe, B. 1974: *Iron-Age Communities in Britain*, London: Routledge and Kegan Paul.

Dacey, M. F. 1973: Statistical tests of spatial association in the locations of tool types, *American Antiquity*, 38, 320–8.

Dalton, G. 1981: Anthropological models in archaeological perspective. In I. Hodder, G. Isaac and M. Hammond (eds), *Pattern of the Past*, Cambridge: University Press, 17–48.

Daniel, G. E. 1962: *The Idea of Prehistory*, Harmondsworth: Penguin.

——, 1963: The personality of Wales. In I. L. Forster and L. Allock (eds), *Culture and Environment; Essays in Honour of Sir Cyril Fox*, London: Routledge and Kegan Paul, 7–23.

——, 1964: *The Idea of Prehistory*, 2nd edn, Harmondsworth: Penguin.

——, 1967: *The Origins and Growth of Archaeology*. Harmondsworth: Penguin.

Darby, H. C. 1956: The clearing of the woodland in Europe. In W. L. Thomas (ed.), *Man's Role in Changing the Face of the Earth*, Chicago: University of Chicago Press, 183–216.

——, (ed.) 1973: *A New Historical Geography of England*, Cambridge: Cambridge University Press.

Dart, R. 1957: The osteodontokeratic culture of *Australopitchecus prometheus*, *Mem. Transvaal Museum*, 10.

Darvill, T. C. et al. (eds) 1978: *New Approaches to Our Past: an Archaeological Forum*. Southampton University: Department of Archaeology.

Darvill, T. C. and McWhirr, A. D. 1982: Roman brick production and the environment. In D. Miles, (ed.) *The Romano-British countryside – Studies in Rural Settlement and Economy*, Oxford, British Archaeological Reports, British Series 103, 137–49.

—— 1984: Brick and tile production in Roman Britain: models of economic organisation. *World Archaeology*, 15, 239–61.

Davidson, D. A. 1980: *Erosion in Greece during the first and second millenia* BC. In R. A. Cullingford, D. A. Davidson and J. Lewin (eds), *Timescales in Geomorphology*, Chichester: John Wiley, 143–59.

—— and Shackley M. L., 1976: *Geoarchaeology; Earth Science and the Past*. London: Duckworth.

Day, M. H. 1977: *Guide to Fossil Man*. 3rd ed, London: Cassell.

De Atley, S. P. and Findlow, F. J. (eds) 1984: *Exploring the Limits: Frontiers and Boundaries in Prehistory*. Oxford: British Archaeological Reports, International Series 223.

de Chardin, P. Teilhard 1955: *The Phenomena of Man*. London: Collins: Fontana reprint 1965.

Deacon, H. J. 1983: Late Quaternary environmental changes and the implication for the archaeological record in southern Africa. *Paper presented at International Symposium on Late Cainozoic Palaeoclimates of the Southern Hemisphere, Swaziland* (unpublished).

Dear, M. and Clark, G. 1978: The state and geographic process: a critical review. *Environment and Planning*, A 13, 1191–6.

Deetz, J. 1977: *In Small Things Forgotten*. New York: Anchor Books.

Deevey, E. S., Price D. S., Vaughan H. H., Brenner M. and Flannery M. S., 1979. Mayan urbanism; impact on a tropical karst environment. *Science*, 206, 298–306.

Deffontaines, P. 1924: Sur la géographie préhistorique. *Annales de Géographie*, 33, 19–28.

Delano Smith, C. and Parry, M. 1981: *Consequences of Climatic Change*. Nottingham: University of Nottingham, Dept. of Geography.

Dennell, R. W. 1972: The interpretation of plant remains: Bulgaria. In E. S. Higgs (ed.) *Papers in Economic Prehistory*, Cambridge: Cambridge University Press, 149–59.

—— 1976: The economic importance of plant resources represented on archaeological sites, *Journal of Archaeological Science* 3, 229–47.

——, 1980: The use, abuse & potential of site-catchment analysis. In F. S. Findlow and J. E. Ericon (eds), *Catchment Analysis*, Los Angeles: Anthropology UCLA, 10, 1–20.

—— 1983: *European Economic Prehistory: A New Approach*. London and New York: Academic Press.

—— 1985: The hunter-gatherer/agricultural frontier in prehistoric temperate Europe. In S. W. Green and S. M. Perlman (eds), *The Archaeology of Frontiers and Boundaries*, Orlando: Academic Press, 113–19.

Devereux, P. and Thomson, I. 1979: *The Ley Hunter's Companion*. London: Thames and Hudson.

Dickens, P. 1977: An analysis of historical house-plans. In D. L. Clarke (ed.)

Spatial Archaeology, London: Academic Press.

Dickinson, R. E. 1969: *The Makers of Modern Geography*. London: Routledge and Kegan Paul.

Dicks, T. R. B. 1972: Network analysis and historical geography. *Area*, 4, 4–9.

Ditchfield, P. H. and Roe, F. 1910: *Vanishing England*. London: Methuen.

Dodgshon, R. A. 1980: *The Origin of British Field Systems: An Interpretation*. London and New York: Academic Press.

—— and Butlin, R. A. eds 1978: *An Historical Geography of England and Wales*, London: Academic Press.

Donkin, R. A. 1979: Agricultural terracing in the aboriginal new world. *Viking Fund Publications in Anthropology*, 56, Tucson: University of Arizona Press.

Donley, L. 1982: House power: Swahili space and symbolic markers. In I. Hodder (ed.), *Symbolic and Structural Archaeology*, Cambridge: Cambridge University Press.

Doornkamp, J. C. and Warren, K. 1980: Geography in the United Kingdom, 1976–80, *Geographical Journal*, 146, 94–110.

Doran, J. 1982: A computational model of socio-cultural systems and their dynamics. In A. C. Renfrew, M. J. Rowlands, and B. A. Segraves, *Theory and Explanation in Archaeology*, New York and London: Academic Press, 375–88.

Dortignac, E. J. and Love, L. D. 1960: Infiltration and surface litter, *Transactions of the American Society of Agricultural Engineers*, 3, 58–61.

Downs, R. M. 1970: Geographic space perception: past approaches and future prospects. *Progress in Geography*, 2, 65–102.

Duncan, J. S. 1980: The superorganic in American cultural geography. *Annals of the Association of American Geographers*, 70, 181–92.

Dunnell, R. C. 1979: Trends in current Americanist archaeology. *American Journal of Archaeology*, 83, 437–49.

——, 1980: Americanist archaeology: the 1979 contribution, *American Journal of Archaeology*, 84, 463–78.

Dyer, C. 1982: Deserted medieval villages in the West Midlands. *Economic History Review*, 2nd Series, 35, 19–34.

Dyson, S. L. 1985: *The Creation of the Roman Frontier*, Princeton: Princeton University Press.

Eagleson, P. E. 1978: Climate, vegetation and soil, *Water Resources Research*, 14, 705–76.

Eisenstadt, S. N. 1963: *The Political System of Empires*. New York: The Free Press of Glencoe.

Ekholm, K. and Friedman, J. 1979: 'Capital' imperialism and exploitation in ancient world systems. In M. T. Larsen (ed.), *Power and Propaganda*, Copenhagen: Akademisk Forlag, 41–58.

Ellison, A. 1983: *Medieval Villages in South-East Somerset*. Bristol: Western Archaeological Trust.

Elwell, H. A. 1981: A soil loss estimation technique for southern Africa. In R. P. C. Morgan (ed.), *Soil Conservation: Problems and Prospects*, Chichester: John Wiley, 281–92.

—— and Stocking, M. A. 1976: Vegetal cover to estimate soil erosion hazard in Rhodesia, *Geoderma*, 15, 61–70.

Embleton, C. and Thornes, J. 1979: *Process in Geomorphology*, London: Edward Arnold.

Emery, F. V. 1969: *The World's Landscapes: Wales*, London: Longman.

English Heritage 1984: *An Analysis of Support from Central Government (DAMHB) and the Historic Buildings and Monuments Commission (HBMC) for the Recording of Archaeological Sites and Landscapes in Advance of their Destruction between 1982 and 1984.* London: Historic Buildings and Monuments Commission for England.

English Heritage Monitor 1984: London: English Tourist Board.

Entrekin, J. N. 1976: Contemporary humanism in geography. *Annals of the Association of American Geographyers*, 66, 613–32.

Ericson, J. E. 1984: Towards the analysis of lithic production systems. In J. E. Ericson and B. A. Purdy (eds), *Prehistoric Quarries and Lithic Production*, Cambridge: Cambridge University Press.

—— and Purdy, B. A. (eds) 1984: *Prehistoric Quarries and Lithic Production*, Cambridge: Cambridge University Press.

Estes, J. E. and Senger, L. W. (eds) 1974: *Remote Sensing: Techniques for Environmental Analysis*, Santa Barbara: Hamilton.

Evans, J. G. and Limbrey, S. 1974: The experimental earthwork on Morden Bog, Wareham, Dorset, England, *Proceedings of the Prehistoric Society*, 40, 170–202.

—— and Cleere, H. (eds) 1975: *The Effect of Man on the Landscape: the Highland Zone.* Council for British Archaeology, Research Report 11.

Evenari, M., Shanan, L. and Tadmor N. 1982: *The Negev. The Challenge of a Desert.* 2nd edn, Cambridge, MA: Harvard University Press.

Eyre, S. R. and Jones, G. R. J. (eds) 1966: *Geography as Human Ecology*, London: Edward Arnold.

Fairburn, R. A. 1980: An excavation of a small nineteenth-century lead mining complex on Alston Moor, *Industrial Archaeology Review*, 4, 245–56.

Falconer, K. 1980: *Guide to England's Industrial Heritage.* London: Batsford.

Fawcett, C. B. 1957: Geography and empire. In G. Taylor (ed.), *Geography in the Twentieth Century*, London: Methuen, 418–432.

Fellows Jensen, G. 1972: *Scandinavian Settlement Names in Yorkshire*, Copenhagen: Akademisk Forlag.

——, 1978: *Scandinavian Settlement Names in the East Midlands*, Copenhagen: Akademisk Forlag.

Finberg, H. P. R. (ed.) 1962: *Approaches to History*, London: Routledge and Kegan Paul.

——, 1964: *Lucerna*, Leicester: Leicester University Press

——, 1972: *The Agrarian History of England*, Vol. I, Part II, AD 43–1042, Cambridge: Cambridge University Press.

Findlow, F. J. and Ericson, J. E. (eds) 1980: *Catchment Analysis: Essays on Prehistoric Resource Space*, Los Angeles: Anthropology UCLA, 10.

Fisher, C. A. (ed.) 1968: *Essays in Political Geography*, London: Methuen.

——, 1977: A confusion of concepts: region and regional, *Geographical Journal*, 143, 89–91.

Flannery, K. V. 1967: Culture history v. culture process: a debate in American archaeology, *Scientific American*, 217, 119–22.

——, 1972: The cultural evolution of civilisations, *Annual Review of Ecology and Systematics*, 3, 399–426.

——, 1973: Archaeology with a capital S. In C. Redman (ed.), *Research and Theory in Current Archaeology*, New York: John Wiley.

——, (ed.) 1976: *The early Mesoamerican Village*, New York and London: Academic Press.

——, 1982: The Golden Marshalltown: a parable for the archaeology of the 1980s, *American Anthropologist*, 84: 265–78.

—— and Marcus, J. 1976: Formative Oaxaca and the Zapotec cosmos, *American Scientist*, 64, 374–83.

Fleming, A. F. and Ralph, N. 1982: Medieval settlement and land-use on Holne Moor, Dartmoor: the landscape evidence, *Medieval Archaeology*, 26, 101–37.

Flemming, N. C. 1969: Archaeological evidence for eustatic change of sea level and earth movements in the western Mediterranean in the last 2000 years. *Geological Society of America Special Paper*, 109.

Flenley, J. R. 1979: The late Quaternary vegetational history of the equatorial mountains, *Progress in Physical Geography*, 3, 488–509.

Fletcher, R. 1977: Settlement studies (micro and semi-micro). In D. L. Clarke (ed.), *Spatial Archaeology*, London: Academic Press.

——, 1981: People and space: a case study on material behaviour. In I. Hodder, G. Isaac and N. Hammond (eds), *Pattern of the Past*, Cambridge: Cambridge University Press.

Fleure, H. J. and Whitehouse, W. E. 1916: The early distribution and valley-ward movement of population in south Britain, *Archaeologia Cambrenis*, 20, 101–40.

Floret, C., Pontanier, R. and Rambal, S. 1982: Measurement and modelling of primary production and water use in a south Tunisian steppe, *Journal of Arid Environments*, 5, 77–90.

Foley, R. 1981: Off-site archaeology: an alternative approach for the short-sited. In I. Hodder, G. Isaac and N. Hammond (eds), *Pattern of the Past*, Cambridge: Cambridge University Press, 157–83.

Fournier, M. F. 1960: *Climat et Erosion*, Paris: Presses Universitaires de France.

Fowler, E. (ed.) 1972: *Field Survey in British Archaeology*, Council for British Archaeology.

Fowler, P. J. (ed.) 1972: *Archaeology and the Landscape*, London: John Baker.

——, (ed.) 1975: *Recent Work in Rural Archaeology*, Bradford upon Avon: Moonraker Press.

——, 1977: *Approaches to Archaeology*. London: Black.

Fox, C. 1923: *The Archaeology of the Cambridge Region*. Cambridge: Cambridge University Press.

——, 1932: *The Personality of Britain*, Cardiff: University of Wales.

——, 1938: *The Personality of Britain*, Cardiff: National Museum of Wales and the University of Wales Press.

——, 1947: Reflections on the archaeology of the Cambridge region. *Cambridge Historical Journal*, 9, 15–16.

Francis, C. F., Thornes J. B., Romero-Diaz, A., Lopez-Bermudez, F. and Fisher, G. C. (in press), Topographic control of soil moisture, vegetation cover and land degradation in a moisture stressed Mediterranean environment, *Catena*.

Freeman, L. G. and Butzer, K. W. 1966: The acheulean station of Torralba (Spain): a progress report, *Quaternaria*, 8, 9–21.

Friedel, D. A. 1981: Civilisation as a state of mind: the cultural evolution of the lowland Maya. In G. D. Jones and R. T. R. Kautz (eds), *The Transition to Statehood in the New World*, Cambridge: Cambridge University Press, 188–227.

Frere, S. S. and St Joseph, J. K. S. 1983: *Roman Britain from the Air*. Cambridge: University Press.

Friedman, J. 1974: Marxism, structuralism and vulgar materialism. *Man*, 9, 444–69.

—— and Rowlands, M. J. (eds) 1977: *The Evolution of Social Systems*, London: Duckworth.

Fritz, J. 1978: Palaeopsychology today: ideational systems and human adaption in prehistory. In C. Redman (ed.) *Social Archaeology*, New York: Academic Press.

Fry, P. S. 1984: *Battle Abbey and the Battle of Hastings*, London: Historic Buildings and Monuments Commission.

Gall, P. L. and Saxe, A. A. 1977: The ecological evolution of culture: the state as predator in succession theory. In Earle T. K. and Ericson J. E. (eds), *Exchange Systems in Prehistory*, New York: Academic Press, 255–68.

Galloway, R. W. 1970: The full glacial climate in south-western USA, *Annals of the Association of American Geographers*, 60, 245–56.

Gamble, C. 1981: Scratches on the palaeolithic record, *Nature*, 291, 533–4.

Garnett, A. 1945: The loess regions of central Europe in prehistoric times, *Geographical Journal*, 106, 132–43.

Garnsey, P. D. A. and Whittaker, C. R. (eds) 1978: *Imperialism in the Ancient World*, Cambridge: Cambridge University Press.

Geikie, J. 1874: *The Great Ice Age and its Relation to the Antiquity of Men*. London: Isbister.

Gell, W. 1846: *The Topography of Rome and its Vicinity*, London: Bohn.

Gelling, M. 1978: *Signposts to the Past*, London: Dent.

Gellner, E. 1982: What is structuralisme? In C. Renfrew, M. J. Rowlands and B. A. Segraves (eds), *Theory and Explanation in Archaeology*, New York and London: Academic Press, 97–123.

Giddens, A. 1979: *Central Problems in Social theory: Action, Structure and Contradiction in Social Analysis*. London: Macmillan.

——, 1981: *A Contemporary Critique of Historical Materialism*. London: Macmillan.

Gifford, D. P. 1978: Ethnoarchaeological observations of natural processes affecting cultural materials. In R. A. Gould (ed.), *Explorations in Ethnoarchaeology*, Alberquerque: University of New Mexico.

Gill, E. D. 1965: The palaeogeography of Australia in relation to the migrations of marsupials and men, *Transactions New York Academy of Sciences*, series 2, 28, 5–14.

Gilman, A. and Thornes, J. B. 1985: *Land Use and Prehistory in South East Spain*. London, Allen and Unwin.

Gittins, L. 1982: Soapmaking in Britain, 1824–1851: a study in industrial location, *Journal of Historical Geography*, 8, 9–40.

Glacken, C. J. 1967: *Traces on the Rhodian Shore*. Berkeley: University of California Press.

Glassie, H. 1975: *Folk Housing of Middle Virginia*, Knoxville, University of Tenessee Press.

Gledhill, J. and Rowlands, M. J. 1982: Materialism and socio-economic process in multilinear evolution. In Renfrew A. C. and Shennan S. J. (eds), *Ranking, Resource and Exchange*, Cambridge, Cambridge University Press, 144–49.

Godelier, M. 1977: *Perspectives in Marxist Anthropology*. Cambridge: Cambridge University Press.

Gold, J. R. 1980: *An Introduction to Behavioural Geography*, Oxford: Oxford University Press.

—— 1982: Territoriality and human spatial behaviour, *Progress in Human Geography*, 6, 44–67.

Goodall, D. W. 1982: The modelling of arid ecosystem dynamics. In D. W. Goodall, and R. A. Perry (eds), *Arid Land Ecosystems*, vol. 2, Cambridge: Cambridge University Press, 385–409.

—— and Perry, R. A. 1981: *Arid Land Ecosystems*, Cambridge: Cambridge University Press.

Gottman, J. 1980: *Centre and Periphery: Spatial Variations in Politics*, Chichester: John Wiley.

Goudie, A. S. 1972: The concept of post-glacial progressive desiccation. *Research Paper Series, School of Geography, Oxford*, 4.

—— 1976: Geography and prehistory: a survey of the literature with a select bibliography, *Journal of Historical Geography*, 2, 197–205.

—— 1981: *The Human Impact*. Oxford: Blackwell.

——, 1983: *Environmental Change*. 2nd edn, Oxford: Clarendon Press.

Gould, P. 1974: Some Steineresque comments and Monodian asides on geography in Europe, *Geoform*, 17, 9–13.

Gowlett, J. A., et al. 1981: Early archeological sites, hominid remains and traces of fire from Chesowanja, Kenya, *Nature*, 294, 125–9.

Graf, W. L. 1979: The development of intermontane arroyos and gullies, *Earth Surface Processes*, 4, 1–14.

Gray, H. L. 1915: *The English Field Systems*, Cambridge, MA: Harvard University Press (reprint, London: Merlin Press 1959).

Green, D. and Haselgrove, C. 1978: Some problems in cross-disciplinary communication as viewed from Archaeology and Geography. In D. Green, C. Haselgrove and M. Spriggs (eds), *Social Organisation and Settlement*, Oxford: British Archaeological Reports, International Series (Supplementary) 47, vii–xxxvi.

—— and Spriggs, M. (eds) 1978: *Social Organisation and Settlement*, Oxford: British Archaeological Reports, International Series (supplementary) 47.

Green, E. L. 1973: Location analysis of prehistoric Maya sites in northern British Honduras, *American Antiquity*, 38, 279–92.

Green, S. W. and Perlman, S. M. (eds.) 1985: *The Archaeology of Frontiers and Boundaries*. New York: Academic Press.

Gregory, C. A. 1982: *Gifts and Commodities*, London and New York: Academic Press.

Gregory, D. 1976: Rethinking historical geography, *Area*, 8, 295–9.

—— 1978a: *Ideology, Science and Human Geography*, London: Hutchinson.

—— 1978b: The discourse of the past: phenemenology, structuralism and historical geography, *Journal of Historical Geography*, 4, 161–73.

—— 1981b: Human agency and human geography, *Transactions of the Institute of British Geographers*, 6, 1–18.

—— 1981b: Alfred Weber and location theory. In D. R. Stoddart (ed.), *Geography, Ideology and Social Concern*, Oxford: Blackwell, 165–85.

—— 1982a: Solid geometry: notes on the recovery of spatial structures. In P. Gould and G. Olsson (eds), *A Search for Common Ground*, London: Pion, 187–219.

—— 1982b: *Regional Transformation and Industrial Revolution: A Geography of the Yorkshire Woollen Industry*, London: Macmillan.

Gregory, K. J. and Walling, D. 1979: *Man and Environmental Processes*, Folkestone: Dawson.

Griffin, J. B. 1967: Climatic change in American prehistory. In W. Fairbridge (ed.), *Encyclopedia of Atmospheric Sciences and Astrolgeography*, New York: Reinholt. 161–71.

Grinsell, L. Rhatz, P. and Warhurst, A. 1966: *The Preparation of Archaeological Reports*, London: John Baker.

Grossman, L. 1977: Man-environment relationships in anthropology and geography, *Annals of the Association of American Geographers*, 67, 126–44.

Guelke, L. 1974: The idealist alternative in human geography, *Annals of the Association of American Geographers*, 64, 193–202.

Gurnell, A. M. and Gregory, K. J. 1984: The influence of vegetation on stream channel processes, In T. P. Burt and D. E. Walling (eds), *Catchment Experiments in Geomorphology*, Norwich: Geo Books, 515–36.

Guyot, A. 1850: *Comparative Physical Geography, or, the Earth in Relation to Man*, London: Gover.

Haas, J. 1982: *The Evolution of the Prehistoric State*, New York: Columbia University Press.

Haggett, P. 1965: *Locational Analysis in Human Geography*, 1st edn, London: Edward Arnold.

——, Cliff, A. D. and Frey, A. 1977: *Locational Models*, London: Edward Arnold.

Haines, G. H. 1973: *Whose Countryside?* London: Dent.

Hall, D. 1974: Survey of Newton Bromswold, Northamptonshire, London: *Deserted Medieval Village Research Group Report*, 10.

—— 1982: *Medieval Fields*. Aylesbury: Shire Publications.

Hall, R. L. 1976: Ghosts, water barriers, corn, and sacred enclosures in the eastern woodlands,*American Antiquity*, 41, 360–4.

Hallam, H. E. 1965: *Settlement and Society*. Cambridge: Cambridge University Press.

Hamilton, F. E. I. (ed.) 1974: *Spatial Perspectives on Industrial Organisation and Decision Making*. London, John Wiley.

—— and Linge, G. J. R. (eds) 1979: *Spatial Analysis, Industry and the Industrial Environment, vol. 1, Industrial Systems*, Chichester: John Wiley.

—— (eds) 1983: *Spatial Analysis, Industry and the Industrial Environment, vol. 3, Regional Economics and Industrial Systems*, Chichester: John Wiley.

Hamilton, W. J. 1842: *Researches in Asia Minor, Pontus and Armenia with some Account of their Antiquities and Geology*. 2 vols, London: Murray.

Hammond, F. 1981: The colonisation of Europe: the analysis of settlement process. In I. Hodder, G. Isaac and N. Hammond *Pattern of the Past: Studies in honour of David Clarke*. Cambridge: University Press, 211–48.

Hammond, N. 1972: Locational models and the site of Lubaantun: a Classic Maya centre. In D. L. Clarke (ed.), *Models in Archaeology*, London: Methuen, 757–800.

Hampshire County Planning Department 1982: *Saving Old Farm Buildings*. Winchester: Hampshire County Council.

—— 1984: *Hampshire's Heritage and a Policy for its Future*. Winchester: Hampshire County Council.

Hanna, M. 1984: *English Churches and Visitors. A Survey of Anglican Incumbents*. London: English Tourist Board.

Harding, A. (ed.) 1982: *Climatic Change in Later Prehistory*. Edinburgh: Edinburgh University Press.

Harris, A. 1961: *The Rural Landscape of the East Riding of Yorkshire 1700–1850*, University of Hull Publications, London and New York; Oxford University Press.

Harris, E. C. 1979: *Principles of Archaeological Stratigraphy*, London and New York: Academic Press.

Harriss, J. C. 1971: Explanation in prehistory, *Proceedings of the Prehistoric Society*, 37, 38–55.

Hart, C. R. 1981: *The North Derbyshire Archaeological Survey to AD 1500*. Chesterfield: The North Derbyshire Archaeological Trust.

Hart, H. 1945: Logistic social trends. *American Journal of Sociology*, 50, 337–52.

Hartshorne, R. 1950: The functional approach to political geography. *Annals of the Association of American Geographers*, 40, 95–139.

Harvey, D. W. 1967: Models of the evolution of spatial patterns in human geography. In R. J. Chorley and P. Haggett (eds.), *Models in Geography*, London: Methuen, 549–608.

—— 1969 *Explanation in Geography*, London: Edward Arnold.

—— 1976: The Marxian theory of the state. *Antipode*, 8, 80–98.

Harvey, M. 1980: Regular field and tenurial arrangements in Holderness, Yorkshire, *Journal of Historical Geography*, 6, 3–16.

—— 1982: Regular open field systems on the Yorkshire Wolds. *Landscape History*, 4, 29–39.

—— 1983: Planned field systems in Eastern Yorkshire: some thoughts on their origin, *Agricultural History Review*, 31, 92–103.

—— 1984: Open field structure and landholding arrangements in Eastern Yorkshire. *Transactions of the Institute of British Geographers*, 9, 60–74.

Harvey, P. D. A. 1965: *A Medieval Oxfordshire Village*, Oxford: University Press.

Hassan, E. A. 1979: Geoarchaeology: The geologist and archaeology, *American Antiquity*, 44, 267–70.

Hawkes, C. 1954: Archaeological theory and method: some suggestions from the Old World, American Anthropologist, 56, 155–68.

Hawkes, J. 1968: The proper study of mankind, *Antiquity*, 42, 255–62.

Hayes, P. P. and Jones, D. A. 1985: The environmental history of the Rocchetta plain. In R. Hodges, and J. Mitchell, (eds), *San Vincenzo al Volturno. The Archaeology, Art and Territory of an Early Medieval Monastery*, Oxford: British Archaeological Reports, International Series 252, 201–12.

Hayfield, C. 1980: *Fieldwalking as a Method of Archaeological Research*, London: HMSO, Directorate of Ancient Monuments and Historical Buildings, Department of the Environment, Occasional Papers No. 2.

Hayter, R. and Watts, H. D. 1983: The geography of enterprise: a reappraisal, *Progress in Human Geography*, 7, 157–81.

Healey, I. N. and Swift, M. J. 1971: Aspects of the accumulation and decomposition of wood in the litter of a coppiced Beech-Oak woodland. *Organismes du Sol et Production Primaire*, Proc. Xth Coll. Soil Zool., INRA, Paris, 417–30.

Heighway, C. M. 1972: *The Erosion of History: Archaeology and Planning in Towns*. London: Council for British Archaeology.

Helmfrid, S. (ed.) 1961: The Morphogenesis of the Agrarian Cultural Landscape, *Geografiska Annaler*, 43.

—— 1972: Historical geography in Scandinavia. In A. R. H. Baker, (ed.), *Progress in Historical Geography*, Newton Abbot: David and Charles, 63–89.

Hibbert, A. R., Davis, E. A. and Scholl D. G. 1974: Chaparral conversion potential in Arizona I Water Yield. United States Department of Agriculture,

Forest Service: *Research Paper*, RM–126.

Higgs, E. (ed.) 1972: *Papers in Economic Prehistory*, Cambridge: Cambridge University Press.

—— and Vita-Finzi C. 1966: The climate, environment, and industries of Stone-Age Greece, *Proceedings of the Prehistoric Society*, 32, 1–29.

—— 1970: Prehistoric economy in the Mount Carmel area of Palestine: site catchment analysis, *Proceedings of the Prehistoric Society*, 36, 1–37.

—— 1972: Prehistoric economies: a territorial approach. In E. S. Higgs (ed.), *Papers in Economic Prehistory*, Cambridge; Cambridge University Press, 27–36.

—— Vita-Finzi, C., Harris D. R. and Fagg, A. E. 1967: The climate, environment and industries of Stone-Age Greece, Part III. *Proceedings of the Prehistoric Society*, 33, 1–29.

Hill, D. 1981: *An Atlas of Anglo-Saxon England*, Oxford: Blackwell.

Hillier, B., Leaman, A., Stansall, P. and Bedford, M. 1976: Space syntax, *Environment and Planning*, B3, 147–85.

Hillman, G. 1973: Crop husbandry and food production: modern models for the interpretation of plant remains, *Anatolian Studies*, 23, 241–4.

—— 1981: Reconstructing crop husbandry practices from charred remains of crops. In R. Mercer (ed.), *Farming Practice in British Prehistory*, Edinburgh: Edinburgh University Press, 123–62.

Hinchliffe, J. and Schadla-Hall, R. T. (eds) 1980: *The Past Under the Plough*, London: Department of the Environment, Directorate of Ancient Monuments and Historic Buildings, Occasional Papers 3.

Hindle, B. P., Hutchinson, P. and Langton, J. 1972: Networks and Roman roads. Comments, *Area*, 4, 137–9; 279–80.

Hirth, K. G. 1978: Inter-regional trade and the formation of prehistoric gateway communities, *American Antiquity*, 43, 25–45.

Hodder, I. R 1972: Locational models and the study of Romano-British settlement. In D. L. Clarke (ed.), *Models in Archaeology*, London: Methuen, 887–909.

—— 1974: Regression analysis of some trade and marketing patterns, *World Archaeology*, 6, 172–89.

—— (ed.) 1978: *The Spatial Organisation of Culture*, London: Duckworth.

—— (1979a) Simulating the growth of hierarchies. In Renfrew, A. and Cooke, K. L. (eds), *Transformations: Mathematical Approaches to Culture Change*, New York and London: Academic Press, 117–44.

—— 1979b: Social and economic stress and material culture patterning, *American Antiquity*, 44, 446–54.

—— 1982a: *The Present Past*, London: Batsford.

—— 1982b: Theoretical archaeology: a reactionary view. In I. Hodder (ed.), *Symbolic and Structural Archaeology*, Cambridge: Cambridge University Press, 1–16.

—— 1982c: *Symbols in Action*, Cambridge: Cambridge University Press.

—— 1984a: Archaeology in 1984, *Antiquity*, 58, 25–32.

—— 1984b: Ideology and power – the archaeological debate, *Environment and Planning*, D2, 347–53.

—— and Orton, C. 1976: *Spatial Analysis in Archaeology*. Cambridge: Cambridge University Press.

Hodges, R. A. 1982: *Dark Age Economics*, London: Duckworth.

—— 1983: New approach to medieval archaeology. In D. Hinton, (ed.), *25*

Years of Medieval Archaeology, Sheffield: Dept. of Prehistory and Archaeology, Sheffield University, 24–37.
—— 1985: San Vincenzo al Volturno and its region between the 5th and 11th centuries. In R. Hodges and J. Mitchell (eds), *San Vincenzo al Volturno. The Archaeology, Art and Territory of an Early Medieval Monastery*, Oxford: British Archaeological Reports, International Series 252, 259–73.
—— Barker, and Wade, K. 1980: Excavations at Santa Maria in Città, *Papers of the British School at Rome*, 48, 70–125.
—— 1984: Excavations at Vacchereccia (Rocchetta Nuova), *Papers of the British School at Rome*, 52, 148–93.
Hooke, D. (ed.) 1985: *Medieval Villages*, Oxford University Committee for Archaeology, Monograph 5.
Hooke, J. M. and Kain, R. J. P 1982: *Historical Change in the Physical Environment*. London: Butterworth.
Hopkins, D. M. 1967: *The Bering Land Bridge*. Stanford: Yale University Press.
Hoskins, W. G. 1955: *The Making of the English Landscape*. London: Hodder and Stoughton.
—— 1967: *Fieldwork in Local History*. London: Faber and Faber.
Hosler, D. H., Sabloff, J. A. and Runge, D. 1977: Simulation model development: a case study of the Classic Maya collapse. In N. Hammond (ed.), *Social Processes in Maya Prehistory*, London: Academic Press, 553–90.
Houston, J. M. 1963: *A Social Geography of Europe*. London: Duckworth.
Howell, C. 1983: *Land, Family and Inheritance in Transition*, Cambridge, Cambridge University Press.
Hudson, N. W. 1957: Erosional control research – progress report on research at Henderson's Research Station, 1953–56. *Rhodesian Agricultural Journal*, 54, 297–323.
Huffman, T. 1981: Snakes and birds: expressive space at Great Zimbabwe, *African Studies*, 40, 131–50.
Hughes, P. J. and Sullivan, M. E. 1981: Aboriginal burning and late Holocene geomorphic changes in eastern New South Wales, *Search*, 12, 277–8.
Hunter, M. 1975: *John Aubrey and the Realm of Learning*. New York: Science History Publications.
Huntington, E. 1907: *The Pulse of Asia*, London: Constable.
—— (1910) The burial of Olympia: a study in climate and history, *Geographical Journal*, 36, 657–86.
Hurst, J. G. 1984: The Wharram Research Project: Results to 1983, *Medieval Archaeology*, 28, 77–111.
Hyslop, J. 1984: *The Inca Road System*, New York: Academic Press.
Iggers, G. C. (ed.) 1975: *New Directions in European Historiography*, Middletown, CN: Wesleyan University Press.
Isaac, G. L. 1978: Food sharing and human evolution: archaeological evidence from the Plio-Pleistocene of East Africa, *Journal of Anthropological Research*, 34, 311–325.
—— 1983: Bones in contention: competing explanations for the juxtaposition of Early Pleistocene artifacts and faunal remains, *In J. Clutton-Brock and C. Grigson (eds) Animals and Archaeology: 1. Hunters and Their Prey*, Oxford: British Archaeological Reports, International Series 163, 3–19.
Iversen, J. 1956: Forest clearance in the stone age, *Scientific American*, 194, 36–41.

Jacobi, R. M. 1980: The Upper Palaeolithic in Britain, with special reference to Wales. In J. A. Taylor (ed.), *Culture and Environment in Prehistoric Wales*, Oxford: British Archaeological Reports, 76, 15–99.

Jacobsen, T. and Adams, R. H. 1958: Salt and silt in ancient Mesopotamian agriculture, *Science*, 128, 1251–8.

Jacobsen, T. W. 1976: 17,000 years of Greek prehistory, *Scientific American*, 234, 76–87.

James, P. E. 1960: Some fundamental elements in the analysis of the viability of states. In C. A. Fisher (ed.), *Essays in Political Geography*, London: Methuen, 33–7.

Jarman, M. R. 1972: A territorial model for archaeology: a behavioural and geographical approach. In D. L. Clarke (ed.), *Models in Archaeology*, London: Methuen, 705–33.

—— Vita-Finzi, C. and Higgs, E. S. 1972: Site catchment analysis in archaeology. In P. J. Ucko, G. W. Dimbleby and R. Tringham (eds), *Man, Settlement and Urbanism*, London: Duckworth, 61–6.

Jarrige, J.-F. and Meadow, R. H. 1980: The antecedents of civilisation in the Indus valley, *Scientific American*, 243, 102–110.

Jequier, J-P. 1975: Le Mousterien alpin. *Eborodunum*, 2.

Jett, S. C. 1964: Pueblo Indian migrations: an evaluation of the possible physical and cultural determinants, *American Antiquity*, 29, 281–300.

Johnson, G. A. 1972: A test of the utility of Central-Place Theory in archaeology. In P. J. Ucko, G. W. Dimbleby and R. Tringham (eds), *Man, Settlement and Urbanism*, London: Duckworth, 769–86.

—— 1973: *Local Exchange and Early State Development in Southwestern Iran*. (Museum of Anthropology, University of Michigan Anthropological Papers 51), Ann Arbor: Museum of Anthropology, University of Michigan.

—— 1975: Locational analysis and the investigation of Uruk local exchange systems. In J. A. Sabloff and C. C. Lamberg-Karlovsky (eds), *Ancient Civilisation and Trade*, Albuquerque: University of New Mexico Press, 285–339.

—— 1977: Aspects of regional analysis in archaeology. *Annual Review of Anthropology*, 6, 479–508.

—— 1978: Information sources and the development of decision-making organisations. In C. L. Redman et al. (eds), *Social Archaeology: Beyond Subsistence and Dating*, New York: Academic Press, 87–112.

—— (1980) Rank–size convexity and system integration: a view from archaeology. *Economic Geography*, 56, 234–47.

—— 1982: Organisational structure and scalar stress. In C. Renfrew, M. J. Rowlands and B. A. Segraves (eds), *Theory and Explanation in Archaeology*, London and New York: Academic Press, 389–421.

Johnston, R. J. 1973: *Spatial Structures*, London: Methuen.

—— 1979: *Geography and Geographers: Anglo-American Human Geography since 1945*, London: Edward Arnold.

—— 1982: *Geography and the State: An Essay in Political Geography*, London: Macmillan.

—— 1983a: *Philosophy and Human Geography*, London: Edward Arnold.

—— (1983b) *Geography and Geographies: Anglo-American Human Geography since 1945*. 2nd ed. London, Edward Arnold.

Jones, B. 1984: *Past Imperfect: The Story of Rescue Archaeology*. London: Heinemann.

Jones, G. D. and Kautz, R. R. (eds) 1981: *The Transition to Statehood in the New World*, Cambridge: Cambridge University Press.

Jones, P. N. 1969: *Colliery Settlement in the South Wales Coalfield 1850–1926*, University of Hull, Occasional Papers in Geography, 14.

Jones, S. B. 1959: Boundary concepts in the setting of place and time. *Annals of the Association of American Geographers*, 49, 241–55.

Kasperson, R. E. and Minghi, J. V. (eds) 1969: *The Structure of Political Geography*, London: University of London Press.

Keatinge, R. W. 1974: Chimu rural administrative centers in the Moche Valley, Peru, *World Archaeology*, 6, 66–82.

Keeble, D. 1977: Industrial Geography, *Progress in Human Geography*, 1, 304–12.

—— 1978: Industrial Geography, *Progress in Human Geography*, 2, 318–23.

Keeley, H. C. M. (ed.) 1984: *Environmental Archaeology: a Regional Review*, London: DAMHB. Dept. of the Environment, Occasional Paper no. 6.

Kehoe, A. B. and Kehoe T. F. 1973: Cognitive models for archaeological interpretation, *American Antiquity*, 38, 150–4.

Kemp, B. J. 1978: Imperialism and empire in New Kingdom Egypt. In P. D. A. Garnsey and C. R. Whittaker, (eds), *Imperialism in the Ancient World*, Cambridge: Cambridge University Press, 7–58.

King, J. L. and Moll, R. G. 1972: Set-theory models: an approach to taxonomic and locational relationships. In D. L. Clarke (ed.), *Models in Archaeology*, London: Methuen 735–66.

Kirkby, M. J. 1976: Hydrological models – the influence of climate. In E. Derbyshire (ed.), *Geomorphology and Climate*, Chichester: John Wiley, 247–67.

—— and Kirkby, A. V. T. 1971: Long-term measurement of debris transport rates using archaeological mounds in semi-arid areas, *Paper presented at British Geomorphological Research Group Symposium*, Durham 25 September.

—— and Morgan, R. P. C. 1980: *Soil Erosion*, Chichester: John Wiley.

—— and Neale, R. H. in press: A soil erosion model incorporating seasonal factors, *Proceedings of the 1st International Geomorphology Conference*, Manchester, September 1985, Chichester: John Wiley.

Koelsch, W. A. 1970: Review of A. H. Clark's *Arcadia*, Economic Geography, 46, 201–2.

Kohl, P. L. 1981: Materialist approaches in prehistory, *Annual Review of Anthropology*, 10, 89–118.

Kraft, J. C., Kayan, I. and Erol, O. 1980: Geomorphic reconstructions in the environs of ancient Troy, *Science*, 209, 776–82.

Kristiansen, K., Larsen, M. and Rowlands, M. J. (eds) 1986: *Centre–Periphery Relations in the Ancient World*, Cambridge: Cambridge University Press.

Kruk, J. 1980: The Neolithic Settlement of Southern Poland. In J. M. Howell and N.J. Starling (eds), *British Archaeological Reports, International Series* 93: Oxford.

Kurzweil, E. 1980: *The Age of Structuralism*, New York: Columbia University Press.

Kus, S. 1981: The context of complexity. In S. E. van der Leeuw, (ed.), *Archaeological Approaches to the Study of Complexity*, Amsterdam: Albert Egges van Griffen Instituut voor Prae-en Protohistorie, 197–227.

—— 1982: Matters material and ideal. In I. Hodder (ed.), *Symbols and Structural Archaeology*, Cambridge: Cambridge University Press.

Lamb, H. H. 1967: Review of 'Discontinuity in Greek Civilisation' by R. Carpenter, *Antiquity*, 41, 233–4.

—— 1968: The climatic background to the birth of civilisation, *Advancement of Science*, 25, 103–20.

—— 1982: *Climate, History and the Modern World*, London: Methuen.

Langton, J. 1979: *Geographical Change and Industrial Revolution: Coalmining in South-West Lancashire, 1590–1799*. Cambridge: Cambridge University Press.

Larsen, M. T. (ed) 1979: *Power and Propaganda: A Symposium on Ancient Empires*, Copenhagen: Akademisk Forlag.

Lattimore, O. 1951: *Inner Asian Frontiers of China*, Boston: Beacon Press.

Le Houerou, H. N. 1981: Impact of man and his animals on Mediterranean Vegetation. In F. di Castri, D. W. Goodall and R. L. Specht, (eds.), *Mediterranean-Type Shrublands*, Amsterdam: Elsevier, 479–517.

Leake, W. M. 1830: *Travels in the Morea*, 3 vols, London: Murray.

Leakey, R. 1981: *The Making of Mankind*, London: Michael Joseph.

Lee, R. B. (1978) What hunters do for a living, or how to make out on scarce resources. In R. B. Lee and I. de Vore (eds), *Man the Hunter*, Chicago: Aldine, 30–48.

Lehni, R. (ed.) 1984: *Actes de Colloques sur les Inventaires des Biens Culturels en Europe* Paris: Nouvelles Editions Latines (Cahiers de l'Inventaire, Numero Special).

Leighly, J. 1963: *Land and Life: A Selection from the Writings of Carl Ortwin Sauer*, Berkley: University of California Press.

Leith, H. 1975: Modelling the primary productivity of the world. In H. Leith, and R. H. Whittaker (eds), *Primary Productivity of the Biosphere*, New York: Springer Verlag.

—— and Box, R. 1972: Evapotranspiration and primary productivity, *Publications in Climatology*, Elmer: Centerton, 25, 37–46.

Leone, M. 1982: Some opinions about recovering mind, *American Antiquity*, 47, 742–60.

Leone, M. 1984: Interpreting ideology in historical archaeology. In D. Miller and C. Tilley (eds), *Ideology, Power and Prehistory*, Cambridge: Cambridge University Press.

Ley, D. 1982: Rediscovering man's place, *Transactions of the Institute of British Geographers*, 7, 248–53.

Ley, D. and Samuels, M. (eds), 1978: *Humanistic Geography: Prospects and Problems*. London and Chicago, Maarouta Press.

Limbrey, S. and Evans, J. G. (eds) 1978: *The Effect of Man on the Landscape: the Lowland zone*, Council for British Archaeology, Research Report 21.

Lloyd, S. 1956: *Early Anatolia*, London: Penguin.

Lloyd, S. 1980: *Foundations in the Dust*. London: Thames and Hudson.

Longacre, W. 1970: *Archaeology as Anthropology*, Tucson: University of Arizona.

Lopez-Bermudez, F., Romero-Diaz, F., Fisher, G. C., Francis, C. F. and Thornes, J. B. 1985: Erosion, y ecologia en la Espana semi-arida, Cuenca de Mula, Murcia. *Cuadernos de Investigacion Geografica*, Logrono, XI, 3–4, 113–26.

Lowenthal, D. 1972: *Environmental Assessment: a Case Study of Boston*. New York: Publications in Environmental Perception, 2, American Geographical Society.
—— 1979: Environmental perception: preserving the past. *Progress in Human Geography*, 3: 549–59.
—— and Binney, M. (eds) 1981: *Our Past Before Us: Why Do We Save It?* London: Temple Smith.
—— and Bowden, M. J. (eds) 1976: *Geographies of the Mind; Essays in Historical Geography in Honor of John Kirtland Wright*. New York: Oxford University Press.
Lukermann, F. E. 1972: Settlement and circulation: pattern and systems. In W. A. McDonald and G. R. Rapp (eds), *The Minnesota Messenia Expedition: Reconstructing a Bronze Age Regional Environment*, Minneapolis: University of Minnesota Press, 148–70.
Lundholm, b. 1976: Domestic animals in arid ecosystems, *Ecological Bulletin* (Stockholm), 24, 29–42.
Lyons, T. R. and Avery, T. E. 1977: *Remote Sensing. A Handbook for Archaeologists and Cultural Resource Managers*, Washington DC: Cultural Resources Management Division, National Park Service, US Department of the Interior.
Lyons, T. R. and Hitchcock, R. K. (eds) 1977: *Aerial Remote Sensing Techniques in Archaeology*, Albuquerque: Reports of the Chaco Center, no. 2.
MacEwen, M. (ed.) 1976: *Future Landscapes*, London: Chatto and Windus.
Macintosh, R. P. 1980: The relationship between succession and the recovery process in ecosystems. In J. Cairns (ed.), *The Recovery Process in Damaged Ecosystems*, Ann Arbor: Ann Arbor Scientific Publications, 11–62.
Mackinder, H. J. 1902: *Britain and the British Seas*. London: Heineman.
—— 1931: Comment on a paper by S. W. Wooldridge, and D. J. Smetham, The glacial drifts of Essex and Hertfordshire, and their bearing upon the agricultural and historical geography of the region, *Geographical Journal*, 78, 243–65.
McBurney, E. B. M. and R. W. Hey, 1955: *Prehistory and Pleistocene Geology in Cyrenaican Libya*, Cambridge: Cambridge University Press.
McGhee, R. 1977: Ivory for the sea woman: the symbolic attributes of a prehistoric technology, *Canadian Journal of Archaeology*, 1, 141–9.
McGimsey, C. R. 1972: *Public Archaeology*, New York: Seminar Press.
—— and Davis, H. A. (eds) 1977: *The Management of Archaeological Resources*. Washington DC: Society for American Archaeology.
McGuire, R. H. 1983: Breaking down cultural complexity: inequality and heterogeneity. In M. B. Schiffer, (ed.), *Advances in Archaeological Method and Theory*, 6, New York: Academic Press, 91–142.
McIntosh, R. J. 1983: Floodplain geomorphology and human occupation of the upper inland delta of the Niger, *Geographical Journal*, 149, 182–201.
McNain, B. 1980: *The Method and Theory of V. Gordon Childe*, Edinburgh: Edinburgh University Press.
McNee, R. B. 1960: Towards a more humanistic economic geography: the geography of enterprise, *Tijdschrift voor Economische en Sociale Geografie*, 51, 201–5.
—— 1974: A systems approach to understanding the geographic behaviour of

organisations especially large corporations. In F. E. I. Hamilton, (ed.), *Spatial Perspectives on Industrial Organisation and Decision Making*, Chichester: John Wiley.

McWhirr, A. D. 1979: Tile-kilns in Roman Britain. In A. D. McWhirr (ed.), *Roman Brick and Tile: Studies in Manufacture, Distribution and Use in the Western Empire*, Oxford, British Archaeological Reports, British Series 68, 97–190.

Maitland, F. W. 1897: *Domesday Book and Beyond*, London: Collins (Fontana reprint, 1960).

Marcus, J. 1973: Territorial organisation of the lowland Classic Maya, *Science*, 180, 911–16.

—— 1974: The iconography of power among the Classic Maya, *World Archaeology*, 6, 83–94.

—— 1976: *Emblem and State in the Classic Maya Lowlands: An Epigraphic Approach to Territorial Organisation*, Washington, DC: Dumbarton Oaks.

Marsh, G. P. 1864: *Man and Nature; or Physical Geography as Modified by Human Action*. London.

Martin, P. S. and Wright, H. E. (eds) 1967: *Pleistocene Extinctions: the Search for a Cause*. New Haven: Yale University Press.

Massey, D. 1973: Towards a critique of industrial location theory, *Antipode*, 5, 33–9.

—— 1979: A critical evaluation of industrial location theory. In F. E. I. Hamilton, and G. J. R. Linge (eds), *Spatial Analysis, Industry and the Industrial Environment, vol. 1, Industrial Systems*, Chichester: John Wiley.

—— and Meegan, R. A. 1979: The geography of industrial reorganisation, *Progress in Planning*, 10, 155–237.

Masters, P. M. and Flemming, N. C. (eds) 1983: *Quaternary coastlines and Marine Archaeology; towards the Prehistory of Land Bridges and Continental Shelves*, London: Academic Press.

Mayhew, A. 1973: *Rural Settlement and Farming in Germany*, London: Batsford.

Maxwell, G. S. (ed.) 1983: *The Impact of Aerial Reconnaissance on Archaeology*. London: Council for British Archaeology, Research Report no. 49.

Meadow, R. H. 1975: Mammal remains from Hajji Firuz: a study in methodology. In A. T. Clason (ed.), *Archaeozoological Studies*, Amsterdam: North Holland Publishing Co., 265–83.

Meentmayer, V. 1978: Macroclimate and lignin control of litter decomposition rates, *Ecology*, 59, 465–72.

Megaw, J. V. S. and Simpson, D. D. A. 1979: *Introduction to British Prehistory*, Leicester: Leicester University Press.

Meirion-Jones, G. 1971: The use of Hearth Tax Returns and vernacular architecture in settlement studies, *Transactions of the Institute of British Geographers*, 53, 133–60.

Meitzen, A. 1895: *Siedelung und Agrarwesen der Westgermanen und Ostgermanen der Kelten, Römer, Finnen und Slawen*, Berlin.

Mellaart, J. 1965: *Earliest Civilisations of the Near East*, London: Thames and Hudson.

Michell, J. 1982: *Megalithomania. Artists, Antiquarians and Archaeologists at the Old Stone Monuments*. New York and London: Thames and Hudson.

Milisauskas, S. 1979: *European Prehistory*, London: Academic Press.

Millar, F. (ed.) 1967: *The Roman Empire and its Neighbours*, New York: Delacorte.
Miller, C. P. 1983: Idustrial archaeology in the U.S.A.: documenting the Pennsylvania Railway Ore Dock at Cleveland, Ohio, *World Archaeology*, 15, 148–60.
Miller, D. and Tilley, C. (eds) 1984: *Ideology, Power and Prehistory*, Cambridge: Cambridge University Press.
Millman, R. N. 1975: *The Making of the Scottish Landscape*, London: Batsford.
Mills, W. J. 1982: Positivism reversed: the relevance of Giambattista Vico, *Transactions of the Institute of British Geographers*, 7, 1–14.
Minchinton, W. 1983: World industrial archaeology: a survey, *World Archaeology*, 15, 125–36.
Mitchell, F. 1976: *The Irish Landscape*, London: Collins.
Mitchell, J. B. 1954: *Teach Yourself Historical Geography*, London: English Universities Press.
Moir, E. 1964: *The Discovery of Britain: the English Tourists 1540–1840*. London: Routledge and Kegan Paul.
Moore, B. and Rhodes, R. 1984: *Geographical Variations in Industrial Costs*, Cambridge: University of Cambridge, Dept. of Land Economy, Interim Research Report.
Moore, H. 1982: The interpretations of spatial patterning in settlement residues. In I. Hodder, (ed.), *Symbolic and Structural Archaeology*, Cambridge: Cambridge University Press.
Moore, P. D. 1973: The influence of prehistoric cultures upon the initiation and spread of blanket bog in upland Wales, *Nature*, 241, 350–3.
Morgan, R. P. C. 1981: Implications. In M. J. Kirkby, and R. P. C. Morgan (eds), *Soil Erosion*, Chichester: John Wiley.
Morris, C. 1972: State settlements in Tawantinsuyu: a strategy of compulsory urbanism. In M. Leone, (ed.), *Contemporary Archaeology*, Carbondale: Southern Illinois University Press, 393–401.
Mosley, M. P. 1982: The effect of a New Zealand beech forest canopy on the kinetic energy of water drops and on surface erosion, *Earth Surface Processes and Landforms*, 7, 103–7.
Mueller, J. W. 1974: The use of sampling in archaeological survey, *American Antiquity*, 39, 1–91.
—— (ed.) 1975: *Sampling in Archaeology*, Tucson: University of Arizona Press.
Munton, R. J. and Goudie, A. S. 1984: Geography in the United Kingdom, 1980–1984, *Geographical Journal*, 150, 27–47.
Murdock, G. P. 1957: World ethnographic sample, *American Anthropologist*, 59, 664–87.
Naroll, R. 1956: A preliminary index of social development, *American Anthropologist*, 58, 687–715.
National Materials Advisory Board 1982: *Conservation of Historic Stone Buildings and Monuments*. Washington DC: National Academy Press.
NCSS (National Council for Social Service) 1971: *Hedges and Local History*, London: published for the Standing Conference for Local History.
Netterberg, E. 1969: Ages of calcretes in southern Africa. *South African Archaeological Bulletin*, 24, 88–92.
Newcomb, R. M. 1968: Geographical location and analysis and Iron Age settlement in West Penwith, *Archaeology*, 7, 5–14.

—— 1971: Celtic Fields in Himmerland, Denmark, *Photogrammetrica*, 27, 101–13.

—— 1979: *Planning the Past*, Folkestone: Dawson, Archon Books.

Newton, R. 1972: *The Northumberland Landscape*, London: Hodder and Stoughton.

Nicolis, G. and Prigogine, I. 1977: *Self-organisation in Non-equilibrium Systems*, New York: John Wiley.

Nicholson, M. 1970: *The Environmental Revolution*, London: Hodder and Stoughton.

Noble, C. A. and Morgan, R. P. C. 1983: Rainfall interception and splash detachment with a Brussels sprouts plant: a laboratory simulation. *Earth Surface Processes and Landforms*, 8, 569–78.

Norton, W. 1984: *Historical Analysis in Geography*, London and New York: Longman.

Noy, T., Higgs, E. S. and Legge, A. J. 1973: Recent excavations at Nahal Oren, Israel, *Proceeding of the Prehistoric Society*, 39, 75–99.

Noy-Meir, I. and Seligman, N. G. 1979: Management of semi-arid ecosystems in Israel. In B. H. Walker (ed.), *Management of Semi-Arid Ecosystems*, Amsterdam: Elsevier, 115–61.

Odum, H. T. 1971: *Environment, Power and Society*, New York: John Wiley.

Okely, J. 1979: An anthropological contribution to the history and archaeology of an ethnic group. In B. Burnham and J. Kingsbury (eds), *Space, Hierarchy and Society*, Oxford: British Archaeological Reports, International Series 59.

Olsson, G. 1980: *Birds in Egg/Eggs in Bird*, Ann Arbor: Department of Geography, University of Michigan.

Olwig, K. R. 1980: Historical geography and the society/nature 'problematic': the perspective of J. F. Schouw, G. P. Marsh and E. Reclus, *Journal of Historical Geography*, 6, 29–45.

Open University 1977: *Values, Relevance and Policy*, Milton Keynes: Open University.

Orme, A. R. 1970: *The World's Landscapes: Ireland*, London: Longman.

Palmer, R. 1984: *Danebury...An Aerial Photographic Interpretation of its Environs*. London: HMSO (Royal Commission on Historical Monuments, Supplementary Series 6).

Park, C. C. 1983: Water resources and irrigation in pre-Hispanic Peru. *Geographical Journal*, 149, 153–66.

Parry, M. 1978: *Climatic Change, Agriculture and Settlement*, Folkestone: Dawson, Archon Books.

—— and Slater, T. R. (eds) 1980: *The Making of the Scottish Countryside*, London and Montreal: Croom Helm and McGill-Queen's University Press.

Parsons, J. 1968: Teotihuacan, Mexico, and its impact on regional demography, *Science*, 162, 872–7.

Paterson, J. H. 1974: Writing regional geography, *Progress in Geography*, 6, 1–26.

Pearce, D. (ed.) 1982: *The SPAB Barns Book*. London: Society for the Protection of Ancient Buildings.

Pearcy, G. E. et al., 1957: *World Political Geography*, New York: Crowell.

Phillips, C. W., Rivet, A. L. F. and Feacham, R. W. 1963: *Field Archaeology: Some Notes for Beginners Issued by the Ordnance Survey*, London: HMSO.

Piggott, S. 1959; 1965: *Approach to Archaeology*, London: Black.

—— 1976: *Ruins in a Landscape*, Edinburgh: Edinburgh University Press.

Pinder, D., Shimada, I. and Gregory, D. 1979: The nearest-neighbour statistic: archaeological application and new developments, *American Antiquity*, 44, 430–45.

Plog, F. 1979: Alternative models of prehistoric change. In A. C. Renfrew and K. L. Cooke, (eds), *Transformations: Mathematical Approaches to Culture Change*, London: Academic Press, 221–36.

—— 1982: Is a little philosophy (science?) a dangerous thing? In C. Renfrew, M. J. Rowlands and B. A. Seagraves, (eds.) *Theory and Explanation in Archaeology*, New York and London: Academic Press, 25–33.

Plog, S. 1980: *Stylistic Variation in Prehistoric Ceramics*, Cambridge: Cambridge Unviersity Press.

Polanyi, K. 1957: The economy as instituted process. In K. Polanyi, C. Arensburg and H. W. Pearson (eds), *Trade and Markets in the Early Empires*, New York: Free Press, 243–70.

Pollard, E., Hooper, M. D. and Moore, N. W. 1974: *Hedges*. London: Collins.

Potts, R. and Shipman, P. 1981: Cutmarks made by stone tools on bones from Olduvai Gorge, Tanzania, *Nature*, 291, 577–90.

Pounds, N. J. G. 1963: *Political Geography*, New York: McGraw-Hill.

Powlesland, D. 1983a: Pots, pits and portables, *Practical Computing*, June 1983, 144–6.

—— 1983b: West Heslerton, *Current Archaeology*, 7, 142–4.

—— 1984: *West Heslerton Parish Project Rescue Excavations 1976–82: An Interim Report*, Unpublished: Dominic Powlesland, The Old Abbey, Yedingham, Malton, Near York.

(The) Prehistoric Society 1984: *Prehistory, Priorities and Society: the Way Forward*. London: The Prehistoric Society.

Price, B. J. 1978: Secondary state formation: an explanatory model. In R. Cohen and E. Service (eds), *The Origins of the State: The Anthropology of Political Evolution*, Philadelphia: Institute for the Study of Human Issues.

Price Williams, D., Watson, A. and Goudie, A. S. 1982: Quaternary colluvial stratigraphy, archaeological sequences and palaeoenvironment in Swaziland, southern Africa, *Geographical Journal*, 248, 50–67.

Prince, H. 1971: Real, Imagined and Abstract Worlds of the Past, *Progress in Geography*, 3, 1–86.

—— 1982: Modernisation, restoration, preservation. . . In A. R. H. Baker and M. Billinge (eds), *Period and Place: Research Methods in Historical Geography*, Cambridge: Cambridge University Press, 33–43

Pritchard, G. A. 1981: *Farming on Ancient Monuments*, Pinner, Middlesex: HMSO for Ministry of Agriculture, Fisheries and Food.

Proudfoot, V. B. 1965a: Archaeological evidence for rates of weathering and erosion in Britain, *Institute of British Geographers Geomorphological Symposium, Rates of Erosion and Weathering in the British Isles*, Bristol, 27–31.

—— (1965b) Bringing archaeology to life, *Advancement of Science*, 22, 125–33.

—— 1981: Archaeological space. *Journal of Historical Geography*, 7, 303–6.

Quaini, M. 1982: *Geography and Marxism*, Oxford: Blackwell.

Rackham, O. 1976: *Trees and Woodland in the British Landscape*, London: Dent.

—— 1980: *Ancient Woodland*, London: Arnold.

Rahtz, P. A. (ed.) 1974: *Rescue Archaeology*, Harmondsworth: Penguin.

Raikes, R. L. 1967: *Water, Weather and Prehistory*, London: John Baker.

Raistrick, A. 1972: *Industrial Archaeology, an Historical Survey*, London: Methuen.

Randsborg, K. 1980: *The Viking Age in Denmark*, London: Duckworth.

Rapp, M. and Lossant, P. 1981: Some aspects of mineral cycling in the garrigue of southern France. In F. di Castri, D. W. Goodall and R. L. Specht (eds), *Mediterranean-Type Shrublands*, Amsterdam: Elsevier.

Rappaport, R. 1971a: Ritual, sanctity and cybernetics, *American Anthropologist*, 73, 59–76.

—— 1971b: The sacred in human evolution, *Annual Review of Ecology and Systematics*, 2, 23–44.

Ratzel, F. 1896: Die Gesetze des räumlichen Wachstums der Staaten: Ein Beitrag zur wissenschaftlichen politischen Geographie. *Petermanns Mitteilungen*, 42, 97–107.

Ravensdale, J. R. 1974: *Liable to Floods*, Cambridge: Cambridge University Press.

Redman, C. Rubertone, P. and Anzalone, R. 1979: Medieval archaeology at Qsar es-Seghir, Morocco, *Journal of Field Archaeology*, 6, 1–16.

Redman, C. and Watson, P. J. 1970: Systematic intensive surface collection, *American Antiquity*, 35, 279–91.

Reed, C. A. (ed.) 1977: *The Origins of Agriculture*, The Hague: Mouton.

Reed, M. 1984: *Discovering Past Landscapes*, London and Canberra: Croom Helm.

Rees, J., Hewings, G. and Stafford, H. (eds) 1981: *Industrial Location and Regional Systems*, London: Croom Helm.

Rees, P. 1980: Excavations at Chatsworth Street Cutting; part of the original terminus of the Liverpool and Manchester Railway, *Industrial Archaeology Review*, 5, 160–70.

Relph, E. 1970: An enquiry into the relations between phenomenology and geography, *Canadian Geographer*, 14, 193–201.

Renfrew, A. C. 1969: Review of 'Locational Analysis in Human Geography' by P. Haggett. *Antiquity*, 43, 74–5.

—— (ed.) 1974: *British Prehistory*, London: Duckworth.

—— 1975: Trade as action at a distance. In J. A. Sabloff and C. C. Lamberg-Karlovsky (eds), *Ancient Civilisation and Trade*, Albuquerque: University of New Mexico Press, 3–59.

—— 1976: Archaeology and the earth sciences. In D. A. Davidson and M. L. Shackley (eds), *Geoarchaeology: Earth Science and the Past*, London: Duckworth, 1–5.

—— 1977a: Space, time and polity. In J. Friedman and M. Rowlands (eds), *The Evolution of Social Systems*, London: Duckworth.

—— 1977b: Alternative models for exchange and spatial distribution. In T. Earle and J. Ericson (eds), *Exchange Systems in Prehistory*, London: Academic Press, 71–90.

—— 1978: Trajectory discontinuity and morphogenesis: the implications of Catastrophe Theory for archaeology. *American Antiquity*, 43, 203–44.

—— 1979: Systems collapse and social transformation: catastrophe and anastrophe in early state societies. In A. C. Renfrew and K. L. Cooke (eds), *Transformations: Mathematical Approaches to Culture Change*, New York: Academic Press, 481–506.

—— 1980: The Great Tradition versus the Great Divide: archaeology and anthropology, *American Journal of Archaeology*, 84, 287–98.

—— 1981: Space, time and man, *Transactions of the Institute of British Geographers*, 6, 257–78.

—— 1982a: Explanation revisited. In A. C. Renfrew, M. J. Rowlands and B. A. Segraves, *Theory and Explanation in Archaeology*, New York and London: Academic Press, 1–3.

—— 1982c: Polity and power: interaction, intensification and exploitation. In C. Renfrew and M. Wagstaff (eds), *An Island Polity: The Archaeology of Exploitation in Melos*, Cambridge: Cambridge University Press, 264–90.

—— 1983a: Geography, archaeology and environment: I, Archaeology, *The Geographical Journal*, 149, 316–23.

—— 1983b: Foreward to L. R. Binford, *In Pursuit of the Past; Decoding the Archaeological Record*, London: Thames and Hudson, 7–9.

—— 1983c: *Towards an Archaeology of Mind*, Cambridge: Cambridge University Press.

—— 1985: *The Archaeology of Cult: The Sanctuary at Phylakopi*. Supplementary vol. no. 18, British School at Athens, London: Thames and Hudson.

—— and Cherry, J. F. (eds) 1986: *Peer Polity Interaction and Sociopolitical Change*, Cambridge: Cambridge University Press.

—— and Cooke, K. L. (eds) 1979: *Transformations: Mathematical Approaches to Culture Change*, London and New York: Academic Press.

—— and Level, E. V. 1979: Exploring dominance: predicting polities from centres. In Renfrew, A. C. and Cooke, K. L. (eds), *Transformations: Mathematical Approaches to Culture Change*, New York: Academic Press, 145–67.

—— Rowlands, M. J. and Segraves,B. A. (eds) 1982: *Theory and Explanation in Archaeology*, New York: Academic Press.

—— and Wagstaff, M. 1983: *An Island Polity: The Archaeology of Exploitation in Melos*. Cambridge: Cambridge University Press.

Rennell, J. 1800: *The Geographical System of Herodotus, Examined; and Explained by a Comparison with Those of Other Ancient Authors and with Modern Geography*, London: Nicol.

Rich, C. J. 1836: *Narrative of a Residence in Koordistan and on the Site of Ancient Nineveh; with journal of a voyage down the Tigris to Bagdad and an account of a visit to Shiraz and Persepolis*, 2 vols, London.

Riden, P. 1973: Post-post-medieval archaeology, *Antiquity*, 47, 210–16.

Ritchie-Noakes, N. 1984: *Liverpool's Historic Waterfront: the World's First Mercantile Dock System*, London: HMSO (Royal Commission on Historical Monuments, Supplementary Series 7).

Roberts, B. K. 1972: Village Plans in Britain, *Medieval Archaeology*, 16, 33–56.

—— 1977: *Rural Settlement in Britain*. Folkestone: Dawson.

—— 1978: The regulated village in Northern England: some problems and questions, *Geographia Polonica*, 38, 245–52.

—— 1979: Village Plans in Britain. *In J. Claude (ed.), Recherches de Géographie Rurale: Hommage au Professeur Franz Dussart*, Liége: Les Soins de Charles Christians et de Jacqueline Claude.

—— 1982a: *Village Plans*, Aylesbury: Shire Archaeology.

—— 1982b: *Rural Settlement: A Historical Perspective*, Historical Geography Research Series, 9, Norwich: Geo Books.

—— and Glasscock, R. E. (eds), 1983: *Villages, Fields and Frontier. Studies in*

European Rural Settlements. Oxford: British Archaeological Reports, International Series 185.

Roberts, N. L., Erol, O. De Messer, T. and Verpmann, H. P. 1979: Radiocarbon chronology of Late Pleistocene Konya Lake, Turkey, *Nature*, 281, 662–4.

Rodwell, W. 1981: *The Archaeology of the English Church*, London: Batsford.

Ronaldshay, Earl of, (Dundas, L. J. L.) 1928: *The Life of Lord Curzon*, London: Ernest Benn.

Roper, D. C. 1979: The method and theory of site catchment analysis: a review. In M. G. Schiffer (ed.), *Advances in Archaeological Method and Theory*, vol. 2, New York: Academic Press, 119–40.

Rosenzweig, N. 1968: Net primary productivity of terrestrial communities: prediction from climatological data, *American Naturalist*, 102, 67–74.

Rostoker, W. et al., 1983: Casting farm implements, comparable tools and hardware in ancient China, *World Archaeology*, 15, 196–210.

Rowlands, M. J. 1971: The archaeological interpretation of prehistoric metal working, *World Archaeology*, 3, 210–24.

—— 1982: Processual archaeology as historical social science. In A. C. Renfrew, M. J. Rowlands and B. A. Segraves (eds), *Theory and Explanation in Archaeology*, New York and London: Academic Press, 155–74.

Rowley, T. 1981: *The Origins of Open Field Agriculture*, London: Croom Helm.

—— and Breakell, M. (eds) 1975; 1977: *Planning the Historic Environment* Oxford: University Dept. for External Studies.

Roxey, P. M. 1938: The terrain of early Chinese civilisation. *Geography*, 23, 225–36.

RCHM (Royal Commission on Historical Monuments) 1968: *West Cambridge-shire*. London: HMSO.

Sackett, J. 1982: Approaches to style in lithic archaeology. *Journal of Anthropological Archaeology*, 1, 59–112.

Sahlins, M. 1974: *Stone Age Economics*, London: Tavistock Press.

—— 1981: *Historical Metaphors and Mythical Realities*, Ann Arbor: University of Michigan Press.

St Joseph, J. K. S. (ed.) 1977: *The Uses of Air Photography*, London: John Baker.

Sanders, W. T. 1972: Population, agricultural history, and societal evolution in Mesoamerica. In Spooner, B. (ed.), *Population Growth: Anthropological Implications*, Cambridge, MA: MIT Press, 101–53.

Sanders, W. T. and Webster, D. 1978: Unilinealism, multilinealism, and the evolution of complex societies. In Redman, C. L. *et al.*, (eds), *Social Archaeology: Beyond Subsistence and Dating*, New York: Academic Press, 249–302.

Santos, M. 1977: Society and space: social formation as theory and method. *Antipode*, 9, 3–13.

Sauer, C. O. 1948: Environment and culture during the last deglaciation. *Proceedings American Philosophical Society*, 92, 65–77.

—— 1952: *Agricultural Origins Dispersal (Bowman Memorial Lectures, Series 2.), New York: American Geographical Society*.

—— 1956: *The agency of man on the Earth. In W. L. Thomas (ed.), Man's Role in Changing the Face of the Earth*, Chicago: University of Chicago Press, 49–69.

—— 1968: *Northern Mists*, Cambridge: Cambridge University Press.
Sawyer, P. (ed.) 1976: *Medieval Settlement*, London: Edward Arnold.
—— (ed.) 1978: *Names, Words, and Graves: Early Medieval Settlement*, University of Leeds: School of History.
Schiffer, M. B. 1972: Archaeological context and systemic context. *American Antiquity*, 37, 156–65.
Schiffer, M. B. and Gumerman, G. J. (eds), 1977: *Conservation Archaeology. A Guide for Cultural Resource Management Studies*. New York and London: Academic Press.
Schoenwetter, J. 1981: Prologue to a contextual archaeology, *Journal of Archaeological Science*, 8, 367–79.
Schumm, S. A. 1965: Quaternary palaeohydrology. In H. E. Wright and D. G. Frey (eds), *Quaternary of the United States*, Princeton: Princeton University Press, 783–94.
—— 1979: Geomorphic thresholds: the concept and its applications, *Transactions of the Institute of British Geographers*, 4, 485–516.
—— and Lichty, R. L. 1965: Time, space and causality in geomorphology, *American Journal of Science*, 263, 110–19.
Seligman, N. G., Tadmor, N. H., Noy-Meir, I. and Dovrat, A. 1971: An exercise in simulation of a semi-arid grassland, *Bulletin de Recherche Agronomique*, Gembloux: Semaine d'étude des problemes méditerranéens, 138–43.
Service, E. R. 1962: *Primitive Social Organisation: An Evolutionary Perspective*, New York: Random House.
—— 1975: *Origins of the State and Civilisation: The Process of Cultural Evolution*, New York: Norton.
Shackley, M. 1985: *Using Environmental Archaeology*, London: Batsford.
Sheail, J. 1976: *Nature in Trust*. Glasgow: Blackie.
Shennan, S. J. 1985: *Experiments in the Collection and Analysis of Archaeological Survey Data: the East Hampshire survey*. Sheffield: Sheffield University, Dept. of Archaeology and Prehistory.
Sheppard, J. A. 1966: Pre-enclosure field and settlement patterns in an English Township – Wheldrake, near York, *Geografiska Annaler*, 48B 59–77.
—— 1974: Metrological analysis of regular village plans in Yorkshire, *Agricultural History Review*, 22, 118–35.
—— 1976: Medieval village planning in Northern England: some evidence from Yorkshire, *Journal of Historical Geography*, 2, 3–20.
Shepherd, R. 1980: *Prehistoric Mining and Allied Industries*. London: Academic Press.
Shipman, P. 1981: *Life History of a Fossil*, Cambridge, MA: Harvard University Press.
Shoard, M. 1980: *The Theft of the Countryside*. London: Temple Smith.
Sielmann, B. 1971: Der Einfluss der Umwelt auf di neolithische Besiedlung Südwestdeutschlands unter besonderer Berücksichtigung der Verhältnisse am nördlichen Oberrhein, *Acta Praehistorica et Archaeologica*, 2, 65–197.
Silvester, R. J. (ed) 1984: *Fenland Research, no. 1. Fieldwork and Excavation in the Fens of Eastern England 1983–4*. Gressenhall, Dereham: Norfolk Museums Service (for the Fenland Project).
Sim, K. 1981: *Jean Louis Burckhardt. A Biography*, London: Quartet Books.
Simmons, I. G. and Tooley, M. J. (eds), 1981: *The Environment in British Prehistory*, London: Duckworth.

Simon, H. A. 1957: *Models of Man*. New York: John Wiley.

Sinclair, G. (ed.) 1983: *The Upland Landscapes Study*. Narberth, Dyfed: Environment Information Services

Small, A. (ed.) 1965: *The Fourth Viking Congress*, Aberdeen University Studies, 149, Edinburgh: Oliver and Boyd.

Smalley, I. J. 1968: The loess deposits and Neolithic culture of northern China, *Man* n. 5, 224–41.

Smith, C. A. 1976a: Regional economic systems: linking geographical models and socio-economic problems. In C. A. Smith (ed.), *Regional Analysis*, London: Academic Press, 3–63.

—— 1976b: Exchange systems and the spatial distributions of elites. In C. A. Smith, (ed.), *Regional Analysis*, London: Academic Press, 309–74.

Smith, C. T. 1967: *An Historical Geography of Europe before 1800*, London: Longman.

Smith, D. 1963: The British hosiery industry in the middle of the nineteenth century: an historical study in economic geography, *Transactions and Papers of the Institute of British Geographers*, 32, 125–42.

—— 1965: *The Industrial Archaeology of the East Midlands*, Newton Abbot: David and Charles.

—— 1966: A theoretical framework for geographical studies of industrial location, *Economic Geography*, 42, 95–113.

—— 1970: On throwing out Weber with the bathwater: a note on industrial location and linkage, *Area*, 2, 15–18.

—— 1971: *Industrial Location: An Economic Geographical Analysis*, New York: John Wiley.

—— 1979: Modelling industrial location: towards a broader view of the space economy. In F. E. I. Hamilton and G. J. R. Linge (eds), *Spatial Analysis, Industry and the Industrial Environment: vol. 1, Industrial Systems*, Chichester: John Wiley.

—— 1981: *Industrial Location: An Economic Geographical Analysis*, 2nd edn, New York: John Wiley.

Smith, N. J. H. 1980: Anthrosols and human carrying capacity in Amazonia, *Annals of the Association of American Geographers*, 70, 553–66.

Soja, E. W. 1971: *The Political Organisation of Space*. Association of American Geographers, Commission on College Geography, Resource Paper 8.

Sparks, B. W. and West, R. G. 1972: *The Ice Age in Britain*, London: Methuen.

Spate, O. H. K. 1960: Quantity and quality in geography, *Annals of the Association of American Geographers*, 50, 377–94.

Specht, R. L. 1972: Water use by perennial evergreen plants in Australia and Papua New Guinea, *Australian Journal of Botany*, 277–92.

Spooner, B. 1972: The status of nomadism as a cultural phenomenon in the Middle East. In W. Irons and N. Dyson-Hudson (eds), *Perspectives on Nomadism*, Leiden: Brill, 122–31.

Spratt, D. 1982: *Prehistoric and Roman Archaeology of North-East Yorkshire*. Oxford: British Archaeological Reports, British series 104.

Spriggs, M., (ed.), 1984: *Marxist Perspectives in Archaeology*, Cambridge: Cambridge University Press.

—— 1984: Another way of telling: Marxist perpectives in archaeology. In M. Spriggs, (ed.), *Marxist Perspectives in Archaeology*. Cambridge: Cambridge University Press, pp. 1–9.

Sprout, H. 1968: Political Geography. In D. L. Sills (ed.), *International Encyclopaedia of the Social Sciences*, New York: Macmillan, 116–23.

Stamp, D. 1974: *Nature Conservation in Britain*. 2nd edn, London: Collins.

Stein, A. 1923: Memoir on maps of Chinese Turkistan and Kansu, *Records of the Survey of India*, 17.

Steponaitis, V. 1978: Location theory and complex chiefdoms: a Mississipian example. In B. D. Smith (ed.), *Mississipian Settlement*, New York: Academic Press, 417–53.

Stoddart, D. R. 1967: Organism and ecosystem as geographical models. In R. J. Chorley and P. Haggett (eds), *Models in Geography*, London: Methuen, 511–48.

Storper, M. 1981: Toward a structural theory of industrial location. In J. Rees, G. Hewings and H. Stafford (eds), *Industrial Location and Regional Systems,* London: Croom Helm.

—— and Walker, R. 1979: *Systems and Marxist Theories of Industrial Location: A Review*, Institute of Urban and Regional Development, University of California, Berkeley, Working Paper, 312.

—— 1983: The theory of labour and the theory of location. *International Journal of Urban and Regional Research*, 7, 1–41.

Sturdy, D. and Sturdy, S. 1977: *Historic Monuments of England and Wales*. London: Dent.

Subbarao, B. 1958: *The Personality of India*, 2nd edn, Baroda: University of Baroda, Department of Archaeology.

Swain, P. J. 1982: *Farming and the Countryside*. Alnwick: Ministry of Agriculture, Fisheries and Food.

Swan, V. G. 1984: *The Pottery Kilns of Roman Britain*, London: HMSO (Royal Commission on Historical Monuments, Supplementary Series 5).

Szafranski, W. 1960: A contribution to the problem of the 'monotheism' in the palaeolithic time, *Swiatowit*, 23, 151–60.

Taagepera, R. 1968: Growth curves of empires, *General Systems*, 13, 171–5.

Taylor, C. C. 1974: *Fieldwork in Medieval Archaeology*, London: Batsford.

—— 1975: *Fields in the English Landscape*, London: Dent.

—— 1983: *Village and Farmstead*, London: George Philip.

—— and Muir, R. 1983: *Visions of the Past*. London: Dent.

Taylor, C. G. 1937: *Environment, Race, and Migration*, Toronto: Toronto University Press.

Taylor, D. 1975: *Some Locational Aspects of Middle-Range Hierarchical Societies*, (PhD. dissertation, City University of New York.)

Taylor, H. M. and Taylor, J. 1965: *Anglo-Saxon Architecture*, Cambridge: Cambridge University Press.

Taylor, M. J. 1984: *Industrial geography, Progress in Human Geography*, 8, 263–74.

Taylor, P. J. 1982: A materialist framework for political geography, *Transactions of the Institute of British Geographers*, 7, 15–34.

—— 1984: Introduction: geographical scale and political geography. In P. J. Taylor and J. House (eds), *Political Geography: Recent Advances and Future Directions*, London: Croom Helm, 1–7.

Taylor, W. 1948: *A Study of Archaeology*, Lancaster, PA; Memoirs of the American Anthropological Association, 69.

Thirsk, J. 1961: Industries in the countryside. In, F. J. Fisher (ed.), *Essays in the*

Economic and Social History of Tudor and Stuart England in Honour of R. F. Tawney, Cambridge: Cambridge University Press.

—— 1964: The Common Fields, *Past and Present*, 29, 3–29.

—— (ed.) 1967: *The Agrarian History of England and Wales*, vol. IV, 1500–1640, Cambridge: Cambridge University Press.

Thomas, W. L. (ed.) 1956: *Man's Role in Changing the Face of the Earth*, Chicago: University of Chicago Press.

Thompson, E. P. 1978: *The Poverty of Theory and Other Essays*, London: Merlin.

Thompson, M. W. 1981: Ruins: *Their Preservation and Display*, London: British Museum Publications Ltd.

Thornes, J. B. 1979: Fluvial process. In C. E. Embleton and J. B. Thornes, *Process in Geomorphology*, London: Edward Arnold, 213–71.

—— 1985: The ecology of erosion, *Geography* 70, 222–34.

Tilley, C. 1981: Conceptual frameworks for the explanation of socio-cultural change. In I. Hodder, G. Isaac, and N. Hammond (eds), *Pattern of the Past*, Cambridge: Cambridge University Press, 363–86.

—— 1982: Social formation, social structures and social change. In I. Hodder (ed.) *Symbolic and Structural Archaeology*, Cambridge: Cambridge University Press, 26–38.

—— 1984: Ideology and the legitimation of power in the Middle Neolithic of Southern Sweden. In D. Miller and C. Tilley (eds), *Ideology, Power and Prehistory*, Cambridge: Cambridge University Press.

Titow, J. Z. 1965: Medieval England and the open field system, *Past and Present*, 32, 86–192.

Tivy, J. and O'Hare, G. 1981: *Human Impact on the Ecosystem*, Edinburgh: Oliver and Boyd.

Tobler, W. R. and Weinburg, S. 1971: A Cappadocian speculation, *Nature*, 231, 40–1.

Tod, J. 1829: *Annals and Antiquities of Rajasthan.* 2 vols, London: Smith, Elder and Co.

Townshend, J. R. G. (ed.) 1981: *Terrain Analysis and Remote Sensing*, London: Allen and Unwin.

Trigger, B. 1970: Aims in prehistoric archaeology, *Antiquity*, 44, 26–37.

—— 1974: The archaeology of government, *World Archaeology*, 6, 95–106.

—— 1978: *Time and Traditions: Essays in Archaeological Interpretation*, Edinburgh: Edinburgh University Press; New York: Columbia University Press.

—— 1984a: Alternative archaeologies: nationalist, colonialist, imperialist. *Man*, 19, 355–70.

—— 1984b: Archaeology at the crossroads: what's new? *Annual Review of Anthropology*, 13, 275–300.

Tringham, R. 1971: *Hunters, Fishers and Farmers of Eastern Europe, 6000–3000 BC*, London: Hutchinson.

Tromble, J. M., Renard, K. G. and Thatcher, A. P. 1974: Infiltration for three rangeland soil-vegetation complexes. *Journal of Range Management* 27, 318–21.

Tuan, Yi-Fu 1974: *Topopohilla: a Study of Environmental Perceptions, Attitudes and Values*, Englewood Cliffs: Hs.

—— 1975: Images and mental maps, *Annals of the Association of American*

Geographers, 65, 205–13.

Turner, J. 1962: The *tilia* decline; an anthropogenic interpretation, *New Phytologist*, 61, 328–41.

Turner, K. M. 1985: Water loss from forest and range lands in California, *Proceedings of the Field Conference on Chaparral Ecosystems Research*, Santa Barbara: UCLA.

Turner, S. 1979: *The Politics of Landscape. Rural Scenery and Society in England Poetry 1630–1660*. Oxford: Blackwell.

Tylecote, R. F. 1962: *Metallurgy in the British Isles*, London: Edward Arnold.

Ucko, P. J. and Dimbleby, G. W. 1969: *The Domestication and Exploitation of Plants and Animals*. London: Duckworth.

Ucko, P., Dimbleby, G. W. and Tringham, R. (eds) 1972: *Man, Settlement and Urbanism*, London: Duckworth.

van der Leeuw, S. E. (ed.) 1981a: *Archaeological Approaches to the Study of Complexity*, Amsterdam: Albert Egges van Griffen Instituut voor Prae- en Protohistorie.

—— 1981b: Information flows, flow structures, and the explanation of change in human institutions. In S. E. van der Leeuw (ed.), *Archaeological Approaches to the Study of Complexity*, Amsterdam: Albert Egges van Giffen Instituut voor Prae- en Protohistorie, 229–312.

VCH Np. 1937: *Victoria County History, Northamptonshire*, London: Institute of Historical Research.

Vidal de la Blache, P. 1902: Les conditions géographiques des faits sociaux. *Annales de Géographie*, 11, 13–23.

—— 1928: *The Personality of France*, London: Christophers.

Vita-Finzi, C. 1969a: *The Mediterranean Valleys: Geological Changes in Historical Times*, Cambridge: Cambridge University Press.

—— 1969b: Fluvial Geology. In D. Brothwell and E. Higgs (eds), *Science in Archaeology; A Survey of Progress and Research*, London: Thames and Hudson, 135–50.

Wade, K. R. 1978: Sampling at Ipswich: the origins and growth of the Anglo-Saxon town. In J. F. Cherry and S. Shennan (eds), *Sampling in Contemporary British Archaeology*, Oxford: British Archaeological Reports, British Series 50: 279–84.

Wagner, F. H. 1976: Integrating and control mechanisms in arid and semi-arid ecosystems. Considerations for impact assessment. *Symposium on Biological Evaluation of Environmental Impact.*, New Orleans, Louisiana.

Wagstaff, J. M. 1972: The Physical geography of the Myrtos region: a preliminary appraisal. In P. Warren, Myrtos. An Early Bronze Age Settlement in Crete, British School at Athens, Supplementary Volume no. 7, London: Thames and Hudson, 273–82.

—— 1973: Physical geography and settlements, *Anatolian Studies*, 23 (special volume on the Aşvan Project), 197–215.

—— 1978: A possible interpretation of settlement pattern evolution in terms of 'catastrophe theory', *Transactions of the Institute for British Geographers*, 3, 165–78.

—— 1981: Buried assumptions: some problems in the interpretation of the Younger Fill raised by recent data from Greece, *Journal of Archaeological Science*, 8, 247–64.

—— 1983: Geography, archaeology and environment: II, A human geographer's view, *The Geographical Journal*, 149, 323–25.

Walker, R. and Storper, M. 1981: Capital and industrial location, *Progress in Human Geography*, 5, 473–509.

Wallerstein, I. 1974: *The Modern World System*, London: Academic Press.

Walther, H. 1939: Grasland, Savanne und Busch der Ariden Teile Afrikas und ihrer ökologischen Bedingtheit. *Jahrbuch für Wissenschaftliche Botanik*, 87, 850–60.

Ward, R. de C. 1909: *The Life of Man in the Temperate Zones*, London: Murray.

Washburn, D. K. 1974: Nearest neighbor analysis of Pueblo I-III settlement patterns along the Rio Pueno of the East, New Mexico, *American Antiquity*, 39, 315–35.

Watson, P. J., LeBlanc, S. A. and Redman, E. L. 1971: *Explanation in Archaeology: an Explicitly Scientific Approach*, New York: Columbia University Press.

Webb, M. C. 1973: The Peten Maya decline viewed in the perspective of state formation. In T. P. Culbert (ed.), *The Classic Maya Collapse*, Albuerquerque: University of New Mexico Press, 367–404.

Webber, M. J. 1972: *The Impact of Uncertainty on Location*, Cambridge, MA: Harvard University Press.

Weber, A. 1909: *Über den Standort der Industrien*, (translated by C. J. Friedrich (1929) as *Alfred Weber's Theory of the Location of Industries*). Chicago: University of Chicago Press.

Webster, D. 1975: Warfare and the evolution of the state: a reconsideration, *American Antiquity*, 40, 464–70.

Webster, D. 1976: On theocracies, *American Anthropologist*, 78, 812–28.

Weide, D. L. and Weide, M. L. 1973: Application of geomorphic data to archaeology: a comment, *American Antiquity*, 39, 428–31.

Wendorf, F. J. 1979: The use of barley in the Egyptian Late Paleolithic. *Science*, 205, 1341–7.

Whallow, R. 1973: Spatial analysis of occupation floors I: the application of dimensional analysis of variance, *American Antiquity*, 38, 266–78.

—— 1974: Spatial analysis of occupation floors II: the application of nearest neighbor analysis, *American Antiquity*, 39, 16–34.

Wheatley, P. 1971: *The Pivot of the Four Quarters*, Edinburgh: Edinburgh University Press.

Wheeler, R. E. M. 1968: *The Indus Civilisation*, Cambridge: Cambridge University Press.

White, P. 1978: The excavation of industrial archaeological sites, *Industrial Archaeology Review*, 2, 160–7.

Whitehand, J. W. R. (ed.) 1981: *The Urban Landscape: Historical Development and Management: Papers by M. R. G. Conzen*, London and New York: Academic Press.

Whittaker, R. H. and Marks P. L. 1975: Methods of assessing terrestrial productivity. In H. L. Leith and R. H. Whittaker (eds.), *Primary Productivity of the Biosphere*, New York: Springer Verlag, 55–118.

Whittaker, R. H. and Niering, J. 1975: Vegetation of Santa Catalina Mountains, Arizona, V, Biomass, production and diversity along the elevation gradient, *Ecology*, 56, 771–90.

Whittlesey, D. S. 1929: Sequent occupance, *Annals of the Association of American Geographers*, 19, 162–5.

Whyte, K. A. 1984: *Register of Research in Historical Geography*. Norwich:

Geo. Books, Historical Geography Research Series, no. 14.

Wiersum, K. F. 1983: Effects of various vegetation layers of an *Acacia auriculiformis* forest plantation on surface erosion in Java, Indonesia. *International Conference on Soil Erosion and Conservation*, Hawaii, 16–22 January.

Wiessner, P. 1983: Style and social information in Kalahari San projectile points, *American Antiquity*, 48, 253–76.

Wigens, A. 1980: *The Clandestine Farm*. St Albans: Paladin.

Wigley, T. M. L., Ingram, M. J. and Farmer, G. 1981: *Climate and History. Studies in Past Climates and their Impact on Man*. Cambridge: Cambridge University Press.

Wilkins, D. E. and Norton, B. E. 1974: Logan: Utah State University, Resource management. *US/IBP Desert Biome Research Memoir*, RM 74–67.

Wilkinson, J. C. 1977: *Water and Tribal Settlement in South-East Arabia: a Study of The Aflaj of Oman*, Oxford: Clarendon Press.

Willerding, U. 1980: Zum Ackerbau der Bandkeramiker. *Materialhefte Ur- & Fruhgesch. Niedersachsens*, 16, 421–56.

Willey, G. R. and Sabloff, J. 1974: *A History of American Archaeology*, London: Thames and Hudson.

Williams, J. 1829: *Two Essays on the Geography of Ancient Asia; intended partly to illustrate the campaigns of Alexander, and the Anabasis of Xenophon*. London: Murray.

Williams, M. 1970: *The Draining of the Somerset Levels*. Cambridge: Cambridge University Press.

Williams-Ellis, C. (ed.) 1937: *Britain and the Beast*. London: Dent.

Wilson, A. G. and Kirkby, M. J. 1975: *Mathematics for Geographers and Planners*, Oxford: Clarendon Press.

Wilson, 1881: *The Survey of Western Palestine*, London: The Committee of the Palestine Exploration Fund.

Wobst, H. M. 1974: Boundary conditions for palaeolithic social systems: a simulation approach, *American Antiquity*, 39, 147–78.

—— 1977: *Stylistic Behaviour and Information Exchange*, Ann Arbor: University of Michigan Museum of Anthropology, Anthropological Paper, 61, 317–42.

Wolf, E. R. 1982: *Europe and the People without History*, Berkeley: University of California Press.

Wood, P. 1980: Industrial geography. *Progress in Human Geography*, 4, 406–16.

Wooldridge, S. W. and Linton, D. L. 1933: The loam terrains of south-east England in their relation to its early history, *Antiquity*, 7, 297–310.

Wright, H. T. 1977: Recent research on the origin of the state. *Annual Review of Anthropology*, 6, 379–98.

—— 1978: Toward an explanation of the origins of the state. In R. Cohen and E. R. Service (eds), *Origins of the State*, Philadelphia: Institute for the Study of Human Issues, 49–68.

—— and Johnson, G. A. 1975: Population, exchange, and early state formation in southwestern Iran, *American Anthropologist*, 77, 267–89.

Wright, H. W. 1968: Climatic change in the eastern Mediterranean region: the natural environment of early food production in the mountains north of Mesopotamia, *Final Report of University of Minnesota, Contract NONR-710 (33) TASK NO. 389–129*.

Zedler, P. H. 1982: Vegetation change in chaparral and desert communities in San Diego County, California. In J. Cairns (ed.), *The Recovery Process in Damaged Ecosystems*, Ann Arbor: Ann Arbor Scientific Publications, 236–53.

Zeuner, F. E. 1958: *Dating the Past: an Introduction to Geochronology*, 5th edn, London: Methuen.

—— 1959: *The Pleistocene Period: its Climate, Chronology and Faunal Successions*, London: Hutchinson (rev. edn).

Notes on Contributors

John Cherry is Lecturer in Aegean Prehistory at the University of Cambridge. His principal interests are in Aegean pre- and proto-history, state formation, island archaeology, archaeological field survey, and the application of computers in archaeology. Recent publications include 'The emergence of the state in the prehistoric Aegean', *Proceedings of the Cambridge Philological Society*, 30 (1984), 18–48; 'Islands out of the stream: isolation and interaction in early East Mediterranean insular prehistory', in A. B. Knapp and T. Stech (eds), *Prehistoric Production and Exchange in the Aegean and East Mediterranean* (Los Angeles, 1985); (with C. Renfrew) *Peer Polity Interaction and Socio-Political Change* (Cambridge, 1986); and (with J. L. Davis and E. Mantzourani) *The Landscape of Northern Keos in the Cyclades* (Cambridge, 1986).

Robin Dennell is a lecturer in the Department of Archaeology and Prehistory in the University of Sheffield. On-going interests include prehistoric subsistence and the early history of agriculture in Europe and the Near East but, as field director of the British Archaeological Mission to Pakistan, much of his time is currently given to the Palaeolithic and Pleistocene history of northern Pakistan. Recent publications include *European Economic Prehistory* (London, 1983); 'The hunter-gatherer/agricultural frontier in prehistoric temperate Europe', in S. Green and S. M. Perlman (eds), *The Archaeology of Frontiers and Boundaries* (London and New York, 1985); and (with H. Rendell and M. Halim) 'New perspectives on the palaeolithic of northern Pakistan', *South Asian Archaeology, 1983*, 9–12.

Peter Fowler is now Professor of Archaeology in the University of Newcastle upon Tyne after serving as secretary to the Royal Commission on Historical Monuments (England). Long associated with rescue and landscape archaeology, his interests also embrace the archaeology of farming, aerial photography and experimental archaeology. Recent publications include *The Farming of Prehistoric Britain*

(Cambridge, 1983); *Farms in England: Prehistoric to Present* (London, 1983); 'The past in public', in Robinson and Gilchrist (eds), *Archaeology, Politics and the Public* (York, 1986); 'Roman fields in Barnsley Park', *Transactions of the Bristol and Gloucester Archaeological Society*, 103 (1985), 77–82; and 'Monuments, inventories and record in England: policy and practice', *Actes du Colloque sur les Inventaires des Biens Cultures en Europe* (Paris, 1984).

Andrew Goudie is Professor of Geography and Head of the School of Geography in the University of Oxford. He is a geomorphologist who has worked closely with archaeologists in India, Pakistan and Swaziland. His recent books include *Environmental Change* (2nd edn Oxford, 1983; *The Human Impact* (2nd edn Oxford, 1986); *The Nature of the Environment* (Oxford, 1984); and (with Rita Gardner) *Discovering Landscape in England and Wales* (London, 1985).

Eric Grant is Senior Lecturer in Historical Geography and Archaeology at Middlesex Polytechnic. His interests lie at the interface of archaeology and geography in such areas as spatial archaeology, landscape archaeology and industrial archaeology, and he is currently preparing a report on his excavation of a medieval site in Somerset. Published work includes an edited volume on *Central Places, Archaeology and History* (Sheffield, 1985).

Ian Hodder is lecturer in Archaeology at the University of Cambridge. His major interests lie in theoretical developments in what he calls *post-processual* archaeology, symbolic interpretation and the application of these ideas to the prehistory of Europe. Recent publications include *Symbols in Action* (Cambridge, 1982); *The Present Past* (London, 1982); and *Reading the Past* (Cambridge, 1986).

Richard Hodges is a lecturer in the Department of Archaeology and Prehistory at Sheffield University. Much of his time is absorbed by the multi-disciplinary projects (including excavation and site survey) at Roystone Grange (Derbyshire) and San Vincenzo al Volturno (Italy). His publications include *Dark Age Economics* (London, 1982) and he has two books in the press (*Markets* and *Archaeology and the Beginnings of English Society*). His is also finalizing his report on the six years of the San Vincenzo Project.

Brian Roberts is a senior lecturer in Geography at Durham University, where he teaches and researches on historical geography, particularly that of England. Recent publications include *Village Plans* (Aylesbury, 1982); *Rural Settlements: A Historical Perspective* (Norwich, 1982); and (with R. E. Glasscock) *Villages. Fields and Frontiers. Studies in European Rural Settlements.* (Oxford, 1983). His forthcoming book,

The Making of the English Village establishes the principles and practice of village plan analysis.

John Thornes is Professor of Physical Geography and Head of the Geography Department in the University of Bristol. His main research interests lie in geomorphology and ecology, and spread into archaeology from an interest in erosion, particularly that around Argaric sites in Spain where he has worked with Antonio Gilman. He has co-authored *Geomorphology and Time* (London, 1977) with D. Brunsden and *Land Use and Prehistory in South East Spain* (London, 1985) with A. Gilman, as well as editing *Process in Geomorphology* (London, 1979) with C. Embleton.

Malcolm Wagstaff is a senior lecturer in geography at Southampton University where he teaches historical geography and the regional geography of the Middle East. His major research interests lie in man–land relationships, particularly settlement patterns and agriculture, in the Near East where his extensive field work has often been carried out in collaborative projects with archaeologists. His recent books include *The Development of Rural Settlements* (Amersham, 1982); (with C. Renfrew) *An Island Polity: The Archaeology of Exploitation in Melos* (Cambridge, 1982); and *The Evolution of Middle Eastern Landscapes* (London, 1985). A second edition of *The Middle East: A Geographical Study* (with P. Beaumont and G. H. Blake) is in preparation.

Index